GHOST GRIZZLIES

A JOHN MACRAE BOOK

HENRY HOLT AND COMPANY
NEW YORK

DAVID PETERSEN

GHOST GRIZZLIES

Henry Holt and Company, Inc.
Publishers since 1866
115 West 18th Street
New York, New York 10011

Henry Holt® is a registered trademark of
Henry Holt and Company, Inc.

Published in Canada by Fitzhenry & Whiteside Ltd.,
195 Allstate Parkway, Markham, Ontario L3R 4T8.

Library of Congress Cataloging-in-Publication Data
Petersen, David.
Ghost grizzlies / David Petersen.—1st ed.
p.   cm.
"A John Macrae book."
Includes bibliographical reference and index.
1. Grizzly bear—Colorado.   2. Grizzly bear—San Juan
Mountains (Colo. and N.M.). 3. Wildlife reintroduction—Colorado.
4. Wildlife reintroduction—San Juan Mountains (Colo. and N.M.).
5. Petersen, David.   I. Title.
QL737.C27P425   1995   94-39987
599.74'446—dc20   CIP

ISBN 0-8050-3117-0

Henry Holt books are available for special promotions
and premiums. For details contact: Director, Special Markets.

First Edition—1995

Designed by Kate Nichols
Illustration by Michael McCurdy

Printed in the United States of America
All first editions are printed on acid-free paper. ∞

10   9   8   7   6   5   4   3   2   1

This book is for my mother and father,
who put the San Juans in my blood . . .

for John A. Murray,
who planted the seed of possibility . . .

and for Doug Peacock,
who nourished its growth.

CONTENTS

FOREWORD:
RETURN OF THE LEGEND

Our legends are quartered in the landscape of dreams. This book documents the resistance with which these legends are retrieved from the peripheries of American frontier culture and brought into the cold light of the late twentieth century.

There's nothing new about grizzlies in Colorado, of course. They were there when humans arrived on this continent. Today's turmoil about grizzlies in Colorado is because we thought we'd gotten rid of them. "The Last Southwestern Grizzly" or "The Last Colorado Grizzly" is a chapter which has been written a dozen times since 1950 and repeatedly throughout these four decades the state's position has been: "no grizzlies left." Each time an "extinct" grizzly shows up—as happened in 1951 and again in 1979—they are once again proclaimed dead and gone forever.

But somehow these animals have persisted; they seem, like the knapweed in the ditch, never to go away altogether.

Thus, the grizzly in Colorado has become a conservation issue no one asked for. The federal agencies were unprepared; they said the bear would cost too much and the feds didn't have the money. Ranchers and loggers thought the mountains were safe and purged of grizzlies, wolves, and similar varmints. Conservationists were preoccupied with issues of human use and access into wilderness areas. After all, how can you organize conservation measures around protection of an animal you don't really believe exists?

Even if one considers grizzlies still roaming wild in Colorado good news, it may be the most unwelcome good news in several decades. This is puzzling. One would have expected public enlightenment in a state like Colorado to be such that verification of a surviving remnant of native grizzlies would have been received with open arms. Human readjustments to the renewed presence of the bear would be small and limited to a few sheep allotments and bear-hunting areas. The agency that sets the public tone is the state of Colorado's Division of Wildlife. Their official opposition to grizzly or wolf reintroduction has been public record; this certainly shows deep and lingering ambivalence. Somehow we expected a more favorable response today. Even the factions within the Division most sympathetic to grizzlies refer to such press as "the continuing furor over the presence/absence of grizzly bears in Colorado." What this means is that the state still sees the issue of the grizzly in Colorado as mostly unsubstantiated loud and uninvited noises made by outside agitators.

This reception is a small, though hardly fatal, disappointment.

At the same time, all this commotion has occurred very recently; the several extinctions and reincarnations of the Colorado grizzly go back only forty years. I can trace most of this history within my own lifetime in the American West.

Thirty years ago, I was a geology student living in south-central Colorado. I had heard about the Colorado grizzly in the usual way I learned about exotic wildlife items, in men's magazines, the *Argosy*s and *True*s of my youth. These last big bears lived somewhere between truth and fiction, unmistakably bigger than life and in the same plausible category as buried treasure and lost gold mines. In 1964 I was working alone doing geological mapping on the west slope of the Sangre de Cristo Mountains above the Great Sand Dunes of the San Luis Valley. Every day I'd scramble up an arid ridge to the thirteen-thousand-foot crest of the range and drop down another to my camp at ten thousand feet. I lived there parts of four months and never saw a human away from camp. I was twenty-one years old and in love with the Rocky Mountains.

The only problem with the place was that it was too dry for quality trout fishing. For that, I'd pack up my flyrod, jump in my jeep, and drive the hundred miles to the San Juan Mountains. I fished the Weminuche Wilderness, near Wolf Creek Pass, and the Needle Mountains farther west. These were the places, according to my magazines, where the Colorado grizzly might still live. Once, in Chicago Basin, I saw bear tracks, big bear tracks about ten inches long, big enough to be a grizzly bear, though in those days I couldn't tell griz tracks from black bear. All the same, the possibility was mythical.

I hung on—the way you cling to a childhood dream—to a chance of grizzlies in Colorado during the late sixties. It carried the potential of legend. In Vietnam, I looked at pictures of Colorado and imagined—again and again, almost daily, in and out of monsoonal seasons for well over a year—the grizzly that might still roam there.

By the 1970s, rumors of grizzlies in Colorado had been demoted to a category beneath actual hope, like stories about Big Foot or Yeti. Wildlife experts in the state and federal agencies had written off the big bear in Colorado. By the end of that decade, I had taken up the cause of grizzlies myself. Every year of the seventies, I visited southern Colorado, passing through to fish, backpack, or visit an Indian ruin but never for a minute seriously expecting to encounter a real griz.

In 1979 a man named Ed Wiseman killed an old, female grizzly in the south San Juan Mountains of Colorado—it was a murky story full of half-truths and loose ends that would dangle inconclusively for fifteen years until Dave Petersen sorted it out. Still, we always knew the bear part of the story was true.

After that, nothing much happened. The Division of Wildlife undertook two futile years of the usual baiting and trapping; then it declared the big bear nonexistent, and the Colorado grizzly faded away once again.

The 1980s, like the presidency that defined it, slept. An occasional rumor of a Colorado grizzly would surface, but, not unlike Sasquatch, no one took it seriously. Toward the late '80s, the frequency of bear reports increased, especially from the south San Juan Mountains. I listened. Artist Martin Ring of Longmont, Colorado, sent me photographs of bear sign. In September 1990, we took a trip and found a bear track that didn't look like that of a black bear.

The rest of the story is told in *Ghost Grizzlies*.

• • •

Dealing with these last surviving grizzlies will require new attitudes among both citizens and game managers because these bears are different. For ordinary residents of southwestern Colorado (or anywhere else), having grizzlies around means renewed alertness, a reawakening to the possibility of other worlds and orders—even dangers. It also means stopping our agriculture at the fence line. In practical terms, this means resisting the extension of a road up the last pristine valley or a trail up into the last untouched basin. It means keeping wild pockets everywhere, even in our backyards, even if we no longer have the big mammals to fill them. Living in grizzly country requires a sort of modesty, an enforced humility. In short, having griz means humans must collectively back off, ceasing our endless domestication of the natural world.

How do we legislate the return of the largest carnivore and most uncontrollable omnivore on the North American continent in this day of aggressive wildlife management and closely administered ecosystems? After all, what Colorado has done all this time is merely keep the door to wildness open—by design or otherwise—by maintaining a blank spot on the map and simply reserving a wild pocket big enough to allow the legends to endure—Faulkner's swamp on the north bank of the Tallahatchie River, the Cabeza Prieta Desert, the Bob Marshall Wilderness, the Shiawassee River Flats of my boyhood: a wilderness of land and mind big enough for the last outlaw bear to hang out, a place for an old renegade to gear up for another legendary raid.

This sort of landscape is hard to come by using conventional land-management theory. Most of what contributes to blank spots on maps is benign neglect. Government agencies aren't good at this; passive management and nonintervention produce few jobs and smaller paychecks. If we give such wastelands undue attention by designating them as "Parks" or "Wildernesses," we necessarily hype the areas. The itch of public curiosity is scratched, and the places get far more attention than they deserve. In Colorado, occupied grizzly habitat has included large private holdings where the owners are sufficiently wealthy or independent to be able to leave the land alone and not squeeze every last grazing or timber nickel out of it.

• • •

Colorado is, in the conventional view, western Middle America, everyone's safe notion of a woodsy backyard, a tame, scenic place to ski and hike as opposed to a wild fortress of formidable beasts like wolves and bears. Most people consider the backcountry of Colorado quite "civilized." Yet the potential is there, lying dormant just under the skin of scenery; Colorado's pine forests aren't paved (like much of Michigan's) nor its prairies plowed under (like Kansas's). What goes on in Colorado would be a microcosm of the entire country and could be a model for all the world: this time, the focus of this change would necessarily be regional ecosystems valued for their own sake, not as resources for humans. In other words, the mere recognition that a grizzly could survive in southwestern Colorado will necessitate changes in attitudes, which will require government agencies and citizens alike to regard portions of Colorado as true wilderness habitat where that last big bear may yet roam.

The untaming of nature, despite the inflexibility of our Western minds and mind-boggling practical problems of land ownership and agency jurisdiction, is nonetheless doable. Western cultural taboos against dismantling the assembled or the materialistic worship of concrete monoliths are not sacrosanct. The blowing of dams, razing of human structures, tearing up of roads, acquiring passage down riparian bottoms or ridges for wildlife migratory corridors, or movement over or under interstate highways is something that could be done. We have the necessary science, biology and engineering.

But even with our advanced technology, restoring wildness is a leap of mind, because it entails fighting to protect the nonagricultural rights of wild animals. This means recognizing that creatures such as wolves and bears have valid worlds and rights beyond our own convenience, that surviving remnants of wolves in Mexico and grizzlies in Colorado exist in defiance of our will and are not passive creatures. Our culture does not yet know why these creatures evolved to what they are and why they continue to exist as survivors. What is clear is that an ancient wisdom is yet at large on the land. The native wildlife of Colorado has been slowly sculpted by natural forces through millennia to fit into the land they lived in, the land we now live in. They were not shoehorned into the habitat by hybrid geneticists. They live apart from our barnyard selections and thus preservation of remnant populations should take precedent over human-stocked reintroductions. The evolutionary and genetic future of native species resides in these wild survivors.

This requisite human value system—sometimes called "biocentric" as opposed to "anthropocentric"—that demonstrates reverence for all life and respects the rights of other species, will be adopted not out of the altruism of our fine breeding but because it is the only way we modern humans can hang on to a life worth living without paving the planet, the sole option for sustaining quality life compatible with entire self-regulating ecosystems and, sometimes, the big, even dangerous animals who also live there, who on occasion kill, injure, or eat human beings and their livestock. In short, it's the only cultural option for sharing the land we live on with grizzly bears.

Welcoming the grizzly back to its homeland in the southern Rocky Mountains is not a pipe dream; it should be seen as part of a practical and feasible process to restore a large section of Colorado to its former biological glory. This means having all the fauna that was present in 1850 again ranging free in southwestern Colorado, including wolves, grizzlies, bison, wolverines, and lynx. These animals would occupy core wilderness areas surrounded by buffer areas of public and private lands linked by travel corridors moving around pockets and communities of human beings.

Modern humans are part of this fauna, and the project of restoring wildness to Colorado will become the "social experiment" Yellowstone National Park has constantly claimed for itself. (This will free Yellowstone to raze those numerous centers of industrial tourism, rid itself of vast parking lots, and become the Denali it should be.)

The return of these legends will stretch our minds. The dream can be here, now.

—Doug Peacock
Cabeza Prieta

PREFACE

November already, and the little death of winter has descended upon the San Juans. Since last night, two heavy wet feet of snow have fallen here in the southwestern Colorado high country, hiding the sun and hazing the last holdout bears into their winter dens. This morning, the thermometer shivered at nineteen degrees.

The snow and cold and abbreviated days have likewise abruptly ended my summer's wilderness roamings and chased me into my own winter den, such as it is—an eight-by-twelve storage shed insulated against the cold and pressed into service as a poor man's study; after this clumsy fashion I imitate the bears, who drag warming mattresses of grass and evergreen boughs into their grottoes. For the next five months or so, I am destined to huddle within these confines and scribble, even as the bears sleep, snore, and dream their wild dreams of "lumbering flatfooted over the tundra," as Galway Kinnell so poetically envisions the essence of grizzly bearness.

In his wilderness classic *Grizzly Years,* my friend Doug Peacock wryly observes that grizzly bear experts these days seem to outnumber grizzly bears. Unfortunately, there's an ironic truth to that statement, prompting me to claim no such academic expertise. At best, I am a bug-eyed student of wild nature, a chaser after its slippery truths.

In the past handful of years, the controversy surrounding the ghost grizzlies of Colorado has escalated from mere rhetorical gainsaying to an ironfisted clash of worldviews. As a full-time resident of the rural San Juan Mountains for many years now, I realized some time ago that here was a story in need of exploring, in need of telling. (It is a story, in fact, so close to home and heart that I simply could not *not* tell it.) Moreover, a great deal of unrecorded, or incompletely and erroneously recorded, grizzly lore still lives hereabouts—oral history with one foot in the grave and doomed, like the San Juan grizzlies themselves, to be lost for eternity if not soon preserved.

Researching this book has been an adventure of discovery, its writing unfolding an event, a trip, a conversation, a chapter at a time and reflecting, I hope, the parallel unfolding of my knowledge, understanding, and views.

Even so, some old-line rural westerners and agency employees, a few of them my friends, may take umbrage at my criticisms of (to offer one example of many) the Forest Service's antiquated, myopic, and unsustainable policy of "multiple use"—a neat little euphemism comprising such decidedly un-neat forest uses as overlogging, overgrazing, sloppy mining, rampant road building, and a litany of boisterous human recreational activities. Similarly, some ranchers, sheepmen in particular, may hold my views of their self-hallowed "traditional western lifestyle" in high scorn. Likewise, some hunters and outfitters, many friends among them, may attack my vigorous endorsement of the recent public condemnation (by vote) of the more egregious aspects of bear "hunting" in Colorado, even as indiscriminate enemies of all hunting will damn my defense of this basically honorable activity.

And fair enough. As my late friend Ed Abbey was wont to say, "If there's anyone still present whom I've failed to insult, I apologize."

San Juan Mountains, Colorado
November 1994

ACKNOWLEDGMENTS

Clarke Abbey, Bruce Baizel, Rick Bass, Tom Beck, Carl Brandt, Cary Carron, Glen Eyre, Cheri Jones, Rick Kahn, Albert LaFarge, Jack Macrae, Rick McIntyre, John Murray, Doug Peacock, Caroline Petersen, Bill Romme, Bob Rouse, Mike Schlarb, Dennis Schutz, Dennis Sizemore, Tim Thier, Jim Tolisano, Arthur Trujillo, Jim Webb, Neal Wedum, Ernie Wilkinson, Ed Wiseman . . . each of these good folk has helped in some significant way to bring this bear of a project to bay, and I thank you all most sincerely.

The prospect of acknowledging the many others who have helped is quite simply overwhelming—the list is that long. To all of you (and you know who you are), I say . . . thank you, friends.

Finally, I'd like to acknowledge *Backpacker, Bugle, High Country News, Northern Lights, Touring America,* and *Wilderness* magazines, in whose pages bits of this book took seminal form.

*Where there was wildness, there was
possibility, chance, genuine life full of promise
and risk and perplexing uncertainty.*

—Harry Middleton

PRELUDE

*Some of life's most exciting moments are
spent near the middle of the food chain
rather than on the top.*

—Richard Nelson

JUNE 1988: YELLOWSTONE NATIONAL PARK

Just after daylight this morning, photographer Branson Reynolds and I
put on Yellowstone Lake at Sedge Bay, our canoe stuffed to the gunwales
and beyond with backcountry supplies. In a lazy morning of paddling,
including a couple of brief stops for short exploratory hikes into the dark
forest, we made about ten miles along the 140-square-mile lake's unroaded eastern shore.

It was late afternoon by the time we landed and made camp here at
Park Point. Tomorrow, we plan to paddle another ten miles or so to Trail
Creek, near the outlet of the Yellowstone River. Ranging out from a base
camp there, we hope to spend several days observing and photographing
moose and other wildlife.

But just now, with the western horizon darkening from gilt to lavender, we're growing a little concerned that we may get a somewhat
closer look at one particular species of Yellowstone wildlife than we've
bargained for.

Of course, we've known from the conception of this little adventure
that the remote Southeast Arm of Yellowstone Lake is grizzly country,
especially this time of year. Still, the chance of meeting with the great
shy bear is slight—a chance, we figured, worth taking. After all, the
opportunity to place oneself in real peril of being mauled, mangled, and

possibly even eaten by a wild animal is rare these emasculated days. Horrifying as it may seem, being made to feel like potential prey is a vitally humbling connection with our species' evolutionary memory. The grizzly is atavism incarnate, and going unarmed into grizzly country is always an adventure.

"Plenty of griz in there," I'd been told by Tom Murphy, a world-class outdoor photographer who lives near the park and leads commercial photo safaris into the Yellowstone backcountry, "but you're not likely to see one."

Just now, with darkness folding the world in close around us, *not* seeing an approaching grizzly is precisely our concern. Somehow, Branson and I, a couple of self-styled rugged outdoor types, have been led through an insidious transition from casual confidence to creeping paranoia since arriving at the park a couple of days ago.

It was probably unwise to reread Stephen Herrero's authoritative and unsettling *Bear Attacks* just before embarking on this little voyage. ("The bear dragged Barbara's body about two hundred feet down a steep bank into heavy alder undergrowth and began to eat it.") That was the start, I guess, though real doubts didn't settle in until yesterday, during our visit to the Lake Ranger Station where we were obliged to stop for boating, fishing, and backcountry camping permits.

When the ranger there learned we were headed here to Park Point and beyond, he studied us for a long moment, as if to fix our features in memory in case he might later be called on to identify our mangled remains, and then volunteered the exciting news that a grizzly sow with cubs had been sighted at Park Point within the last couple of days. Other bears were said to be operating in that area as well.

The ranger then cautioned us to take the standard bear-country camping precautions: suspend all food from a tree well above the ground, camp at least a hundred yards upwind of the food cache, avoid getting fish or food odors on our bodies or clothing, keep a clean camp, no food in the tent, et cetera. Old news, all of this—until he added, "And don't leave the immediate area of your camp."

That was a bit much. "Why not?" I asked.

"Fish," the ranger answered. "Yellowstone cutthroat trout are spawning in the mouths of the creeks that empty into the lake all along the Southeast Arm. And the grizzlies are there in numbers to feed on them, using the Thorofare trail as a runway from creek to creek. We've had to close the trail to hikers. Looks like it'll be just you two fellows and the bears up there."

Well, we do hate crowds.

More unsettling news came that same evening over dinner at Canyon Lodge, where we bumped into an acquaintance of Branson's, a tall, trail-grimy park wrangler just returned from the vicinity of our destination. Branson's dusty cowboy friend eagerly informed us that grizzly activity was so intense in the Trail Creek area, where we planned to make our base camp, that a trail maintenance crew of a dozen workers he'd packed in the day before had just radioed a request for immediate evacuation.

The wrangler went on to explain that special precautions such as the closing of the hiking trail paralleling the lakeshore, the impending evacuation of the work crew, and our being warned not to wander from camp were intended not so much to protect people from bears but to protect bears from people.

"The grizzlies need those fish, and they don't need people disturbing them," he concluded.

Right. Fair enough. No argument.

"But why, then," I probed, "are they letting us go in there at all?"

"Beats me," offered the cowboy, grinning broadly now. "Guess they figure two unarmed guys in a canoe present no significant threat to the grizzlies."

Certainly not. No threat whatsoever. Not to the grizzlies.

Finally, while enjoying a break at the mouth of Clear Creek during our paddle in this morning, far enough along the closed hiking trail for it to come as a surprise, up strolled a lone park ranger. The clean-cut fiftyish gent explained that he was staying in a patrol cabin just around the next bend in the lakeshore, tending a fish-counting trap. He had heard our canoe grinding over the beach gravel as we landed, then our voices; fishing was prohibited in the spawning creeks, and he'd come to check us out.

"Where you fellows headed?" he asked.

"Park Point tonight."

The ranger's relaxed smile sagged to an official scowl. "Best watch out for grizzlies. One grumpy old sow has made a nuisance of herself around there the past three summers, barging in and rooting around for food, treeing campers."

Pause for effect, underscored by a meaningful look.

"But don't let that spoil your fun. Chances are you won't see her."
Yes. Chances are.

And so it is, after having been force-fed all this discomfiting food for thought, our imaginations now are working overtime and our worries waxing as the daylight wanes.

Against official proscription, Branson and I decide to take a little evening stroll to see what lies within the nearby forest. After we've wormed our way a quarter mile or so into the lovely gloom, we come to the off-limits Thorofare trail. A long, narrow sedge meadow typical of the Yellowstone backcountry opens beyond the trail. We inspect the trail, looking for fresh grizzly tracks, but see only horseshoe prints headed out. We are surprised and a bit disappointed not to spot elk or deer or even a family of bears feeding nearby.

We return to camp.

In the remaining daylight, Branson assesses nearby trees for climbability, then wanders down to the lakeshore to collect enough driftwood for a prolonged fire. Meanwhile, I begin a nervous watch with my big, light-sensitive binoculars, scanning the shadowy edges of the forest down the lakeshore from where our camp is set, a hundred yards or so up from the water.

Watching, I'm overtaken by a childish bogeyman fantasy in which a growling Pleistocene monster emerges from the darkling forest and shambles toward me as I lie sleepless beneath the stars. His nostrils are flared, his lips drawn back in a hungry snarl, and I hear the metallic clacking of ivory teeth and feel hot ursine breath washing foul across my sleepy face. I burst in panic from my sleeping bag and dash for the nearest tree. Nearing safety, I leap for the trunk and climb. But not quite fast enough; I gasp in pain as finger-length claws rip deep into the flesh of my trembling legs, dragging me down . . . down.

No good, thinking this way! I kindle a generous fire, turn my back to the mounting flames, and resume my nervous watch.

Too soon, like a self-fulfilling prophecy, I spot a blur of movement close along the dark tree line near the lakeshore, maybe seventy yards to the south. I strain to see but can determine only that something big is out there, moving slowly our way.

Ho boy.

I alert Branson, who reconfirms the location of his refuge tree. I move away from the fire, out into the shadows for a better look. There I focus my binoculars and see . . . a lovely little mule deer doe, nibbling at dandelion flowers glowing an eerie gold in the failing light.

Total darkness engulfs us. Now even my low-light optics are useless. Branson and I hunker close to the fire and exchange bear-scare stories from Herrero's book, as if such verbal bravado will somehow protect us. Time passes.

By and by, the moon makes a show—a fat yellow orb waxing toward fullness, shining bright as hope through scattered clouds. It sheds no direct light on us, though, since our camp lies back within the dark forest's edge. Cold, insouciant waves rattle rhythmically against the gravelly lakeshore. Eventually, conversation gives way to private thought, leaving our ears free to prowl the invisible void beyond our little cave of firelight.

Sometime past midnight, Branson leans back and gives in to sleep. I am left alone with my timid and self-deprecating thoughts, feeling small and weak, my he-manhood seriously challenged. What would friend Peacock (he who goes fearless amongst the grizzlies) say if he could see me now? Damn glad he can't.

The fire flares and pops. Branson snores softly. Bats circle the flickering perimeter of light. The long night grinds on. No bears show.

Come morning, I feel relief and something akin to disappointment. Still, I know that with the next darkness, and the next, the same unreasonable, unfathomable, wholly primal *fear* will return—a fear made instinctive through thousands of generations of humans huddled close in the fastness of the timeless night . . . listening, listening.

But I know also that in the coming weeks, back home in the beautiful but comparatively boring San Juan Mountains of southwestern Colorado, I will think back on this experience with grateful nostalgia and cross my fingers for the continued existence and prosperity in the lower forty-eight of North America's most beautiful monster, *Ursus arctos horribilis.*

1

"WHERE THE
LAST GRIZZLIES ROAM"

The San Juan Grizzly Project

On a postcard-perfect Colorado evening in June 1991, in a wooded grove of a private ranch situated midway between Wolf Creek Pass and the bustling tourist village of Pagosa Springs, a stout, scruffy man in his late forties addresses an equally scruffy audience gathered round a pine-scented campfire.

Douglas Arapaho Peacock—writer, documentary filmmaker, and a leading authority on the behavior of grizzly bears—addresses a dozen or so listeners, among them wildlife biologists, a conservation ecologist, an attorney, ranchers, outfitters, and journalists.

Speaking quietly, Peacock says that information gathered with his own eyes during recent treks into the remotest backcountry of the south San Juans, and bolstered by a muscular body of "external" evidence, has convinced him that a remnant population of native grizzly bears still exists hereabouts.

While I would never second-guess Peacock's sixth sense for grizzlies, which verges on the preternatural, what he is proposing here strikes me initially as . . . well, maybe just a little too hopeful.

After all, as recently as the early 1980s, the Colorado Division of Wildlife's bear biologist, Tom Beck, spent two summers directing a search for grizzlies in the south San Juans. The Beck study had been necessitated when a healthy adult grizzly sow was killed by, and had almost killed, a local hunting outfitter named Ed Wiseman in the South

San Juan Wilderness in 1979. The Beck study turned up "lots of black bears but no grizzlies," and that has been the official Division stance on the matter ever since.

Tom Beck had concluded his "Job Final Report" by suggesting that his crew's "failure to catch a grizzly bear does not mean a definite absence of bears." Beck recommended that the Division assume that a few grizzlies might be left and take at least modest precautions to protect them: minimize human disturbances in the most likely grizzly redoubts, warn livestock owners and herders that grizzlies might turn up and of their protected status, advise hunters likewise. To its credit, the Division did add a brief warning to its bear-hunting brochures to the effect that killing a grizzly bear in Colorado is illegal. Yet, sending strongly mixed signals, the agency has continually assured the public that the Wiseman bear was probably the last grizzly in Colorado.

"No more grizzlies" had also been the Division's pronouncement back in 1952, when it declared the great bears extinct statewide following a centurylong campaign against large predators waged by ranchers and tax-funded government trappers working on behalf of those ranchers.

But back to the program. "In September of 1990," Peacock begins, "I made a quick search for bear sign in the south San Juans. With me on this trip were artist Martin Ring of Longmont, Colorado, and writer Rick Bass of Troy, Montana. Both of these men have extensive experience in the outdoors and with bears. We were interested in four specific sites where possible sightings of grizzlies or their sign had been recently reported.

"On September 26, we bushwhacked out of an untrailed valley at eleven thousand feet and stumbled across three sets of bear tracks. Two of the three were clearly black bear, but the third was different: a rear track measuring eight and three-quarters inches from heel to toe, with the toe prints closer together and in a straighter line than the smaller sets."

A track that size, I reflect, could belong to either a grizzly or a large black bear, of which we have plenty hereabouts, though the configuration of the toes suggests the former.

Peacock goes on to explain that within weeks of the discovery of that big grizzlyish track, a highly respected local rancher named Dennis Schutz had watched for nearly half an hour at fairly close range as a gigantic sow and three huge half-grown cubs fed and played in an alpine meadow on the ranch Schutz manages on the old Tierra Amarilla Mexican land grant, just a handful of miles below where the last "confirmed" (that is, dead) Colorado grizzly had lived. Schutz was positive they were grizzlies.

Now Peacock introduces Schutz, who summarizes his sighting for us, saying that even the three "little" bears were larger than any full-grown black bear he's ever seen in his four decades of tramping through these mountains. Back at home the evening of the sighting, he studied photos of grizzly bears in books and concluded, "Yes, that's definitely what I saw."

A week after Schutz's sighting, Glen Eyre, a Division district wildlife manager from Pagosa Springs, returned with him to the site of the observation and, sure enough, found the snow tracked with huge bear prints. Unfortunately, a herd of elk had obliterated most of the tracks, and melting had dulled the sharp edges of the few untrampled prints.

Peacock assures his audience that he firmly believes Schutz saw exactly what he says he saw, concluding that a few uncharacteristically shy native grizzlies are still likely to be hanging on, holding out "up there" —he points to the jagged wall of mountains looming like a ruined castle wall in the near south.

Having heard all this, I reflect that should it someday be proved that a few native Colorado grizzlies still exist in the wild, and if those survivors are shown to be a distinct subspecies (which many biologists feel would likely be the case), the San Juan grizzly will instantly become the most endangered mammal in North America. A very big deal. In the ensuing agency turf battles, the Colorado Division of Wildlife will at times be at odds with the U.S. Fish and Wildlife Service (FWS) over how best to handle the situation, and who best to handle it, with the U.S. Forest Service caught in the middle. Intra- as well as interagency quarrels may well erupt. Extremist animal rights groups will demand a complete shutdown of portions of the San Juans to all human activity. (In fact, based on the scantiest of evidence, one such group already has done just that.) This will put ranchers, loggers, and other businesspeople who rely on Colorado public lands for their incomes up in arms against the agencies, against the "radical environmentalists," and, by default, against the grizzly for fear that their livelihoods are at stake. And in some cases they could be.

In short, every public-lands special-interest group in the state will come howling out of the woods, a media circus will ensue, the general public as well as affected parties will become interested and involved, and the bears that started it all could easily get abandoned on the sidelines.

How much simpler for the agencies just to bury their heads and wait for the "problem" to go away on its own. Which, it would seem, is exactly what they've chosen to do all these many years.

As the editor of a Division-published wildlife magazine recently put it to me, "The Division of Wildlife has pretty much concluded that there aren't any [grizzlies left] in Colorado and the Wildlife Commission is not inclined to authorize reintroduction at this time. The bottom line is that there are other endangered species that are more likely to be candidates for reintroduction in Colorado and that is where funds will be put for recovery efforts."

In other words, the topic remains officially taboo despite the almost feverish level of public interest in the status of grizzlies in Colorado.

Be that as it may, the editor's comment had raised an interesting question: Why is the state willing to attempt to restore some of its roughly two dozen other endangered species and not the grizzly? Let me count the whys: restoration programs for smaller animals—river otters, black-footed ferrets, lynx, wolverines, fish, and birds—cost less, are easier to manage, and, the biggie, don't threaten economic interests, including especially grazing, logging, and commercial recreation.

And why is it that the governor-appointed advisory board known as the Colorado Wildlife Commission "is not inclined to authorize [grizzly] reintroduction at this time"? Could it have anything to do with the fact that the Commission—which sets the policies the Division must follow—traditionally is heavily stacked with representatives of the livestock industry? From a Commission resolution unanimously adopted in 1982:

WHEREAS, the growth of the human population has impinged upon the habitat needed by the grizzly bear and the gray (timber) wolf within Colorado, and

WHEREAS, any introduction of wolves or grizzly bear is in potential conflict with huntable species of wildlife, the livestock industry, and the human welfare, and

WHEREAS, a population of gray (timber) wolves or grizzly bear introduced into Colorado could become a management problem, when not contained within its designated management area, and,

> WHEREAS, the human welfare, and the value of Colorado's live-
> stock and wildlife resources is of considerable importance,
> NOW THEREFORE BE IT RESOLVED, that the Colorado Wild-
> life Commission hereby establishes and declares its opposition to
> . . . the introduction of either the gray (timber) wolf or the griz-
> zly bear as free-roaming populations within the State of Colorado.

Even without the Commission's opposition to anything remotely smelling of grizzlies or wolves, the Division's reluctance to champion the grizzly bear in Colorado is understandable. Why, the agency bosses must be thinking, should they invite the political headaches, financial burden, and federal meddling attendant to enforcing Endangered Species Act protections for, and trying to recover, the grizzly bear in yet another western state?

Enter Doug Peacock—demonstrating again why he has become for many the St. Jude of environmentalism, the patron saint of apparently hopeless causes—who vows to help concerned citizens do what he feels the Division and the FWS should have been doing all along. The time has come, Peacock tells his campfire listeners, for a Colorado grizzly hunt.

"The importance of this search," he says in closing, "has as much to do with the future and the quality of Colorado wilderness as it does with trying to prove the existence of a few grizzly bears in the San Juans. At the heart of this project lies an insistence that Colorado's wildness command greater respect from those who manage her lands and natural resources.

"In the national mind there lingers an image of the backcountry of Colorado as a recreational landscape as opposed to a biological treasure. Consequently, southwestern Colorado has considerable areas of 'desig- nated wilderness' with too little wild left in them; official government- built and unofficial outfitter-cut trails penetrate nearly every basin and drainage. In terms of real wilderness potential, and as a reservoir of wild biodiversity, Colorado is a shadow of its former self.

"I believe it's time for the American public to stamp its mark on the wildlands of Colorado. The recognition that a grizzly could survive in today's southwestern Colorado will necessitate changes in attitudes prompting government agencies and citizens alike to regard the San

Juans as true wilderness habitat, where the last Colorado grizzlies may yet roam."

Thus was born the San Juan Grizzly Project.

Over the following months, Peacock—a man with many irons in many fires—having kicked the ball into play, gradually backed off to a position others in the group jokingly but respectfully describe as "spiritual leader." Active control of the San Juan Grizzly Project (SJGP) now rests with the nonprofit education and research group Round River Conservation Studies, headquartered in Salt Lake City.

Round River was founded and is headed by bear biologist Dennis Sizemore, the man who first piqued Peacock's interest in the fate of the San Juans' ghost grizzlies. Round River's board of directors includes Sizemore, New Mexico ecologist Jim Tolisano, Pagosa Springs rancher and environmental attorney Bruce Baizel, and Doug Peacock. In addition to the Colorado grizzly, Round River is investigating the status of the Mexican wolf in southern Arizona, the jaguar in Costa Rica, cougars in the canyon country of southeastern Utah, and clear-cutting in British Columbia's coastal rain forests.

Also deserving of credit is Betty Feazel, matriarch of an old-line Pagosa-area Quaker family and owner of the ranch where Peacock's organizational meeting took place and which now serves as the primary staging area for all SJGP expeditions. Betty believes in the existence of the great bears and wants them here badly enough to have formed a happy alliance with scruffy, foul-mouthed intellectual Peacock and his like-minded crew of conservationist cohorts.

Anyone who follows the Project comes quickly to realize that it is driven by more than merely a desire to prove that grizzlies still roam the San Juans, more even than a wish to preserve those unique animals. It is, bottom line, a commitment to help protect the mountainous ecosystem that has allowed so feared, misunderstood, and ultimately delicate a species as the grizzly to survive with near invisibility all these years.

There will be resistance.

On the whole, westerners view our public lands not as precious preserves of beauty, biological diversity, and national pride but merely as a resource to be chain-sawed, blasted, and grazed for profit and, in leisure hours, a place to hunt, fish, tear around on dirt bikes, ATVs, and snowmobiles, and otherwise indulge in raucous, often destructive play.

Grizzly bears are anathema to this sagebrush-scented, fiercely anthro-pocentric, "people first" worldview.

Another concern for Round River is that if and when the agencies ever acknowledge the existence of living San Juan grizzlies, among their first acts will be to send in platoons of research biologists to bait, trap, radio-collar, and electronically hound-dog any and every grizzly they can find—exactly as the Division had hoped to do in the early 1980s. Their justification will be to "document the range, activities, and critical habitat of the endangered population, so that sound management deci-sions can be formulated," or some such.

Round River counters that we already know, close enough for gov-ernment work, the bounds of the habitat supporting any remaining griz-zlies—the South San Juan Wilderness, the Tierra Amarilla, perhaps a few isolated pockets of the Weminuche Wilderness and contiguous national forest, private and Indian tribal lands.

While hands-on monitoring may be necessary to protect both bears and people in places such as Yellowstone and Glacier country, where large numbers of these competing dominant species are concentrated on the same restricted turf, such drastically intrusive measures seem unnec-essary, even detrimental, here in the San Juans. Experience shows that handled bears are disadvantaged bears. After being snared, tranquilized, pricked, probed, ear-tagged, lip-tattooed, radio-collared, and released, those animals that survive the ordeal will no longer be the ultimately wild, supremely secretive creatures they now are. They will have been technologically raped, demystified, their anonymity stolen away, their very grizzlyness impoverished.

These and other obstructions notwithstanding, as soon as the high-mountain snows allowed backpack access following Peacock's June 1991 organizational meeting, the San Juan Grizzly Project got down to busi-ness. Employing a small crew of enthusiastic, if loosely organized, volun-teer searchers, SJGP began combing promising corners of the South San Juan Wilderness and the Tierra Amarilla for grizzly spoor. It was a start.

By the summer of 1992, the volunteers had been replaced by an equally enthusiastic but much better organized team working under the leadership of an experienced professional. For one exhilarating week, I was a tagalong member of that team.

2

THE SEARCHERS

Afield with the San Juan
Grizzly Project

As I scribble these notes, I'm sprawled indolently amid wildflowers and
lichen-stained rocks beneath a warm turquoise sky, looking out across
the headwaters canyon of the "White"—a stream whose identity I dis-
guise out of respect for the privacy of the place and its wild inhabitants. I
am thoroughly enjoying the unsullied solitude and unmolested scenery
only untrailed wilderness can provide. As befits such an earthly heaven,
getting here was not at all easy.

On the topographic maps, the hike into this subalpine redoubt looks
like a cakewalk: a short stroll along an almost level Forest Service trail, a
ford of the narrow White, a gently undulating side-hill bushwhack a few
miles upstream to the confluence of a feeder creek near the White's
headwaters, ford again, hump the far slope . . . home.

So easy appeared the hike on paper, in fact, and so swollen was my
ex-Marine, mountain-man machismo that I was mildly miffed to learn
that Jim Tolisano would be hiking down from the San Juan Grizzly
Project base camp to guide me and three others in.

I'd spoken with Tolisano briefly at Peacock's Pagosa congress the
previous summer, quickly sizing him up as a likable fellow with credentials aplenty for his job as Round River's field director: master's degree in

forest and watershed management; contract forest ecology researcher for the U.S. Forest Service, United Nations, USAID, Peace Corps, World Wildlife Fund. And more.

A dark, compact man hardened by a life lived actively out of doors, Tolisano greeted us amiably and led out briskly: loping upstream along a gravelly riverbank, winging over a foaming white-water race on a spray-slicked blowdown log, scrambling up a near-vertical scree slope, striding down and huffing back up half a dozen steep lateral drainages—a very brief breather—then a final plummeting switchback descent down a muddy elk trail into the rocky bowels of what had become a mini–Grand Canyon of a river gorge, a numbing-cold ford of the swift, knee-deep headwaters, a rope-assisted ascent of the facing cliff wall . . . and we'd arrived.

In point of fact, it had been a long, breathless, sweat-soaked day of double-time scrambling over terrain that held no resemblance whatsoever to the Pollyanna stroll the topo map had seemed to promise. My forty-six years, moderate Camel habit, and fifty-pound pack hadn't made it any easier. No bloody mosquitoes, though; guess they couldn't take the lightning, thunder, wind, and hail that dogged us most of the way. Or maybe they just couldn't keep up. Some cakewalk.

In the long view from where I now sit—looking a mile or so to the south, across the gaping, water-eroded gorge of the White—rises a chalky wall of naked sedimentary cliff striped here and there with platinum ribbons of falling water. Above each fall a brief, sparkling brook issues from a patch of shaded snow. The raw beauty of this place is heartbreaking.

Behind me, Tolisano's camp—a few scattered tents and a communal fire circle set at the edge of a big mountain park—is surrounded by a mixed old-growth forest of spruce, fir, ponderosa pine, and quaking aspen. This ecotonal wildlife paradise is situated within the busy overlap between the montane life zone below and the subalpine above.

Amid such splendor, I've passed much of my time here prowling the shadowy forests, alone mostly, searching for bear spoor. With the thought that even one last grizzly could be haunting this remote place, these familiar old "safe San Juans" have taken on a whole new excitement.

Safe *south* San Juans, to be specific. The Forest Service has chosen, for administrative purposes, to split the San Juan Mountains into two forests

—the Rio Grande on the east, the San Juan on the west—with the generally north-south meander of the Continental Divide scrawling the dividing line. Locals take it one step farther and use the east-west blacktop of U.S. Highway 160 over Wolf Creek Pass to separate the south San Juans from the San Juans proper.

And truly, they are two different places. The southern mountains are somewhat lower (thus less glaciated), more vulcanized (thus less mineralized and mine scarred), less alpine, wetter, less lacerated by roads and trails (thus more remote and inaccessible), less popular among outdoor enthusiasts because they have fewer big parks and lakes and fourteeners and other such photogenic destinations.

In all, the south San Juans are more compact, less accessible, less well known, less peopled, and in every way generally less messed-over than the northern mountains. And this 159,100-acre South San Juan Wilderness—loosely circumscribed by the towns of Pagosa Springs to the west, South Fork on the north, Platoro eastward, and Chromo in the south—is the vibrant heart of the place.

The balmy June morn has matured into a warm afternoon perfect for bear hunting. Into my day pack I toss snacks, canteen, flashlight, compass, topographic map, notebook, and several zippered plastic bags.

I slip out of camp and move quietly up a wildflower-carpeted mountain slope. A light breeze puffs warm and sweet in my face, florid as Grandma's garden. On this trip so far, I've identified lipstick-red Indian paintbrush, several varieties of flowering vetch (bear food), giant cow parsnips with huge compound umbels of tiny white blossoms (bear food), mountain bluebells (bear food), harebells, long-legged Rocky Mountain iris, knee-high bouquets of purple lupine, candy-striped Richardson's geraniums, low-slung spring beauties (bear food), delicate crimson columbines, a single clutch of ephemeral fairy slippers (also called Calypso orchids, among the rarest and most lovely of conifer-forest wildflowers), wild strawberries (bear food), Wyeth biscuitroot (bear food), droopy-headed virgin's bower (like the Flying Nun with a hangover), monkshood, plus at least a dozen more whose names I do not know.

It's a bruin's Garden of Eden up here—a veritable supermarket for bears. Notwithstanding all the fierceness the grizzly can muster as a predator, it is primarily an omnivore, an opportunistic forager whose diet consists overwhelmingly (roughly 90 percent) of greens. And the majority of what little meat grizzlies do eat comes from insects and carrion. In addition to the rich forage, these relatively unmolested mountain slopes offer abundant thermal and hiding cover and plenty of fresh running water.

Abundant food, clean water, thick cover for hiding and thermal protection, room to roam—the Big Four of productive wildlife habitat and balanced ecologies.

After walking quietly for some time, nearing the top of the undulating slope, just below a battlement of conglomerate rimrock, I encounter a huge downfallen spruce with its rotted guts ripped out—the debris of a bear's calamitous search for ants, larvae, and other bits of squirming protein. I inspect the broken wood and the ground nearby but can find no bear hair or scats. Damn the luck. What with all the booty Tolisano and his crew are bagging daily, I, the self-styled local Old Man of the Mountains, don't necessarily wish to return to camp crapless. (Bear hair, not scats, is what the searchers ultimately are after. But scats are a lot easier to spot and frequently contain hairs ingested during self-grooming or attached as the scat makes its exit.)

Finished with my fruitless log inspection, I glance around and spot a wide place in a game trail traversing the slope just below. I move down for a closer look. It's a bed all right, but what manner of beast has rested here I can't rightly say. There is, however, one intriguing clue: a single, age-bleached deer leg bone projects upright from the front edge of the bed, as if it had been stabbed into the soft duff there. Odd. I've seen hundreds of beds and bones in dozens of forests, but this intriguing combination is a new one for me. I extract the bone and examine it; the dark stains on the lower portion indicate that it has been thus situated for a good long while.

I replace the little monument (to what?) and move on, following the game trail along the sidehill.

Just yards farther on I spy another bed, this one perched on a narrow shelf just below the game runway. Rising like a backrest from this bed is the hollowed bole of a fallen tree, the detached trunk having found repose a ways down the slope, where it lies in rotting fecundity. On examination, I see that the punky innards of the ancient ponderosa stump have been dug out and flung downslope, creating a talus of wood chips extending several yards below.

This is, I'm betting, almost certainly a bear bed and stump excavation. Midway down the chip talus I spy a double handful of tubular black dung that looks half horse and half human, confirming my hunch. I dig into my pack for a plastic bag and ease down the slope to capture the prize—and then I spot two more of the same. (By George, bears *do* shit in the woods.)

I invert the bag and use it as a glove to retrieve the evidence, desiccated and odorless from long exposure to harsh montane elements. The dirty work done, I fish out topo map and notebook and sit down to record the coordinates and topography of the site—details I'll need back at camp to fill out an SJGP "bear occurrence report."

Done, I lean back into the slope and survey my surroundings.

The bear bed and latrine (the two tend to occur together, naturally) immediately overlook a shallow, brushy ravine—a perfect bruin travel corridor. Arcing claw marks in parallel rows of three, four, and sometimes five scar the soft white bark high up several nearby quaking aspens —the work of young black bears, the original small scars having blackened and stretched as the trees grew.

A nap ambushes me, and next thing I know, the afternoon has fairly slipped away, replaced by the gathering gloom of evening, that just-a-little-spooky twilight time when shadows grow long, the nocturnal world begins to wake, and people unaccustomed to the wilds are susceptible to the willies.

I'm rarely uneasy in the woods. But with grizzly bears on my mind continually since packing in here, these familiar old San Juans are feeling fresh and new. And just now, with the advent of evening, even a little exciting.

Nothing, of course, like the adrenaline rush attendant to backcountry travel in Yellowstone, Glacier, Canada, or bear-happy Alaska. In those places, the certain knowledge of a constant lurking grizzly presence creates a surreal twilight zone of excitement that "elevates the mountains, deepens the canyons, chills the winds, brightens the stars, darkens the forests, and quickens the pulse," as my friend John Murray so eloquently bottles the essence in his grizzly anthology *The Great Bear.*

The magic I'm feeling now is far more subtle, reflecting only a hopeful maybe. Still, I *am* feeling something different, more intense than I'm accustomed to hereabouts.

I've not been merely strolling through this ancient dark forest, but creeping around cautious as a hungry cat—striving to see without being seen, to hear without being heard, to scent without being scented, to discover without being discovered. Hunting, as it were.

Every fall, I push aside most of the rest of my life in order to become the best animal I can—an upright cougar. Armed with a simple "stick" bow (sans pulleys or other mechanical aids), handmade cedar arrows, and a level of concentration verging on religious trance, I experience an intensity of immersion in wild nature that I long believed has no equal.

The challenge in traditional bowhunting is not just to collect meat or antlers (though both are welcome rewards for the monumental effort involved); rather, the ultimate satisfaction to be found in this ancient ceremony comes from slipping cougar close, undetected, to deer or elk—the keenest self-defense mechanisms evolution and predation have ever sculpted.

Yet I have in recent years gradually become aware of a way to participate actively in wild nature that's even more intense and personal than playing the predator. When I venture unarmed into grizzly country, the old familiar hunter-prey roles are upended: weaponless in grizzly country, I am no longer the lion—here, I am the deer. No other outdoor experience frightens me so thoroughly, humbles me so deeply, or makes me feel more alive and joyful than just being in grizzly wilderness.

In *Grizzly Years,* Doug Peacock writes that he needs to "confront large fierce animals that sometimes make meat of man to help recall the total concentration of the hunter. Then the old rusty senses, dulled by urban excesses, spring back to life, probing the shadows for shapes, sounds, and smells. Sometimes I am graced by a new insight into myself, a new combination of thoughts, a metaphor, that knocks on the door of mystery."

Granted, there are times—for most of us the *majority* of times—when we don't need, don't *want* the sort of knee-knocking excitement attendant to sharing the woods with six-hundred-pound walking appetites. But for such timid times we have forty-three entirely grizless contiguous states, as well as the bulk of the remaining five (Montana, Wyoming, Idaho, Washington, probably Colorado) in which to wander essentially unthreatened by nature red in tooth and claw. In such emasculated nominal wilderness, there's little more to fear than giardiasis, mosquitoes, cliffs, and the occasional wacko human.

Measured against a Glacier or a Yellowstone or a Bob Marshall Wil-

derness, the too-tame "wilderness experience" available in most of today's overgrazed, mine-poisoned, logging-road-slashed, trail-tortured,
ski-slope-scarred, condo-littered Colorado mountains is a big fat yawn.

Colorado's silver San Juans are far too sublime to languish among
that harness-broke majority. They are, in fact—as Round River biologist
Dennis Sizemore puts the case—another Yellowstone waiting for permission to happen. The bear habitat here is in fact *superior* to that in Yellowstone.

These things considered, and based on what I've seen and heard so
far, I endorse the San Juan Grizzly Project. Win or lose in their efforts to
effect an ecological salvation, important work is getting done. The educational aspect of the Grizzly Project alone, this trip has convinced me,
justifies all.

Beginning in the summer of 1992 and continuing for as many summers as necessary, small teams of highly motivated, tuition-paying student searchers will be prowling the remotest niches of this sublime old
rock pile under the auspices of Round River—hiking hard and high in
snow, rain, crashing lightning, and blistering sun, sleeping on the firm
sweet bosom of the rocky mountain earth, eating communal mush, slapping mosquitoes, making biotic maps, and collecting bear turds—the
good life.

After this rugged fashion, Round River students achieve intense
personal involvement with not only the San Juan Grizzly Project
but the San Juan ecology. And they can earn honest college credit in
the deal—provided they work hard, maintain constant good humor,
religiously attend their instructors' campfire lectures, successfully
complete an individual research or writing project, and pass a
comprehensive final exam.

Student tuition, in turn, helps to meet Round River's growing oper-
ational overhead—food, transportation, insurance, and such—plus laboratory expenses.

Success at the wildlife forensic lab, in fact, is one of SJGP's primary
interim goals. Toward that end, one of the basic activities of the searchers, myself included for these few days, is collecting bear scats. This
summer's pungent prizes—three bags of which I'm proud to have in my
pack at this very moment—will be lugged out and sun-dried, then
picked through with tweezers and magnifying glasses by students in the
biology lab at Fort Lewis College in Durango. Bear hairs thus collected

will be forwarded for species identification to a credible wildlife laboratory or two.

Analysis of the 1991 take—the work was done by the Wyoming Game and Fish Department laboratory at the University of Wyoming, Laramie—revealed that two of the submitted hair samples were "similar to known grizzly bear" hair.

Those hairs, it would seem, provide exciting physical evidence that grizzlies still roam the San Juans. But legally—given that Dr. Christopher Servheen, the federal grizzly bear recovery coordinator, has decreed that "hair by itself . . . does not constitute positive proof of grizzly bears"—they *prove* nothing.

What, then, *will* meet the test? In a May 1992 letter to SJGP, Colorado FWS supervisor LeRoy W. Carlson listed five possibilities, the first of which seems contradictory to Servheen's "hairs don't count no more" proclamation:

1. Hair positively identified by an expert as grizzly bear, particularly coupled with other proof, could be definitive.
2. A carcass would be positive proof. . . .
3. A positively identified track, verified by an expert.
4. Photographs which provide positive identification from an expert.
5. Analysis of DNA cells which provides positive identification of a grizzly bear by an expert.

Additionally, Carlson noted that "another issue which will require verification, should positive documentation of a grizzly bear occur, is to prove that the report, sample, photograph, or even carcass came from the San Juan Mountains."

That's the kicker, and it ties in directly to a worry expressed to me by Tom Moore, the Wyoming lab's senior forensic analyst and the man who literally wrote the book on wildlife hair identification. Repeatedly during our brief phone conversation, Moore used the term "highly suspect" when explaining his concern that the SJGP hair samples he identified as possible grizzly were essentially undamaged, as opposed to being crinkled and otherwise shopworn, which he supposed they should be after passing through the lengthy digestive tract of a bear. The not-so-subtle implication was clear: known grizzly hairs could have been collected elsewhere and planted among the Colorado samples.

Notwithstanding the fact that bears have exceedingly poor digestive systems and often pass plant materials essentially unmolested, and certainly could do so with hairs, I put Moore's concern to Dennis Sizemore, the Round River bear biologist who had tweezed the hairs from the '91 scats and sent them to the lab. He acknowledged that "a degree of procedural tightening-up" was necessary, especially given the political hot-potato status of the grizzly. Such tightening had already begun, he assured me, as evidenced by the fact that the '92 scats would be picked through not by Sizemore or anyone else from Round River or SJGP but by disinterested college students.

"But what about the others?" I asked Dennis, playing the critic's advocate. What about Tolisano; Peacock, who probably has buckets full of the stuff; Bass, who lives in Montana grizzly country (Rick had found one of the two '91 scats that turned out to contain likely grizzly hair); even me (I have an envelope of known Colorado grizzly hair in a file cabinet at home)? Virtually anyone who goes afield with the grizzly searchers could conceivably plant bogus grizzly hairs. How, I asked Dennis, do you put such suspicions to rest?

"There is no foolproof way to eliminate all sources of doubt," he responded. "Nor do we want to get too involved in a game of 'Yes it is/ No it isn't.' That would only drag us away from our primary goal of encouraging people to work toward maintaining the San Juans as a wild place, a balanced and healthy ecosystem. If *that* goal isn't realized soon, any grizzlies still here now won't last much longer. Frankly, I was doubtful myself when I first got involved. I had to be convinced. So will others. We accept that."

Moreover, Sizemore confided, Round River had plans to shift its emphasis from hairs to genes—mitochondria DNA. As the group's attorney, Bruce Baizel, reasons, "If the courts can put people in prison based on DNA testing, we can use the same procedures to prove the existence of living native grizzly bears in Colorado."

Yes—assuming you can raise the umpteen thousands of dollars such testing costs. Here's where the FWS could help . . . *if* they wanted to find grizzlies in the San Juans.

A shimmering tangerine twilight deepens through lavender, edging toward night. Another day's useless journey is done. Time to hike the two or three miles, all downhill, back to camp, where my fellow flop finders are probably even now assembling.

There's Rick Bass, who's spending time with Peacock, Sizemore, Baizel, and others, and writing a book about these extraordinary men and their Round River Conservation Studies; good-natured "Big George" Fischer, a restless computer software designer from Salt Lake City and a star of the '91 search, having lugged out a bulging backpackful of fresh moist bear dung, which, George admits, was "some heavy shit"; handsome, silk-voiced Scott Carrier, an audio professional here to record some "good tape" for a National Public Radio feature on SJGP; Jim Sharman, a former Peace Corps volunteer whom Tolisano met in the Philippines and adopted as his protégé; and a half-dozen student searchers (four men, two women), most of them here in eager response to a small notice placed in an environmental magazine.

I rise, pull on my pack, and slouch back down the mountain. Along the way, following a zigzag elk trail, I spot another bear pie and bag it. Like the others, it's probably the work of a black bear, but that's for the experts to determine. In any case, I've done my bit—four scats collected in one afternoon—and of that I am proud to the point of boastfulness.

But no sooner do I hit camp than I am humbled by the news that Rick Bass has upstaged not just me but the entire crew. A small crowd is gathered around the black plastic tarp upon which the expedition's entire take is spread for drying.

I kneel for a close look at the "Bass scat." The massive heap lies coiled back on itself and would fill a dinner plate. Its mild aroma suggests that its former owner has been enjoying a healthy all-veggie diet of late. (Conversely, the scats of a bear that has been feeding on meat smell like—well, like shit.) The prize fairly dwarfs all the other three dozen or so samples on the tarp and anything I've ever seen laid by a black bear.

In his characteristically quiet voice, Rick tells me that he decided today to climb to the top of a high divide we'd surveyed through binoculars while hiking together yesterday. He'd commented then that the place "looked good for bear." At 11,200 feet, he found this mother of all bear scats. Rick says that three virtually identical scats decorated one corner of that high meadow up there, much too much to lug back to camp in his day pack. And something else, too—big, alive, unidentifiable, lurking back in the trees—had stared briefly at Rick, then crashed away. He had caught only a fleeting glimpse of something big and hairy and subtly ominous.

I congratulate Rick and shuffle over to the campfire, where the crew are just finishing their one-pot supper. I have my own food and am not tempted to join them.

With the tin plates wiped, the grizzly hunters reassemble for Tolisano's evening lecture. This night, he kicks off with a review of the tenets of biodiversity, then goes on to detail the distinctions between keystone, indicator, flagship, and restoration species, concluding an hour or so later with a Socratic exploration of potential methods for awakening local folk to the unique value of the San Juan ecosystem.

While Professor Jim lectures, his serious-faced students take notes by strobing firelight, and I contemplate the lot. There's carrot-topped Dan, at nineteen the youngest member of the expedition and the only one of us who can outpace that leaping gnome Tolisano at thirty-nine; Sara, who signed on, she tells me, in order to take advantage of this unique opportunity to immerse herself simultaneously in nature and intense academics; Steve, a quiet, gentle giant of a fellow who seems to be searching for his place in the world; Beth, a Cornell student and budding artist; Chad, a sober, snuff-dipping young hunter and trapper, here in an effort, he says, to better understand the workings of nature; and barefoot Martin, at twenty-nine the most worldly of the crew.

The Project's ultimate goal, Tolisano reiterates in conclusion, is to create a popularly supported vision for the San Juans wherein a long-term conservation strategy is built into all public-lands management plans. Proving the existence of a few surviving grizzlies up here—"big, sexy critters that get people excited"—would go a long way, he and his Round River compatriots are convinced, toward exciting both local and agency support for that goal.

I'm not so confident. I fear that if those whom ecophilosopher Dave Foreman has dubbed the "bumpkin proletariat" (i.e., welfare ranchers and their Animal Damage Control flunkies, loggers, miners, and other old-line public-lands profiteers) continue to get their way, which they're accustomed to getting and plenty willing to fight for, then Round River's kinder, gentler approach to reforming wildlands management is likely to be ridden out of Colorado on a rail of derision and intimidation. Bullying to get your way, after all, is the code of the West.

But then, I must admit, local popular support for wilderness preservation has been growing hereabouts of late, strengthened by a rising tide of emigration from California and other places already spoiled by over-population and "progress." Ironically, by their very numbers and expectations, these refugees from paradise are transplanting here many of the selfsame problems they'd hoped to leave behind.

Battle lines are forming.

At a public meeting held recently at Fort Lewis College in my hometown of Durango—part of Round River's philosophy of attempting to involve locals in the action—Rick Bass told of the bitter war of wills, words, and worldviews being waged between preservationists and commodities extractionists in his adopted northwestern Montana logging community. Into the eye of the storm, Bass advised the fifty-odd San Juan locals in attendance, there has been thrust the grizzly bear—a scapegoat for much larger problems. Exactly, he cautioned, as it could become here.

"Neither side wins with hard-line confrontation," Rick warned. "Keep your channels of communication open and *don't let hate take over.*" Sound advice indeed, but division and derision are second nature to the rural western character, while objectivity and reason too often are shrouded under clouds of emotion and (perceived) financial necessity.

Sadly, when I think of grassroots support for wilderness, I think of my old friend A. B. Guthrie, Jr., the Montana philosopher and Pulitzer-winning author of *The Way West* and *The Big Sky,* a wilderness classic that gave his state its nickname and much of its fame—and his long fight for wilderness and the grizzly. As reward for his efforts, Guthrie won "local support" in the form of hometown ostracism, including—most painful —the open scorn of his own rancher son.

Nor, likely, will agency support for noneconomics-based wildlands management come much easier. I'm thinking now of the intrinsic resistance of all bureaucracies to reform. And of Dave Foreman's terrifying experience at the hands of a blindly zealous Reagan-Bush FBI, whose pistol-packing status quo enforcers swore to teach that eloquent rabble-rouser a lesson. And did. Ask Dave Foreman—one of the finest minds in the West—about "agency support" for wilderness preservation.

Even my own timid attempts to defend the natural world have generated sometimes uncomfortable heat. There are people hereabouts who have never even met me but nonetheless use my name with hatred—my reward for speaking out in support of the natural world and openly chastising its enemies. ("Criticizing the bad," advised Ed Abbey, "is our duty to the good.")

Lacking the moral courage of a Dave Foreman or a Bud Guthrie or a Doug Peacock or an Edward Abbey, I sometimes grow weary and wonder: Why make myself a pariah in my own community? Why keep on fighting an increasingly bitter and apparently losing battle to preserve a bit of the best of what little is left of the natural world?

Well, I know how old Cactus Ed would answer: "And why the hell *not?*"

3

"BRING 'EM IN, REGARDLESS OF HOW"

The Colorado Grizzly Wars

What we call the progress of Western Civilization from the ant's eye level is but the forward stride of the great exterminator.

—J. Hillman

Grizzly bears have been critically endangered for half a century in Colorado, as a result of more than a century of methodical, relentless, ruthless shooting, trapping, and poisoning—the Colorado Grizzly Wars. But for untold millennia, before the arrival of whites and our overbred, defenseless livestock, human residents of the San Juans enjoyed a relationship of mutual respect with their tooth-and-claw neighbors.

The first peoples to explore and exploit the San Juan Mountains are known today only by the generic name of Paleo-Indians. Physical evidence, including stone tools, fire pits with bits of bone, and various so ons, establishes that Paleo-Indians arrived in the Four Corners region (where Arizona, Utah, Colorado, and New Mexico meet) eleven or twelve thousand years ago, perhaps earlier. Untold generations of these intrepid ancients explored the nearby San Juans as thoroughly as the retreating ice fields of the final great glaciation would allow.

East of the Continental Divide, the San Luis Valley is virtually wrapped around by the San Juans and adjoining ranges. Here, evidence has been found of the late Clovis culture—chipped stone fragments in association with mammoth bones—dating to between 10,900 and 11,200 years ago.

Then came the Folsom habitation of the San Luis Valley and surrounding mountains, between 10,500 and 10,900 years ago, which was apparently continual during those phases when the valley wasn't flooded. The San Luis Folsom folk earned their living primarily by hunting a now-extinct species of bison near small water holes scattered throughout the valley, as evidenced by the numerous bison kill and processing sites unearthed in recent decades.

But the Folsoms also ventured high into the San Juans. Northeast of Creede, in a pass through the high divide separating the San Luis and Gunnison basins, one Folsom site has been found at an elevation of 10,900 feet. At that time, more than ten thousand years ago, that was far above timberline (which is now at about twelve thousand feet), meaning these Stone Age people were living, at least temporarily, out on the alpine tundra.

While afield with the San Juan Grizzly Project during their June 1992 exploration of the headwaters of the "White River" in the south San Juans, I crawled from my tent one morning and came face to quartzite with about two inches of the broken tip of a heavy spear or knife point. I judged it to be Folsom and returned it to the meadow grass in which it had for so very long reposed. How did the man who ventured up here armed only with stone weapons such as this perceive the grizzly? Was it a god to be revered? A monster to be feared? Most likely a mix of both.

By two thousand years ago, Archaic peoples had moved into the Four Corners. Prominent among these were the Anasazi—the name is a Navajo word with two translations: "ancient people" and "ancestral enemies." The Anasazi are thought of primarily as sedentary farmers, artful potters, and skillful stonemasons who built huge mesa-top pueblos and, later, cliff-hanging cities. But for centuries before acquiring the skills and seed that allowed them to become successful farmers (which in due time led to overpopulation, depletion of natural resources, and eventual societal bankruptcy; the old story), Anasazi hunters and gatherers probed high into the San Juans.

Dr. Phil Duke, professor of archaeology at Fort Lewis College and a widely respected authority on the Anasazi, reports that Anasazi pottery shards have been found throughout the San Juans, high and low. It is unknown whether these delicate vessels were carried into the mountains by their makers or traded to other early residents. Probably both.

Although the Anasazi made their permanent homes out on the piñon-juniper mesas and in the sandstone canyons southwest of the mountains, they established at least one major outpost in the San Juans proper. Chimney Rock is a familiar southern Colorado landmark, rising just south of U.S. Highway 160 a few miles west of Pagosa Springs. In the high saddle between Chimney Rock and a sister column, at an elevation of about 7,400 feet, the Anasazi built mysterious stone structures that scholars believe served as an observatory of significant astronomical and religious import.

Yet when I look at Chimney Rock, as I often do in passing at highway speed, I think not of Anasazi sachems and solstice ceremonies but of grizzly bears. Specifically, I am reminded of a life-size diorama tucked away in a second-floor cul-de-sac at the Denver Museum of Natural History. In this lifelike reproduction, the stuffed remains of two adult grizzlies and a tiny cub are posed in a replicated autumn meadow similar to hundreds throughout the San Juans. The smaller of the two adult bears is a fat young male killed in 1913 along the upper Navajo River in the south San Juans. In the background rises Chimney Rock, making the scene both realistic and, for those who know the country, poignant.

By the mid-1870s, whites had wrested control of the land from Indians, and the San Juans were stocked and overstocked with free-ranging cattle. Half a decade later arrived a plague of domestic sheep—the insatiable "hooved locusts" of the West. Certainly, a great many Colorado grizzlies were killed by early nineteenth-century explorers and "sportsmen." But many more were eliminated by stockmen, who viewed as their patriotic duty the pot-shooting of every "varmint" they crossed trails with. Huge and highly visible, Colorado grizzlies took a heavy hit from these insidious forms of persecution. Even so, they could and would have lasted much longer had it not been for the intercession of the federal government.

Finding the hit-and-miss process of predator eradication too slow, cattlemen and sheep ranchers banded together to post bounties on the scalps of wolves and bears, monetary bait intended to lure professional predator hunters. At the same time, the stockmen began clamoring for state and federal assistance in their war on wolves and bears. As usual, these highly organized and politically savvy businessmen got what they wanted: a bloody pogrom funded in largest part not by the stockmen it served but by federal, state, and local governments. The actual killing was carried out by professional hunters and trappers, many of them living relics of that hardy breed of wildlife exploiters we glorify today as the "mountain men."

Of that sanguine lot, Ben V. Lilly (1856–1936) was the Southwest's most infamous. Working primarily in Arizona and New Mexico, Lilly trapped or hounded to bay and killed untold scores of grizzlies. While many another "grizzly man" devoted his adult life to exterminating bears, none was so tenacious, deadly, and ultimately notorious as the eccentric Mr. Lilly. To his admirers, Lilly's skill as a hunter, his fierce independence, and his disdain for roofs and walls—he almost never slept indoors, no matter the season or weather—made him a hero. I've been unable to adopt that view.

In any event, Colorado stockmen had to do without Mr. Lilly, though they had in their service scores of his compatriots from the U.S. Fish and Wildlife Service's Predator and Rodent Control branch. PARC was, and remains today, albeit under a different name, a federal agency sworn and blindly dedicated to the extermination of predators for the perceived economic betterment of ranchers, especially sheepmen. PARC's motto—openly espoused through the middle decades of this century, covert but still operative today—was and is "Bring 'em in, regardless of how."

The PARC tradition in America stretches back to 1913, when Congress first began providing direct predator control assistance to western stockmen. In those formative days, the agency had to make do with "only" three hundred trappers.

In 1931 Congress codified the war on predators with the passage of the Animal Damage Control Act. Still in force today essentially unaltered, the act created a federal agency charged with the "eradication, suppression or bringing under control . . . of animals injurious to agriculture . . . and to conduct campaigns for the destruction or control of such animals."

Across the six decades of its existence, PARC has been known variously as the Division of Wildlife Services, Predator and Rodent Control, and, in recent years, Animal Damage Control. In 1993 ADC reverted to the earliest and most euphemistic of that titular litany, becoming once again Wildlife Services—an unpopular change, it seems, among detractors as well as supporters, with both groups clinging to the more familiar and telling title of Animal Damage Control. ADC currently operates under the Animal Plant and Health Inspection Service, a branch of the U.S. Department of Agriculture—in effect, leaving the fox to guard the chicken house.

PARC/ADC/Wildlife Service's methods of "destruction or control" of "problem" wildlife traditionally have included steel leghold traps, leg and neck snares, trailing hounds, aerial gunning, calling and shooting, and "denning" (wherein infant predators are gassed or incinerated in their dens, or snagged and dragged out with meat hooks and clubbed to death).

One particularly sadistic early antibear device was the keg trap, a favorite with amateur bear slayers as well as professionals since it could be knocked together in minutes at a cost of pennies. Dozens of spike-sized nails were driven at a downward angle into a heavy wooden beer keg. A smelly bait was dropped into the bottom and the trap placed in the woods. When a bear poked its head into the keg to whiff or take the bait, it became snagged on the spikes; the harder the trapped animal attempted to pull out, the deeper the spikes dug in. Even today, the remains of keg traps are occasionally found in Colorado, on public lands as well as private.

An infinitely more humane killer, when it finds the right target, is the "coyote-getter." The original version of this small, inexpensive, easily portable, reusable toxic cannon consisted of a tubular barrel with a baited trigger and a .38 shell with a load of cyanide in place of a bullet. When an animal bit on the bait, it was rewarded with a blast of cyanide square in the mouth. Death followed within seconds. The coyote-getter proved so useful that it was modernized, renamed the M-44, and still enjoys great popularity among ADC trappers today, though its use on national forest lands is forbidden.

This unholy love affair between PARC/ADC trappers and poisons—the nastier and more untenable the toxin, the better—prompted one writer a few years ago to nickname this brutal breed of men "toxic Johnny Appleseeds." Back when PARC/ADC was under U.S. Fish and Wildlife Service jurisdiction, the preferred in-house moniker was "gopher chokers."

Both shoes fit.

• • •

I walked on shore with one man. about 8. A.M.
we fell in with two brown or yellow bear; both of
which we wounded.
—from the journals of Meriwether Lewis,
Monday, April 29, 1805,
along the Missouri River

That we tend to kill the very things we most love is the message in A. B. Guthrie, Jr.'s classic saga of the early nineteenth-century mountain men, *The Big Sky,* a theme repeated in his later western novels. The mountain men of that era, beginning with the Lewis and Clark expedition, led the charge to decimate the ferocious "white bears" and "red Indians" who stood in the way of the pending white invasion. And by so doing— simply by indulging in the wild and unfettered frontier lifestyle they so loved—these men helped to kill the very frontier upon which their lifestyle depended.

Two decades before the opening of the heyday of the fur trappers, Lewis and Clark led an expedition of exploration up the Missouri River, through the untamed heart of present-day Montana, and on to the fog-shrouded Pacific Northwest ("Ocian in view! O! the joy!") and back again. During their twenty-eight months in the western wilderness— May 1804 to September 1806—the captains and their men killed at least forty-three grizzlies, most often with no provocation beyond "falling in with"—that is, encountering—the great bears.

Thus the opening volley in America's grizzly wars was fired the moment the first Americans to explore the Far West saw their first grizzlies.

No one knows exactly when the first grizzly bear was killed by a non-Indian in the southern Rocky Mountain wilderness destined to become Colorado, though many fur-flying encounters with silvertips must have taken place during the early Spanish explorations, beginning with the Don Juan Maria de Rivera expedition of 1765.

In 1776 the Franciscan padres Francisco Atanasio Dominguez and Francisco Silvestre Valez de Escalante led an extensive exploration of the West Slope of Colorado, naming natural features as they went— including such major local rivers as the Dolores (Sorrows), Piedra

(Stony), Los Pinos (Pine), Florida (Flowery), the San Juan itself—and that stream destined to become a heavy-metals disposal drain for the mining industry, El Rio de las Animas Perdidas (the River of Lost Souls), known today as the Animas.

We do, at least, have a precise date for and a detailed accounting of the first known deadly encounter between white American invaders and a Colorado grizzly. Tuesday, November 13, 1821, just wasn't Lewis Dawson's day, notwithstanding it bestowed upon him a double entry in local history—as the first white American to be killed by a Colorado grizzly and, consequently, the first white American to be buried in Colorado soil.

On that chilly late-fall day, while encamped with the Jacob Fowler expedition en route from Fort Smith, Arkansas, to Santa Fe, New Mexico, Dawson was mauled by a grizzly just east of what is now the town of Las Animas, out on the Front Range plains at the head of a north-flowing Arkansas River feeder called the Purgatoire. From their riverside encampment, looking west by northwest, the Fowler party could see for the first time in their long journey the jagged purple rise of the Rocky Mountains.

In those pristine times, grizzlies roamed in abundance not only throughout mountainous western Colorado but all along the Front Range, where mountains meet plains that roll out eastward toward Kansas. Mountain-born grizzlies wandered onto those pancake grasslands, dispersing as far east as the Kansas border and beyond. Of necessity, such adventurous bruins would have restricted their travels primarily to riparian stream corridors, where they were assured of finding food, water, and shelter. Just such a place is where Lewis Dawson met his clawsome fate. From the journals of expedition leader Jacob Fowler:

> While Some Ware Hunting and Others Cooking Some Picking grapes a gun Was fyered off and the Cry of a White Bare Was Raised We Ware all armed in an Instent and Each man Run His own Cors to look for the desperet anemel—the Brush in Which We Camped Contained from 10 to 20 acors Into Which the Bare Head [had] Run for Shelter find[ing] Him Self Surrounded on all Sides—threw this Conl glann With four others atempted to run but the Bare being In their Way and lay Close in the brush undiscovered till the[y] Ware With in a few fet of it—When it Sprung up and Caught Lewis doson

and Pulled Him down in an Instent Conl glanns gun mised fyer or he Wold Have Releved the man But a large Slut Which belongs to the Party atacted the Bare With such fury that it left the man and persued Her a few steps in Which time the man got up and Run a few steps but Was overtaken by the bare When the Conl maid a second atempt to shoot but His [rifle] mised fyer again and the Slut as before Releved the man Who Run as before—but Was Son again in the grasp of the Bare Who Semed Intent on His distruction—the Conl again Run close up and as before His gun Wold not go off the Slut makeing an other atack and Releveing the man—the Conl now be Came alarmed lest the Bare Wold pusue Him and Run up Stooping tree—and after Him the Wounded man Was followed by the Bare and thus the[y] Ware all three up one tree-but a tree standing in Rich [reach] the conl steped on that and let the man and Bare pas till the Bare Caught Him [Dawson] by one leg and drew Him back wards down the tree. While this Was doing the Conl Sharpened His flint Primed His gun and Shot the Bare down While pulling the man by the leg be fore any of the party arived to releve Him—the Bare soon Rose again but Was Shot by several other Wo Head got up to the place of action—it Is to be Remarked that the other three men With Him Run off—and the Brush Was so thick that those on the out Side Ware Som time getting threw.

Still conscious, Dawson was carried back to camp. There Fowler examined his wounds and wrote, "It appeers His Head Was In the Bares mouth at least twice . . . the teeth Cutting the Skin to the bone Where Ever the[y] tuched it."

Dawson's shredded scalp was "Sewed up as Well as Cold be don by men In our Situation." Throughout, Dawson "Still Retained His under Standing but Said I am killed that I Heard my Skull Brake." Dawson spoke "Chearfully on the Subject" until the afternoon of the following day, when he "began to be Restless and Some What delereous—and on examening a Hole in the upper part of His Wright temple Which We beleved only Skin deep We found the Brains Workeing out."

The "unfortnet man died at day Brake" on the morning of November 16, three days after the mauling, and was buried "as Well as our meens Wold admit . . . near the Bank With a Strong Pen of logs over Him to prevent the Bares or Wolves" from feasting on man-flesh.

That done, Fowler and his men "turned our atention [to] the Bare and found Him a large fatt anemel." The boar was skinned and butchered, but the men found "the Smell of a polcat so Strong that We Cold not Eat the meat." Fowler pried the grizzly's mouth open and "found that three of His teeth Ware broken off near the gums Which We Sopose Was the Caus of His not killing the man at the first Bite—and the one not Broke to be the Caus of the Hole in the Right [temple] Which killed the man at last."

Even though the bear's meat was "skunky" after three days of neglect, Fowler's hunters "killed two deer Cased the Skin[s] for Baggs We dryed out the Bares oil and Caryed it with us the Skin Was all so taken Care of."

From Fowler's account it sounds as if one of the hunters spotted and shot at the grizzly, possibly wounding him and sending him into hiding in the dense brush. Apparently Dawson was simply unlucky enough to stumble upon the wounded bear. Ironically, in another week or two, perhaps another day or two, that old grizzer would have been snoring peacefully in den.

The Colorado grizzly wars had begun.

From the time of the Dawson incident, in singles and not infrequently in family groups of a mother and cubs, Colorado's grizzly population was gnawed at by the insatiable maw of encroaching civilization. Habitat was usurped, denaturalized, and denied to wildlife. Natural prey species were depleted and in some areas wiped out, *forcing* large predators to prey on livestock—for which "sin" they were vilified and exterminated.

During the 1870s and 1880s, when open-range cattle and sheep were devouring rich native grasslands, destroying critical riparian habitat, and prompting extensive water pollution and soil erosion all across the West, the grizzly wars escalated to a historic peak. These were the boom days of the freelance wolfers and bear men. So fiercely did these men pursue their work that the last active wolf pack in Colorado, led by the infamous bandit Old Three Toes, abandoned the increasingly hostile San Juans in 1927, fleeing southeast into the Carson National Forest of northern New Mexico. There Old Three Toes continued killing livestock until 1929, when he finally blundered into a trap and became at long last a "good" wolf.

Wolves, while they lasted, were always at the top of PARC's most-wanted list. But the agency had come on the scene a bit late to enjoy the bumper-crop days of wolfing; its lot was to clean up the remnants left by stockmen and freelance bounty trappers. PARC records show that its trappers killed "only" 133 Colorado wolves during the five years 1916 through 1920. After that, the pickings got even slimmer: a lone wolf in 1927, another in 1930. Down in the south San Juans, Archuleta County heard its last wild howl in 1939, while neighboring Conejos County surrendered Colorado's last known native wolf in 1945.

Grizzlies fared only slightly better. Take, for instance, Old Clubfoot, who got his namesake disfigurement by ripping the toes off one paw in a successful attempt to escape the toothy jaws of a steel trap. After a distinguished career of rustling cattle, Old Clubfoot finally met his bloody end north of Delta on October 24, 1902.

On May 26, 1907, another Colorado bruin celebrity was killed by hunters on Lone Cone Mountain, a peak rising west of Telluride in the San Miguel Range of the northwestern San Juans. Accused of extensive cattle killing, this old boar was long hunted before finally being put out of business. The Lone Cone grizzly's weight at death was estimated at between eight hundred and a thousand pounds, with fore-claws averaging four inches in length, and hind feet measuring twelve and a half inches long by seven and a half inches wide across the toes. Ironically, on the day he was killed, the Lone Cone bear's stomach reportedly contained not beefsteak but just a couple of handfuls of ants and the larvae of a few wood-boring beetles.

Old Four Toes, of Montrose-area fame, was killed in 1903; Old Saddleback, described in reports of the time as "a very large old silvertip . . . so called because of an area of light-colored fur near the middle of the back," who ranged near Grand and Strawberry Lakes in northeastern Middle Park, perished in 1905.

But biggest and baddest of all was Old Mose, who earned a national reputation and the honorary title "King of the Grizzlies" (bestowed in his *Denver Post* obituary). Old Mose stood accused of killing hundreds of cattle and sheep and as many as three men. His most unbearlike habit of laconic "moseying"—as opposed to shuffling shambling rambling galumphing or otherwise motivating briskly—earned him his moniker.

Old Mose's outlaw career spanned at least twenty years, during which he terrorized citizens and their livestock throughout Fremont,

Park, and Chaffee Counties. But the heart of Mose's range lay northwest of Cañon City, where he was thought to have denned on Black and Thirty-nine Mile Mountains.

After finally being "controlled" on the last day of April 1904, an eviscerated Old Mose was widely reported to have weighed nine hundred pounds, though much higher estimates exist. And this was in the spring, just after emerging from the winter starvation den. Estimates of this bear's live weight in fall (prime) condition range from twelve to fifteen hundred pounds, the latter figure stretching the limits of morphological possibility. The most modest reports I've uncovered are six hundred pounds gutted, half a ton on the paw. A lot of grizzer bear, no matter how you slice him. And slice him they did, with Colorado butcher shops far and wide advertising "Old Mose, ten cents a pound."

Old Mose's other measurements are less in dispute. His dried skull was carefully measured and recorded at fourteen inches across by fifteen long—the largest known skull ever for a Colorado grizzly. His hide measured ten feet, four inches long and nine feet, six inches wide. That's *a hundred square feet* of bear. The hide still exists, I hear, stashed in the biological specimen vault at the University of California, Berkeley. (The Denver Museum of Natural History, I submit, should request the immediate repatriation of Old Mose's mortal cloak.)

So huge and powerful was Old Mose in life, he was said to have smashed casually through a pole fence sturdy enough to contain a half-ton bull, then waylay said bull with a single devastating swipe of claw and one crushing bite to the neck.

All attempts to trap Mose came to naught; he would variously abjure the baited steel altogether, flip-trip the trap then dine in leisure on the bait, or magically finesse the bait from the very jaws of death without upsetting the trigger pan. On the only occasion when Old Mose was known to have stepped into a steel trap—set underwater, where it could be neither seen nor scented—the King of the Grizzlies joined the stoic ranks of Old Three Toes, Old Clubfoot, and other trap-mutilated Colorado martyrs by tearing free. The cost was two toes from his right rear paw. Later, when some clever fellow tried to take Old Mose with a keg trap baited with ripe fruit, he found the heavy wooden barrel smashed to splinters and fruitless.

Traps having failed, dozens of hunters vowed over the years to give Old Mose a lethal dose of lead poisoning. As proof of their frequent near misses, when Mose's corpse was necropsied, it contained numerous old bullet wounds—a commonly reported number is twenty. One slug had lodged in the bear's spine. An injury of this sort would instantly paralyze most animals, no matter how large, but it apparently had no lasting effect on the King.

Of the three human deaths charged to this beautiful monster, only one, the 1882 mauling of Jake Ratcliffe, was witnessed. According to the testimony of Ratcliffe's hunting partner, Jake shot Old Mose at close range, prompting an immediate counterattack. With no time to get off another shot, Ratcliffe smashed the butt of his rifle across the charging bruin's gigantic conk, but to no effect. The worst of Ratcliffe's many ugly wounds were to the back of his neck—Mose had caught him in the quintessential predator's death grip. Additionally, one arm had been torn away from the body at the shoulder and "macerated," one leg was broken (twice), and both thighs were "shredded."

The evidence linking the other two deaths to Old Mose is circumstantial at best: the skeletons of the missing men were found near where the legendary beast was thought to den.

In retrospect, while Old Mose was in fact a man-killer, his one verified attack came only in desperate self-defense. And though he was an incorrigible rustler of cattle, the number of livestock losses laid at his claws no doubt was greatly exaggerated.

Old Mose finally met his match in James W. Anthony, a professional bear slayer down from Idaho and Wyoming. Anthony's secret weapon was an exceptional pack of trailing hounds. So good were his dogs, boasted Anthony, that for any bear whose trail they struck, "it was either tree, fight, or get killed." Generally all three.

In spite of the talented noses of his hounds, it took Anthony, his dogs, and his hunting partner—a local rancher named Wharton Pigg— nearly a month of sniffing around before finally cutting Old Mose's trail, which was by then too old and cold for the dogs to work. After three days of sight tracking, Anthony's pack finally struck a trail hot enough to nose into.

As soon as the hounds got excited, Mr. Pigg, living up to his name, dashed ahead in hopes of beating his partner to the prize. Anthony remained with his hounds. This loyalty soon paid off when the pack ran down and cornered their quarry. Pigg, meanwhile, had taken a wrong turn somewhere and was out of the running.

Alone and armed only with a small-bore rifle, but infinitely confident, Anthony dismounted and cautiously approached the cacophony of roars and barks. When within "four rods" of the gargantuan bear, figuring that to be plenty close enough, the bounty hunter aimed at the embattled King's head. Apparently even the experienced Anthony was somewhat shaken to be so close to such a legendary beast as Old Mose, because his bullet missed the bear's head and instead struck its throat. As they were trained to do, Anthony's hounds backed off at the crack of his rifle, and the profusely bleeding grizzly simply turned and moseyed away.

But not far. When directly downhill and little more than a dozen yards from his attacker, Old Mose unexpectedly whirled and charged. Anthony responded by firing "two or three" more shots, almost point-blank. One of these connected, grazing the bear's neck and breaking the charge.

Now Old Mose decided to abandon the fray. But as the twice-wounded bear was leaving, Anthony ran up close and shot him behind the right shoulder. The bullet passed through the lungs and exited the breast at "the sticking spot" (in the lower throat, where a butcher "sticks" a pig to bleed it out).

Old Mose, now carrying three of Anthony's bullets—in throat, neck, and engine room—again turned and charged. Again the hunter was ready and fired a point-blank coup de grâce, "unjoining [Old Mose's] neck at the junction with the skull and following down the spinal marrow." Even then, like some ursine Terminator, Old Mose fought every inch of his slow slump groundward, tried to rise again and failed, then lay panting for "some time" before breathing his historic last.

Had Anthony's rifle jammed or misfired, as weapons of the day were inclined to do, the deadly contest would have ended differently. As it was, the hunter's reward for a month and more of laborious pursuit in miserable weather and almost becoming bear scat was a paltry sixty-dollar bounty paid by "the ranch men."

Writing in the *Denver Post*, Dr. E. G. Lancaster, then chairman of the biology department at Colorado College, in Colorado Springs, who participated in the necropsy of the huge corpse (his piece of the action was the fifteen-ounce brain), eulogized Old Mose thusly:

[Old Mose] did not love or hate, probably, and was mild and peaceable if left alone. If frightened or injured or hungry, his instincts said run, crush, or kill, and he did it.

[Old Mose] couldn't be moved by reason or high motives. He would do the things that would satisfy his appetite and passions. When pursued, he would follow his instincts for self-preservation.

He was the biggest and the baddest, but Old Mose was not the last Colorado grizzly whose adventures earned it a name and place in local lore. That dubious honor fell to Bigfoot Mary, who worked the rangelands south of Grand Junction. Mary managed to elude a veritable army of pursuers, surviving until October of 1925. Having been a professional cow thief for nigh on a quarter of a century, Mary had acquired fat enough to yield 166 pounds of lard when her carcass was unceremoniously hacked apart and rendered.

And so it went. A Division report dated February 8, 1971, and titled "A Selected List of Predatory Animals Taken in Colorado by Control Agents of the Division of Wildlife Services [PARC/ADC], Fiscal Years 1916–17 through 1969–70," tallies the deaths of an incredible 5,148 Colorado bears. A footnote adds: "Grizzly and Black Bear could not be separated; it is believed that a number of bear taken in the early years were grizzly."

And several in the later years as well. PARC's banner bear year in Colorado was fiscal 1946–47, when 304 scalped ear pairs were turned in as proof of work well done. Killing of grizzlies in the state was not outlawed until 1953 and no doubt continued illegally long after. A former ADC western-states administrator, now dead, told a reliable mutual friend that shortly after the passage of the Freedom of Information Act, he and other Denver ADC bosses spent "several days" sorting and shredding records of ADC killings of Colorado grizzlies. Why?

In addition to Old Mose and his fellow celebrity bruins, brief records of the deaths of several other, nameless, twentieth-century San Juan grizzlies survive today, in Division files and elsewhere. And in many cases, remains of the bears themselves have been preserved: skulls, hides, a paw, partial and full body mounts. The most visible and poignant of this latter lot is the aforementioned Denver museum mount of a young male, along with the vaulted hides of a near twin that was probably its sibling and an older, larger female who was likely the pair's mother, all killed on April 19 and May 5, 1913.

A local man named William Weisel accomplished that piece of work, just a few miles northeast of the tiny burg of Chromo, along a stretch of the Navajo River canyon commemorated on the maps as Weisel Flat, Weisel Canyon, and Bear Meadow.

And so it went for Colorado's grizzlies. In his 1911 *Biological Survey of Colorado,* federal biologist Merritt Cary summarized:

> At present grizzly bears are uncommon, if not rare, in the northern mountains, but are occasionally seen in the wilder mountains of southern Colorado, particularly in the San Juan, La Plata, and San Miguel Ranges. . . .
>
> Small numbers are found in the San Juan Mountains north of Pagosa Springs and Vallecito, and . . . an average of one or two had been killed north of Pagosa Springs each spring until 1907, when none were killed. . . . [G]rizzlies were quite common in the higher San Juan Mountains as late as 1873. . . .
>
> I have no data respecting the recent occurrence of this bear along the eastern slopes of the Front Range, and it appears to be now extremely rare or entirely absent.

By early in the century, most Coloradans had already forgotten, or simply didn't care, that *Ursus arctos horribilis* had so recently been a major player in the local ecology. Yet grizzlies continued to live, and die, in Colorado.

For instance: In October of 1939 a cattle rancher named Leonard Wellman went elk hunting with friends along Trout Creek, near the town of South Fork in the Rio Grande National Forest, on the eastern flank of Wolf Creek Pass. Wellman saw movement behind some brush and fired. What he had killed turned out to be not an elk but a grizzly bear, which Wellman and his buddies skinned. Wellman later had the hide made into a rug, which remains in the family to this day.

In 1953—the year grizzlies received nominal protection in Colorado —the same rancher was out "riding cattle" on his Forest Service grazing allotment. While passing through a place called Raspberry Gulch, not far from where he'd killed the 1939 bear, Wellman spotted two grizzlies.

He went for his rifle and blazed away, later boasting to friends of having "seriously messed up" one of the pair before they escaped.

Several days later, Wellman returned with a pack of trailing hounds, located the carcass of the "messed up" bruin, and confirmed that it was in fact a grizzly. Since the corpse was putrid and the hair was slipping, and considering that he already had one bear rug and it was now illegal to kill a grizzly in Colorado, Wellman left the carcass to scavengers. Somehow, the rancher escaped punishment. Moreover, no effort was made by any agency to retrieve the skull of the dead bear for species identification, nor did a report of the existence of the second, surviving grizzly ever find its way into official records.

Five years earlier, in 1948, while it was still legal, a local hunter named Jack Semler had killed a grizzly in the Mosca Creek drainage—an isolated, unroaded, and untrailed chunk of de facto wilderness in the San Juan National Forest, south of Granite Peak and west of Bear Mountain.

Three decades later, in 1979, while hunting Mosca Creek, local outfitter T. Mike Murphy came upon a hind bear track in fresh snow on flat ground that he described as being "longer and wider than my hunting boot." He thought little of it at the time, knowing the area held "lots of gigantic black bears," a few in the four-hundred-pound range. But that's not the end of the Mosca Creek saga. In 1989, near the head of the same wild drainage, Division game warden Cary Carron also came across a huge bear track. "It was," he told me, "the biggest I've ever seen." It was also the only time Carron has seen any evidence in the San Juans that raised the possibility in his mind of a living grizzly.

Rancher George Ward of the Saguache area killed a second Colorado grizzly in 1948. The story was recounted for me by George's son Larry, who was with his father at the time. The two men had ridden out one morning to check on a cow and newborn calf. "The calf," said Ward, "looked to have been killed just minutes before we got there, and this old bear was standing right on top of it." Given that George Ward was a PARC trapper who had killed at least one other grizzly, back in '43, "this old bear" had picked the wrong time to kill the wrong man's calf. George Ward raised his rifle and fired. His son still has the hide.

In August of 1951, a sheepherder named Alfonso Lobato killed a young male grizzly near Blue Lake, now within the South San Juan Wilderness. Lobato is long dead, but his son-in-law, Roberto Garcia, passed the story along to me. According to Garcia, Lobato and two other men were herding more than twenty-five hundred sheep grazing in the subalpine parks along El Rito Azul (Blue Creek) fork of the Conejos (Rabbit) River. Several sheep had recently been killed by some unseen nocturnal predator, so when a bear appeared near the herd one evening, Lobato popped it with a little .22 Special. The herder skinned his bear, estimated to have weighed around three hundred pounds on the paw, and eventually packed the hide down the mountain to the nearest human settlement, the tiny log-cabin mining camp of Platoro. There he sold the fresh hide to Ken Wiley, owner of the Skyline Lodge.

It was several days before Wiley found time to drive over the mountains to Monte Vista and deposit the hide with taxidermist Ernest Wilkinson. Wiley wanted a rug, but the pelt had been too long neglected, had never been salted, and was largely spoiled. All Wilkinson could rescue were the head and claws. He tanned the head and neck hide, stretched it over a skull form, and mounted it on a wooden plaque. He then cleaned and arranged the claws on a separate plaque to hang below and complement the head mount.

For years, the head and claws hung in the Skyline Lodge. But Platoro is a summer-only town, its twenty-some miles of gravel access road closed by snow in winter. One cold day, some hoodlums arrived on snowmobiles, broke into the boarded-up lodge, and stole, among other things, the grizzly claws.

Ken Wiley is gone now and the Skyline Lodge has new owners (gregarious Texans catering to gregarious Texans), but the head of Alfonso Lobato's grizzly hangs there yet, perhaps helping to spur frequent reports that grizzlies still roam the wilds above Platoro. And maybe they do.

But then, the frequency of grizzly reports emanating from the Platoro area could also be at least partly due to an innocent collusion between the numerous blond-phase black bears thereabouts and the many people, especially tourists, who harbor a strong desire to see a wild grizzly where none are supposed to be. Retired Division game warden Dick Weldon once showed me a home video, given to him by a Platoro summer resident, of what is clearly a blond-phase black bear, and no giant at that, feeding among the brush alongside the Platoro road. On the video sound track, the excited cameraman's voice pants, "It's a *grizzly!* I'm about a hundred percent sure it's a grizzly!"

Unfortunately, he was about a hundred percent mistaken.

But back in 1951, less than a month after the Blue Lake grizzly had showed itself and died, Monte Vista taxidermist Ernest Wilkinson, who was coincidentally a PARC trapper at the time, killed a second subadult male grizzly that could have been the Blue Lake bruin's twin; Wilkinson in fact has always suspected that the two bears were siblings. Wilkinson's grizzly, another accused mutton muncher, died several score miles north of Blue Lake, in an alpine park above the Rio Grande headwaters called Starvation Gulch—which, however, in no way negates the sibling theory.

The man long credited with having killed the last grizzly in Colorado was Pagosa Springs PARC trapper Lloyd Anderson, the Ben Lilly of the San Juans. In a thirty-six-year career lasting through 1972, Anderson legally killed at least seven grizzlies and hinted to acquaintances that there may have been more. Anderson also eliminated an estimated five hundred black bears. The ranchers he served must have worshiped Lloyd Anderson as a Siva shepherd, their personal destroyer-guardian.

In September 1952, Anderson was called up to the headwaters of Los Pinos River, where purportedly thirty-five sheep had recently been killed by a bear or bears. Anderson built a "cubby"—an open-ended, V-shaped log corral with a bait (often the remains of a "depredated" sheep) jammed back into the narrow apex. A big steel trap was then secreted just inside the opening.

And sure enough, like the wayfaring cat in the old song, the Los Pinos griz came back, she couldn't stay away, the griz came back the very next day. And when she did . . .

To prevent a bear from escaping with a leghold trap, it was standard procedure to chain the hardware to a nearby tree or, lacking that, to a "toggle," or drag log. Anderson used a green spruce toggle eight feet long and one foot in diameter. If a trapped bear tried to run for it, the long heavy toggle would get snagged on trees and brush, slowing or stopping the getaway, at least in theory. In this case, the trap-bound grizzly dragged its improvised ball and chain five rugged mountain miles. A cryptic note in the Division nongame files documents the chase: "Anderson followed [the trapped grizzly] with mule and horse. Mule was spooky, then horse reared. Bear stood up in willows. Bear shot once in viscera and once in head. Anderson salvaged 4 claws and skull. . . . After this, Anderson was restricted from killing grizzly."

For nearly three decades, until September 1979 when the Wiseman bear appeared like some hoary specter from out of the local woodwork, Anderson's 1952 sow was cited by the Division as having been the last grizzly in Colorado and, thus, the last grizzly in the Southwest. Odd reckoning, this, given that the trapper himself had reported that the sow had two big cubs with her, both of which had escaped unharmed and were old enough to survive on their own.

Moreover, Anderson's ability to tell a grizzly from a black bear—from reading spoor as well as by visual identification—was considered by all who knew the man, including his many Division friends, as unimpeachable . . . yet Anderson reported a litany of post-1952 grizzly sightings that were essentially ignored by the Division until shortly before his death.

(In its early years, the Division of Wildlife was called the Colorado Department of Game and Fish, which was later amended to Department of Game, Fish, and Parks, and finally altered to the present name. For simplicity's sake, I use the familiar "Division" throughout, no matter the time period being discussed.)

The first of Anderson's recorded ghost-grizzly encounters occurred in November 1957. While he and a friend were elk hunting, they spotted an adult grizzly and tracked it into a thicket of spruce somewhere up Fourmile Creek, north of Pagosa Springs. The brief Division report of this sighting included the note: "Was hunting with Calvin Perkins, who forbid Anderson from taking this bear." Then, in 1962, the trapper spotted a boar grizzly "on Calvin Perkins' range . . . east of Sugarloaf Mountain." Division notes go on to register that the "bear killed 20 sheep on this range," and that this boar resembled the grizzly Anderson and Perkins had encountered along Fourmile Creek five years before.

Anderson's third phantom grizzly manifested itself in April of 1964, when he, in company with two other men and a pack of trailing hounds, "started" what he felt certain was a silvertip, running it from six that morning to seven in the evening. The chase opened near the head of McCabe Creek, ranged across Fourmile Creek, and ended only when the bear finally shook off the hounds and escaped into the Piedra River drainage northwest of Pagosa. The bear never went to tree but frequently "would back against a rock wall and fight dogs (could not climb). Saliva was seen around these spots," according to the Division's shorthand rendition of Anderson's report. By nightfall, the pack had scattered far and wide, a few of the valuable hounds running lost for as long as two weeks.

The next year, 1965, Anderson identified fresh grizzly tracks along the upper Navajo River, very near where the Wiseman grizzly would appear in 1979. Anderson's attempts to track this bear were foiled when it "went into rock and grass [and he] could not follow."

Also in 1965, Leonard Wellman—the hunter who had killed the "elk" grizzly along Trout Creek back in 1939, a second down in Raspberry Gulch in 1953, and watched a third escape—sighted a fourth grizzly in the same area. "There was absolutely not a shred of doubt in his mind," Leonard's daughter Willa Lee Dickey told me. "It most definitely *was* a grizzly." Over the next several years, Wellman saw the same bear several more times. And even today, some locals believe a few grizzlies still haunt the Trout Creek area of the Rio Grande National Forest, whose heart, as of late 1994, appears about to be cleaved open by a new logging road and a major timbering operation.

The last grizzly sighting reported by ADC trapper Lloyd Anderson came in 1967, when he spent twenty minutes watching a sow with two cubs "within shooting range" as they fed peacefully between Rock and Ute Creeks, up north in the Weminuche.

Other reports of grizzly sightings, and even of grizzlies being killed, a few marked "confirmed," are noted in Division files during the two decades following the killing of the professed "last" San Juan grizzly in 1952.

Still others are known but not noted. For example, two sheep-ranching brothers "over on the Gunnison side" of the San Juans once admitted to a Division official—figuring they were long past the expiration of the statute of limitations—that back during the mid or late 1950s, they had trapped an alleged sheep-killing bear. When they came up on the furious animal, they immediately recognized it as a grizzly. But, as they explained to my informant, "with a bear in a trap and badly wounded, unless you've got a tranquilizer gun, what can you do but shoot it?" So shoot it they did, then buried the incriminating corpse in accordance with the time-tested stockman's grizzly remedy of "shoot, shovel, and shut up."

By 1970 Lloyd Anderson's grizzly sighting reports, along with other anecdotal evidence of living silvertips, finally prompted the Division to launch a long overdue San Juan grizzly search. During the summers of 1970 and 1971, several likely areas in the San Juans, north and south, were temporarily closed to bear hunting while Division employees put out baits (geriatric horses, led out and shot in situ), which were then monitored by motion-sensitive 8mm movie cameras and trip wire–activated 35mm still cameras.

This caper netted lots of poor-quality footage of what appeared to be black bears but nothing that could be positively identified as a grizzly. And not surprisingly: This was before the advent of infrared surveillance cameras, and floodlighting was unworkable since few bears of any species were likely to remain in or return to a brightly lit area. Consequently, the cameras filmed in daylight only, during which high-risk hours no clever survivalist grizzly was likely to come in. Moreover, the movie cameras proved untenable, taking hundreds of frames of empty sky, their motion sensors having been set off by ravens, the wind, forest spirits.

There was, however, one exciting, albeit inconclusive, occurrence during the 1970s grizzly survey. According to Hal Burdick—at the time the Division's chief biologist for the southwest region and the man who wrote the final report of the study—between observations that came just thirty-six hours apart, a horse carcass that weighed thirteen hundred pounds was dragged three hundred yards by a bear. No one involved in the project had ever seen such a feat of strength performed by a black bear, and Burdick says they all doubted the existence of a San Juan blackie big enough to have pulled it off.

Since this event took place down in the south San Juans not too far from the Navajo headwaters, it may have been the work of the Wiseman grizzly, which at that time had several more years to live and would have been in her prime. But then, at the time of her death in 1979, she was estimated to have weighed only 400 to 450 pounds, perhaps not quite large enough to move more than half a ton of dead meat several hundred yards.

In the end, this question, like so many others concerning the grizzly in Colorado, can never be answered with certainty.

In the conclusion of his "San Juan–Rio Grande Grizzly Bear Inventory, 1970 Progress Report," Burdick wrote: "It is my opinion, based on the results to date, that this type of procedure [ground baiting] will not produce grizzlies regardless of their presence. I say this because I feel the high population of black bear throughout the area will devour the baits prior to a grizzly becoming interested. This is based on the assumption that grizzlies do not normally become interested until the bait gets extremely ripe. In each of the recent cases, the blacks had obliterated the baits prior to this time."

The 1971 search proved no more fruitful. Given the number of horses killed over a two-summer period within a very few miles of where the Wiseman grizzly died and no doubt had always lived, without ever a photo of her being taken or her prints being recorded in the smoothed dirt "track pads" maintained around the baits, Burdick was probably correct in doubting the efficacy of ground baiting, perhaps even forecasting the failure of Tom Beck's crew a decade later to bait a grizzly into a snare. Unless, of course, it was the Wiseman grizzly, or another of her race, who had dragged off that hefty horse carcass. But even then, the mystery bruin had managed the feat without leaving a track or getting its picture taken. Ghost grizzlies.

Why had the Division, after nearly two decades of burying its head in the sand re the existence of grizzlies in Colorado, finally reversed itself and gone to the considerable trouble and expense of trying to document with photos and tracks the presence of the great bear in the San Juans?

According to the official report of a May 1970 "Grizzly Bear Restoration Planning Meeting" attended by several key Division personnel, including then-director Harry Woodward and world-class grizzly expert Dr. John Craighead: "It would be highly important in a restoration program to verify or refute reports of grizzlies in the state. If this species currently exists, public acceptance of a restoration project would undoubtedly be considerably different than if animals were introduced where they had not existed for a number of years."

Farther along, the same report documents that "[Director] Woodward stated that he wished to proceed with introduction plans and that he wanted the Forest Service to be directly involved with the Division on this project."

In other words, in the early 1970s, the Division was blessed with a boss who was hoping to find proof of living grizzlies in Colorado to facilitate his desire to implement a reintroduction program. The report goes on to outline not only the planned grizzly "inventory" but such details of reintroduction as choice of release sites, timing, type of animals ("First choice would be a sow with cubs about six months old"), sources for acquiring grizzlies, transportation, publicity ("The less publicity the better"), responsibility and liability, funding, and so on through four single-spaced typed pages.

When no conclusive proof of grizzlies could be found after two summers of looking, Division interest in pursuing San Juan grizzly restoration waned and, with a change of administrators, winked entirely out. Of course, the Wiseman grizzly (at the least) had been there all along. When that old sow appeared and promptly died, the only element of the Great Colorado Grizzly Extirpation Myth to be changed was the date, jumped forward twenty-seven years from 1952 to 1979.

But there were still reports of sightings, some originating from within the Division itself. To wit: In October of 1983, while riding a high drainage in the extreme south San Juans, an outfitter, in company with Division warden Dick Weldon, found the frozen, partially eaten carcass of an elk. In the snow all around the elk were tracks that both men felt sure were grizzly. They also found several silver-tipped bear hairs. The incident was reported, but nothing came of it.

Dick Weldon, recently retired from the Division, also speaks of having come upon a spot up near timberline in the south San Juans, around 1990, that contained "dung and diggings" he felt certain were grizzly spoor. In addition to the "huge quantity" of scat, Weldon thought it mighty odd that his horse, who'd been around a lot of black bears, dead and alive, and had never before acted up, "was *extremely* nervous" on this occasion—as had been one of the outfitter's animals back in '83. "He flat wanted to leave the country," Weldon told me. "The bear had moved a lot of earth and a couple of pretty good sized boulders; looked like he was trying to dig out a whistle pig [marmot]. I think it may have been a grizzly, but of course I can't say for sure."

Then there's the highly credible sighting of a sow and three cubs by Banded Peak Ranch foreman Dennis Schutz in October of 1990. And the hair samples collected that same year by San Juan Grizzly Project searchers and later laboratory-identified as grizzly. And a good deal more.

The history of the Colorado grizzly is still being written.

During the first few years Caroline and I lived here, we had a most pleasant habit of walking or snowshoeing a couple of miles down the mountain to spend Sunday mornings lazing around an antique woodstove drinking coffee and chatting with an octogenarian rancher friend named Helen.

Helen has spent her entire long life on the verdant riverside spread where she was born in 1905. She is living local history and a captivating storyteller. Among my favorites is her "Tale of the Naked Fat Man."

In the summer of 1913, when Helen had just turned eight, her father went hunting along the tight little creek valley where my hillside cabin now squats. There, "in blow-down timber so thick you couldn't ride a horse through," Helen's father killed an exceptionally large bear that could have been the dead-last grizzly in these parts. With helping hands and horses, the hunter wrestled the bruin home and hoisted it by the hind legs into a sturdy tree, then skinned it in preparation for butchering. (Few country folk in those lean and pragmatic days wasted fresh meat of any kind, and "woods pork" was widely considered a delicacy.)

It was then, with the bare bear hanging there and her father standing beside it, bloody knife in hand, that young Helen wandered onto the scene; horrified by what she saw, she burst into tears and fled. Eighty years later, Helen laughed when she recalled how the flayed bear "looked like a naked fat man hanging there. I thought Dad had killed somebody and was fixing to cut him up and feed him to us. I haven't been able to stomach bear meat since."

Story spawns story.

Some years ago, while exploring a secluded bench aspen grove a vigorous hike up the mountain from my cabin, I stumbled upon a hidden spring. Abundant spoor announced that deer, elk, bears, turkeys, and other wildlife visited the place regularly to drink from the little pool, to browse the lush vegetation watered by its brief overflow, and, I like to think, just to be there. Shadowy and quiet and almost a little spooky at twilight, the place exudes a preternatural ambience. I visit this sylvan shrine often; it has become my local refuge from Babylon. And among the most significant elements of the spirit of this place are its bear trees: across the decades, the soft white bark of several of the larger aspens ringing the spring have collected hundreds of blackened bear-claw tracks.

This in itself is hardly unique; I've seen scores of bear-scarred aspens near dozens of secluded spring pools throughout the Rockies. Most often, it's black bear cubs that do the climbing and whose needle-sharp claws scratch and gouge the impressionable bark, leaving distinctive curved parallel signatures. As the aspens grow, these modest tracks harden, blacken, stretch, and puff up, eventually coming to look as if they were made by the most monstrous of bruins.

But two special aspens near "my" spring wear a different sort of signature entirely: heavy, widely spaced vertical claw marks more than a foot long and at just the right height, allowing for several decades of subsequent growth, to suggest that an exceptionally large bear once stood upright, stretched as high as possible and raked its claws heavily downward. Exactly as grizzlies are wont to do. Like my friend Helen, these storybook aspens have survived for nearly a century rooted firmly in this lovely little corner of the silver San Juans. I find it a deeply poignant experience to sit quietly in that enchanted refugium and study those crude autographs and imagine them being scribbled by Helen's Naked Fat Man himself. As perhaps they were.

On one of the last occasions Caroline and I visited Helen, I found myself admitting to her that I was terribly envious of the simple, self-sufficient, quietly satisfying life she'd known growing up and living on a working ranch in the good old days of a still-wild West. "I'd give anything," I confessed, "to have lived your life."

"Hell," said Helen, "you can have my life. I wish I'd been born fifty years earlier."

Surprised, I asked why.

"So I wouldn't be around today to see what the sons of bitches are doing to these mountains."

The thing you've got to watch out for with progress, my old friend Bud Guthrie was quick to point out, is that once you've got it, there's no going back. Helen is teetering on ninety now and no longer guides elk hunters and fly fishers into the wilderness or plants a big garden or keeps chickens or hauls hay out to feed snow-stranded cattle or drives a horse-drawn sleigh thirteen miles to town in January blizzards. No more grizzlies hereabouts, either. Instead, we have ever more new roads slicing like daggers into the heart of what was recently wildness, with ever more urban refugees arriving daily and building ever more houses along those new roads. My magical bear trees are in mortal danger of being "harvested" for the pulp mill that makes the waferboard used to build those new houses. Wal-Mart is coming.

And all that remains of that once-ferocious San Juan grizzly slayer Lloyd Anderson—who, ironically, in his final years lobbied the Division for the restoration of the great bear before it completely disappeared from the San Juans—all that's left of old Lloyd is his name carved on a few heart-rotted quakies here and there in his beloved San Juans.

Of all the old Colorado grizzly war vets, in fact, only Ernie Wilkinson, killer of the 1951 Starvation Gulch boar, still haunts the San Juans in the flesh.

4

THE LAST GRIZZLY SLAYER

Ernie and His Bear

> *We will consume the world out of a sense of desperation, and never get the nourishment we most need.*
>
> —Jonathan White

The last grizzly slayer—the only living former federal trapper to have legally killed a great bear in Colorado—takes up his hand-hewn staff and leads out briskly. We lope past the Weminuche Wilderness boundary sign and start up the long switchback trail toward the Continental Divide and, beyond, Starvation Gulch . . . so named, I'm told, by old-time miners who prospected the place, found nothing, and financially "starved out."

After maybe a quarter mile, my guide suddenly stops and turns, like a man who's just remembered that he's forgotten something. "Dave," he says, "maybe you should take the lead. I might set too fast a pace."

I smile and step to the front. After all, I'm well into my forties, while my guide, who fears he might leave me in the dust, is barely sixty-nine.

I first heard about Ernest Wilkinson—who he is and what he's done and the fact that he's still kicking hard—from John Murray's seminal *Wildlife in Peril.* But I didn't meet the man until this past June, when I phoned ahead for an appointment, then drove 125 miles to Ernest's Taxidermy on the outskirts of Monte Vista.

Ernest's Taxidermy. The walls and floors, the parallel rows of shelves, every cranny and nook of the place is occupied by the indigenous living dead—lifelike mounts of just about every species of wildlife that has ever walked, flown, or finned through the southern Rockies.

I worked my way to the back of the store, where a worn wooden counter is anchored at one end by an ancient manual cash register. Behind the counter, in an open doorway leading back into what I took to be the workshop, stood an attractive older woman with long silver hair pulled back in thick braids. She introduced herself as Meg. We talked for a while, and I learned that she and Ernie have been together for more than forty years. Like her husband, Margaret Wilkinson has lived her entire life in the San Luis Valley.

After we'd gotten to know each other a bit, Meg waved me back into her husband's cluttered quarters and returned to her work—she fashions leather garments and beadwork so fine that Indians come to *her* for costumes and instruction in these traditional crafts.

Apparently oblivious to my entrance, Ernest Wilkinson sat on a backless stool, his flat stomach pressed against a splintered workbench on which rested the in-progress head mount of a five-point bull elk.

As I glanced about at the furry clutter of backlog crowding the workshop, it struck me that Ernest's taxidermy skills were in high demand. "Either you do good work," I ventured as an opener, "or your prices are right."

Wilkinson looked up. "Both," he said, smiling shyly.

As soon as he'd tied off the stitch he was lacing, Wilkinson extended a leathery hand with deeply split brown nails—a hand, I mused as we shook, that had been stained by the blood of three Colorado grizzlies: his own 1951 Starvation Gulch bear, the Blue Lake boar killed a month earlier, and the '79 Wiseman grizzly, whose gorgeous pelt Wilkinson had prepared for the Denver Museum of Natural History.

Ernie is not a large man—five-nine, maybe, 150 pounds, but possessed of a mesomorphic youthfulness that belies his seven decades. His face is round and friendly, the smiling eyes overshadowed by heavy brows, the skin tan and not nearly so wrinkled as the corrugated mountains in which he's spent his life. I found him unaffected and soft-spoken, easily likable.

Ernie dragged up a rickety wooden chair for me, I hauled out my cheap tape recorder, and we launched into the interview I'd come for. As we talked, my host continued his work.

Born in 1924 on a ranch near Monte Vista, Wilkinson grew up hunting and fishing and trapping. When he came out of the army following World War II, he hired on as a government trapper with PARC, "taking care of coyotes and bears where they were doing damage to livestock."

It was work he could do, in country he knew and loved. And back then, when the Rocky Mountain West was still something of a frontier, killing predators that preyed on livestock was considered necessary and honorable work. There was a job to be done, and here was a man to do it.

During the nine years he worked as a federal trapper—seven full-time, two part-time—Wilkinson killed hundreds of coyotes but "not too many" bears. I asked how many was not too many.

"Twenty-six, twenty-seven maybe. Not too many."

Notwithstanding his skill and effectiveness as a predator killer, Ernie told me he had lacked the blind dedication to his work shared by so many federal trappers, and was openly critical of at least a couple of PARC's policies.

"Most government trappers," he complained, "were big on using poisons. They'd dope animal carcasses and in winter scatter strychnine-soaked tallow balls from horseback or drop them by the paper bagfuls from airplanes wherever sheep and cattle were to be grazed the following spring. Any animal or bird that ate one of those baits—coyote, bear, lion, eagle, raven, pine martin, ranch dog, you name it—died. And whatever scavengers that came along to feed on the corpses of the poison victims, they died too. I never went for that. Too indiscriminate."

Wilkinson's disenchantment with PARC's "toxic Johnny Appleseed" techniques and body-count mentality, together with his marriage in 1952 to Margaret, prompted him to take an early semiretirement, becoming a weekends-only government trapper. "Even then," he quietly boasted, "I usually caught more problem bears than most guys who worked full-time; I knew the country so much better than anyone else." After a couple more years, Wilkinson quit PARC for good, preferring to stay home with Meg and develop his fledgling taxidermy business. By then, the Wilkinsons had built the modest house and shop they still occupy today.

Times were hard back then, so in the winters Ernie ran a trapline for furs and food—the Wilkinsons are masters of economizing and will eat almost anything edible and wild, including bobcat. To rake in a few extra dimes during the summer tourist season, they built a small zoo adjacent to the shop and filled it with indigenous wildlife. Ernie soon discovered that he had a talent for training wild animals and before long was providing four-footed actors—black bears, cougars, badgers, bobcats—for movies and television.

"If you've seen John Wayne's *Chisholm Trail,*" Ernie told me, "or the TV shows *Wild Kingdom, Wild World of Animals,* or *American Sportsman,* you've seen my animals."

With such compliant models at hand, it was only natural that Ernie should get into wildlife photography as well.

Today, the little zoo is empty, grown up in weeds, and wears a weathered "Closed" sign. Ernie's actors all grew old and died, and he never bothered to replace them; too much time required for the training, he explained.

Wilkinson can't recall exactly when he began writing, but since 1968 his locally syndicated "Outdoor Tips and Tales" column has appeared in area newspapers. He has published articles in national outdoor magazines, authored a book called *Snow Caves for Fun and Survival,* and in his "spare time" has completed the first 151 pages of the autobiography of a modern-day mountain man.

Additionally and amazingly, the old mountaineer, together with a partner, runs a school called Trail Skills, Inc., through which Ernie teaches survival and primitive skills workshops and leads wilderness backpack treks. This summer, he told me, is typical, with four weeklong hiking expeditions scheduled back-to-back. The first involves guiding a group of "senior citizens" (his term) through some of the loftiest and most spectacular of Rio Grande backcountry.

The years have been, as they say, kind to Ernie. His winter traplines have gotten no shorter, still covering up to twenty miles through terrain so physically challenging that most people eschew it even in summer. The old adventurer crams everything into a big backpack and cross-country skis when possible, snowshoes when necessary. Never carries a tent, preferring to bivouac under a tree or dig a snow cave.

Our conversation turned to bears.

Back in the summer of 1951, his twenty-seventh year, Ernie was responsible for predator control for fifty-three sheep camps scattered from the headwaters of the Rio Grande east all the way to Creede and south as far as Wagon Wheel Gap. His base camp that season was at Brewster Park, a broad willow flat along the river.

Over the years, Ernie had come to know the names and personalities of all of his client shepherds—young Mexicans, Basques, and Indians. "Herding sheep in the mountains is lonely work," he explained. "The herders would always welcome me into their camps in a big way, offering coffee and their favorite treat, canned jam on camp-made bread. It's an experience a lot of people will never have," he reflected, monumentally understating, "riding every day, learning every wrinkle of the land, camping alone every night, living out of a packsaddle."

Ernie's patrol circuits were anywhere from three to thirteen days long, then he'd return to Brewster Park to replenish his supplies and check his "complaint list"—in his absence, Forest Service rangers or sheep ranchers would sometimes drop by and leave notes telling him where they were having predator trouble. When that happened, he'd "pack up some grub and ride right back out again."

I asked if he had practiced the so-called preventive control so popular with federal trappers then and now—killing predators before they cause trouble, assuming that sooner or later they will.

"I worked on coyotes all the time," he said. "But I took bears only when they acted up. Many's the time while out riding, I'd see a bear; he'd be right there, and I could easy have pulled out the 250/3000 Savage rifle I carried in my saddle scabbard and shot him. But I didn't. And sometimes on a deal like that, it wouldn't be but a week and I'd have to go back in there because that same bear had turned to killing sheep. Other times, bears would hang around a camp all summer and not bother a thing. Some trappers would kill every bear they came across, whether it was causing trouble or not; there was a lot of pressure on us for numbers. But I couldn't see it. Just like the poisoning—I didn't like it, and I didn't do it."

I asked about the grizzly.

"I got word they were having trouble up at Starvation; a bear had gotten into a herd of a thousand or so sheep a rancher named Hutchinson was grazing there; it's a pretty big place, once you get in there. The day before I arrived, the herder had moved the flock up out of the gulch, away from where the bear had come out of the trees during the night to kill several sheep. But there were carcasses still lying around, only partially eaten, and I figured the bear would come back to work on them some more. So that's where I set up to get him."

His "set up" done, Wilkinson rode south over Hunchback Pass, around Ute Mountain, and down into Ute Creek—a day each way plus working time—"to take care of some coyote problems." Before pulling out, he asked the herder—Amarante Roybal is the name he recalls—"to go down into the gulch every day and check to see if the bear had gotten into the trap."

When Ernie returned to Starvation three days later, on September 5, he asked Roybal if he'd seen the bear. "Oh no," said the herder, whose halting English Ernie dramatically recreated for me. "Me no go down there alone. It *dark* down there."

"Amarante, like most herders, was scared to death of bears," Ernie explained. "So I rode on down off the ridge and into the gulch, and there was the bear, dead, rolled over on his back with his legs sticking up in the air. The days had been warm, and he was already bloated."

I wondered how the bear had died so quickly in a leghold trap, but didn't ask.

It was a male, two or three years old, 250 or 275 pounds, and heavily muscled. The pelt was in fall prime, colored dark brown with yellow and silvery guard hairs. The part-time taxidermist thought it would have made a beautiful rug, but flies had already blown the flesh, the hair was slipping, and the corpse stank too much to mess with. Only the right front paw, sticking up in the air away from the putrescent carcass, was unspoiled. Noticing the extraordinarily long claws, Ernie cut off the paw, fleshed it out, and rubbed it down with salt. He still has it today, trotting it out to show students in his wilderness skills classes the difference between black bear and grizzly tracks.

At this juncture, Wilkinson led me out into the storefront and produced the paw for my inspection. The fur was chocolate brown with pale yellow guard hairs. The gray palm and toe pads, though rough like a dog's, were still pliable after forty-two years. The palm pad measured three inches front to back and four inches across. Taken together, the toes were slightly wider than the palm, fused at their bases, and arranged in a nearly straight line—not separated by hair and arced like a black bear's. The claws were only slightly curved and yellowish, with the longest measuring almost three inches. The claw tips were only slightly worn, suggesting that the young bear had not been doing a lot of digging, had not yet prepared his winter's den.

When I asked how he'd gone about trapping the animal, Ernie thought a long while before answering.

"Well, you generally want to build a log pen, or cubby, near the trail the bear has been using to come in at night . . . if you get up on a high point right at daybreak, you can see where the bear has walked through the grass the night before and knocked the dew off. So you build your cubby near the trail and drag a sheep carcass over and stuff it in the back. Then you conceal your trap at the entrance so that the bear will have to step into it when he goes for the bait. That way, you're fairly sure of getting the right bear, the one that's been causing the trouble; they usually come back to clean up their leftovers."

What kind of trap had he used?

"In bear traps, I like either a No. 5 or a No. 15 Victor, the only difference between the two being that one has teeth and the other doesn't. Some journalists have said I used a No. 6 Newhouse to catch that grizzly, but I didn't. Those things were too big and heavy to haul around, even on horseback; weighed more than forty pounds. Besides, I didn't know it was a grizzly that had been into the sheep; just naturally assumed it was a black bear. And the No. 5 is plenty big enough for black bear. Just chain it to a tree so's your bear can't drag it off."

Did he know it was a grizzly as soon as he saw it?

"No. It just struck me as a big bear with pretty fur and long claws. There was a lightning storm, and all I was thinking about was taking care of things as quick as possible and getting down out of there before I got fried. So I didn't pay too much attention. I just cut off that one paw and scalped the ears—as was required for the monthly kill count—to take to my boss, district supervisor Lee Bacus down in Monte Vista."

When Ernie showed Bacus the scalp and paw, the older man immediately recognized the long claws and light guard hairs as grizzly. "Lee asked about the skull," Ernie recalled. "He wanted to know if I'd brought it out. I told him no, that the corpse was stinking and a storm was on and I hadn't even thought about it. But I was headed back up there in a couple of weeks to go elk hunting, so I offered to pick it up then."

Ernie tried to make good on that offer, but scavengers had picked the carcass clean and had broken and scattered the bones like shells on a beach. The skull was nowhere to be found.

"Wish I could have located it," Ernie reflected. "It would be worth something today, with grizzlies so rare and all."

Had he ever given any thought to the possibility of grizzlies being around before the Starvation bear turned up? Hadn't there been some gossip—local people with stories about seeing grizzlies or grizzly sign?

"No on both counts," said Ernie, explaining that back then, there *were* no local people. "Just a few sheepherders in summer, and most of them didn't speak English."

When word got out about the Starvation grizzly, the Division of Wildlife "got all excited," designated the upper Rio Grande as a grizzly bear management area and made it illegal to kill the great bears there. Two years later, laws were passed protecting the grizzly throughout Colorado. At least on paper. If any could still be found to protect.

"As part of the deal," Ernie chuckled, "the Division sent a man up to look around for more grizzlies. He spent two summers up there but didn't find a thing so far as I know. Spent a lot of time down here at the shop, too, studying the differences between grizzly and black bear hair and paws, trying to figure it out as he went along."

At this point, I turned the conversation to the Blue Lake grizzly, from whose spoiled hide Wilkinson had salvaged the head mount still on display at the Skyline Lodge in Platoro.

"Like my own bear," he said, "it was a male, big compared to most blackies but small for a grizzly. In fact, I've always suspected that the two were twins. They were both the same age, about two and a half, same size, same color, right down the line. They could have been just recently turned out by their mother, which would help explain why they both got into trouble with sheep at about the same time."

Entirely plausible. It's subadult males of all mammalian species, predators in particular, that do the most wandering and, thus, fall into the most trouble. They've been pushed out of their childhood territories, either by a mother ready to breed again or by a mature male that sees them as competition, and have to go in search of a new home. They're inexperienced and, consequently, often hungry and desperate.

"A young bear like that could cover the distance between Starvation

Gulch and Blue Lake in a couple of days or less," my host suggested.

As tactfully as I could manage, I asked Ernie how he feels today about having killed one of the last grizzlies in Colorado.

"Can't say I'm proud of it. But if a predator was killing sheep, it was my job to take care of him."

"Yes," I agreed, "it was your job, and killing grizzlies was legal then, and it was an accident to boot—you had no way of knowing and no reason to suspect it would be a grizzly. But still, what are your feelings about it now, since grizzlies have been almost entirely wiped out in the lower forty-eight? Would you change anything if you had it to do again?"

"Well," he mused, "I guess I could have done a better job of documenting the circumstances of the kill; should have been more precise about keeping records. And I wish I'd taken pictures."

I gave up. The retrospective remorse I was probing for just wasn't there. Ernest Wilkinson simply does not view any aspect of his grizzly slaying as deserving of guilt. It was his job. It was an accident. It was legal. It was just something that happened. I didn't argue. There was nothing to argue about.

I had not come to Ernest's Taxidermy expecting to make a new friend. My intent was simply to get the story of the Starvation grizzly's death, then leave. But after talking with Ernie for a few hours and getting to know him and finding myself enjoying his company, I suggested that we hike into Starvation together. I wanted to see the place, and I'd need a guide to find the exact spot. Ernie allowed as how he wouldn't mind visiting Starvation again. It had, after all, been forty-two years.

Peaking at a relatively measly 10,833 feet, Timber Hill is more or less the midpoint, though far short of the high point, between the old mining towns of Silverton to the northwest and Creede to the east. According to the plan we'd hatched back in June at his shop, Ernie and I rendezvoused at the Lost Trail Ranch above Rio Grande Reservoir, where he conducts his wilderness skills classes. We left his old pumpkin-colored van parked under a shade tree there and bumped the last spine-shattering miles up to Timber Hill in my four-by pickup.

I can't imagine having endured Stony Pass in a stagecoach or on the hard plank seat of an ore wagon, which the rocky old roadway was built to accommodate more than a hundred years ago, with few improvements since. In several places, rocky talus slides and deep stream crossings make it nearly impassable, even for my high-slung truck.

By the time we made the slow drive up and arrived at camp, only a couple of hours of light remained and electric blue storm clouds threatened; July is the most pyrotechnic of months in the southern Rockies. We set about dragging in an evening's supply of firewood, from which Ernie selected several match-sized sticks of "squaw wood" and deftly arranged a tepee in the center of some previous roadside campers' fire ring. Beneath this, he inserted a splintery "fuzz stick" whittled on the spot, and struck a one-match blaze.

As the flames grew, Ernie produced a "billy can"—in this case, a gallon vegetable tin—filled it with creek water, and dropped in the dinners he had generously volunteered to provide: military-issue "meals ready to eat" in foil bags. After these feasts had simmered for five minutes, chef Ernie fished them out and asked if I wanted a cup of coffee, nodding at the boiling billy water.

I studied the greenish scum floating on top and hesitated.

My companion shrugged. "That's just the ink that boiled off the food pouches. Don't taste so bad. I drink it all the time."

By way of compromise, I filtered a cupful of the glaucous liquid through a paper towel and added a big spoonful of instant caffeine.

Over dinner, Ernie explained his plan of attack for the morning: We would leave my truck there and scramble down into the canyon of the Rio Grande, carrying fly rods and waders in addition to lunches and rain gear. At the river, we would don the waders and ford the icy water, cache waders and fishing gear on the far bank, and claw our way up through the near-vertical terrain, cliff upon cliff, into the dark timber. There we could "probably" pick up an elk trail leading into the bottom of the gulch. Then it would be a straightforward hump of a final mile or so up through the belly of the beast to its head, near where the grisly grizzly deed had been done, oh so long ago.

When I surveyed Starvation Gulch with the naked eye from our Timber Hill camp—looking out across the six-hundred-foot ditch of the Rio Grande and up endless rows of stepped cliffs and through a mile or more of spruce-fir forest as thick and black as a moonless midnight (and sure to be stacked neck-high in blowdown)—the place seemed as remote and foreboding as Detroit.

On the topographical map, it's only about three miles straight-line from the head of the gulch down to the river. On the ground, however, there are no straight lines, effectively doubling the distance. Naked alpine peaks, most of them rising above thirteen thousand feet, guard the gulch on three sides, with the forest and river canyon forming a challenging barrier against approach from below. The spot Ernie had marked on the map as our goal—about where he figures he'd killed the bear—waited at 11,400 feet. Viewed from Timber Hill, it seemed obvious why Starvation Gulch had been among the last grizzly holdouts in the entire Southwest.

I reacted to this maniacally ambitious plan with a fearful groan. Considering distance, altitude gain, and nastiness of topography going up, then allowing God only knows how much time to poke around trying to find the exact spot where Ernie had slain the bear—eat lunch, take pictures—then the steep scramble back down, fording the river and grunting out of the canyon back up to camp (with maybe an afternoon lightning and hail storm tossed in for added excitement), not to mention Ernie's desire to do some evening fishing down in the canyon . . . to attempt all of that in the space of just one brief day, I tactfully suggested, might be pushing things just a *wee* bit, even by Wilkinson's mountain-man standards.

Still, I confessed, I was willing to give it a go, if there was no other way. As an afterthought, I asked how people managed to get sheep in and out of there, and how he'd done it on horseback.

"Oh," said Ernie, "there's other ways in. I suppose we could drive up to Beartown at first light—assuming the road wasn't washed out during the spring melt-off—hike east across the Divide, and drop down into Starvation from the top. Trouble with that route is that we'd have to climb back over the Divide to get out. You might be tired by then."

Indeed.

"And if we go in that way, we won't get to fish coming out."

Unfortunate.

With dinner finished and our greenish swill swallowed, we admired the last violet streaks of an alpine sunset fading beyond the jagged horizon. Heat lightning strobed in the distance. Ernie noted that it would probably be a good idea to go ahead and make up our beds, in case a sudden storm should come up. "Tag along," he suggested, grinning that shy sly grin of his. "You might learn something."

Dragging an eight-foot aspen pole behind him—I'd wondered why he wouldn't let me break it up for firewood—Ernie wandered around for a minute before selecting an open spot beneath a fat, low-limbed spruce. "Time me," he said.

I glanced at my watch—9:18 P.M. Getting dark.

Without appearing to rush, Ernie positioned the aspen limb on the ground parallel to the slope and about three feet out from the spruce, anchoring it in place with several fist-sized rocks wedged in below. Then, dropping to his knees, he began raking up the decomposing spruce needles that littered the ground beneath and around the tree, tossing them into the cavity formed between the trunk above and the aspen-limb dam below.

As he worked, Ernie explained that the thick cushion of needles he was piling up would level the slope, make a soft mattress, provide insulation from the ground, and, should it rain, allow water to flow beneath, keeping his bed high and dry. Finally, he spread his nylon rain poncho over the needle mattress, unrolled a small sleeping bag encased in a weatherproof Gore-Tex bivy sack Meg had sewn up for him, and . . . "How long?"

I checked—9:22. "Four minutes. Flat."

Determined to show Ernie up, I walked over to my pickup, unrolled and blew up my expensive "self-inflating" sleeping pad, unrolled and spread out my sleep sack. I'd just made a one-minute berth in the covered bed of my truck, but the victory was hollow.

A leak was taken, a splash of whiskey was poured (Ernie declined), the fire was stirred and fed wood enough to last another hour or so, and quiet conversation ensued until sack time. Up the mountain somewhere to the west, a bull elk sang out one lusty bugle—like a bent high note on a saxophone. July 24: a full month earlier than I'd ever heard that magical autumn sound before.

Overnight, the clouds had moved on without dropping the feared rain. The morning is clear and cool, ideal for a vigorous hike into the unknown territory of natural and unnatural history. Walking in the lead, I set the pace, taking it easy, in no particular hurry, conserving my energies—though for what, I can't yet say. That's why I'm conserving.

Our daybreak drive up to Beartown was, well, *interesting*. We splashed across the Rio Grande near its headwaters, where the flow looked only a foot deep in the flat morning light but proved to be twice that, then crawled up the Bear Creek "road" to the old Beartown site: 11,162 feet into the sky, a century dead, and not so much as a plank left of what was once a booming mining camp and top-of-the-world stage station.

While side-hilling up one particularly steep stretch of trail, I hear, just ahead, the distinctive *chunk . . . chunk . . . chunk* of a fleeing mule deer; muleys don't run so much as they bound, like some displaced species of African antelope. I stop and scan the forest for a glimpse of the animal but see only trees. Just three leaps had been sufficient to conceal the nervous muley behind a bushy wall of Engelmann spruce, subalpine fir, and a dense understory of waist-high forbs and ferns. Had the animal merely stood still as a statue, or ghosted silently away as bears are wont to do, we would probably have walked right past without ever knowing it was there. Forest hikers would be surprised to know how often they pass close by not only deer but bears, those masters at seeing without being seen, of coming and going without being heard.

Grizzly bears are said to be capable of identifying the upwind odor of humans at nearly a mile and can hear normal conversation at more than three hundred yards. These keen senses, combined with their genetic shyness and inclination to flee from humans at speeds up to thirty miles an hour, account for the rarity of grizzly sightings in the wild. Unless, of course, you are hiking in silence into the wind and bump into one at close range. In such instances, while a black bear will almost always either remain hidden until the danger passes or run away, a grizzly is less predictable.

Now the trail dips into the narrow cut of a glassy snowmelt brook. Just yards below where the little stream slides over the trail, its course is dammed by the moss-shrouded corpse of a huge fallen tree. In and around the resultant small marsh grow sedges, skunk cabbages, and a dazzling profusion of mountain bluebells.

Ernie takes this gorgeous little garden as a cue to launch into an impromptu wilderness skills class, describing which parts of which wild plants are edible and when, and how best to prepare them; warning of the extreme toxicity of the skunk cabbage, more properly called false hellebore or corn lily (*Veratrum californicum*, not to be confused with *Lysichitum americanum*, the innocuous yellow skunk cabbage of the Pacific Northwest and Montana); informing me that pregnant elk cows seek out lush growths of bluebells like this in which to "throw" their June calves and that elk and bears and domestic sheep and cattle all hanker after the tasty pink-blue beauties.

Farther along, Ernie stops and bends down to examine a big dry puffball projecting from the dark mountain soil. "If you've got a bad cut or a bleeding wound of any kind," he says, "find one of these and bust it open"—he pricks the rust-colored fungus with a quick finger and a billion spores rise like brown smoke—"hold it against the wound; it'll staunch the bleeding and prevent infection."

And so it goes through a most informative morning's hike.

By and by the switchbacks line out, the old-growth forest falls behind, and we enter a narrow strip of krummholz, the eerie pygmy "bent wood" forest that occurs just below timberline. The open tundra lies just ahead, just above. When we attain the crest, Ernie stops to survey the scene. A faint path, hardly even a proper game trail, skeins out to our left, weaving through tufts of grass and low-growing alpine wildflowers, tracking north along Indian Ridge. "This way," says my guide, dodging around me to take the lead.

The hike so far, though vigorous, hasn't been bad. And now that we're on top and hiking off-trail, the way is almost level and almost easy, even at a little better than twelve grand.

We walk for a while into the late morning sun before spying the sparkling many-fingered headwaters of Starvation Creek, only a mile or so away and six hundred feet below. Thanks to Ernie's four-decade memory, we have come in blind and wound up exactly where we want to be.

Viewed from above, Starvation Gulch is revealed as a verdant, sloping subalpine park ringed by dark timber and set about by the ten primary peaks of Ute Ridge. This place, gentle and welcoming, bears no resemblance whatsoever to the impenetrable hellhole I worried over from below last evening. Along its grassy edges, the meadow is interrupted here and there by stubby fingers of conifers—one of which marks the last stand of a certain well-fed young Colorado grizzly.

We angle down toward the cirque and come to another clear rill of icy water. Ernie kneels at its edge, removes his ancient grime-stiffened felt hat—at sixty-nine, he still has a full head of hair, damn him—dips the hat in, raises it, and drinks deep from its flooded brim. Water diamonds drip from his chin as he grins at me and says, "Beats carrying a canteen."

Now the old trapper stands and points to a small knoll a few hundred yards below us and overlooking the head of the gulch. I agree with Ernie's suggestion that it's an ideal aerie from which to inspect the park's opposite shore, and we angle steeply down toward it.

As we walk, we spot a serpentine line of tan dots emerging from the gully of Snowslide Creek, out near the center of the gulch. The animals are taking their sweet old time single-filing toward an avalanche chute sandwiched between two timber fingers directly opposite. We stop and raise our binoculars: elk.

Long after we have reached the knoll and plopped down in the cool grass to glass, the elk still come. When the last of the stragglers finally disappears into the timber, we agree that the herd comprised at least eighty of the big deer. Ernie says he's run into batches of two hundred and more up nearby Pole Creek. No doubt he has, but this is the largest gathering of elk I've ever been blessed to see—discounting, that is, the herds of hundreds that winter, docile as cattle, along the Animas River north of Durango. (Or used to; most of the best of that former ranch pasture was recently transmogrified into Durango's third golf course, replete with a tacky gaggle of greens-side trophy homes for the pretentious wealthy. Progress.)

Directly below us, almost within a rock's toss, stands an island of spindly spruce-fir, bunched tightly together as if for mutual security. Around this oblong of trees wraps a broad marsh grown waist-high in a tangle of subalpine willow. Moose nirvana. In fact, the local game warden asked me to watch for a moose cow and calf that were thought to have wintered up here and haven't been seen since fall. Nor, I'm afraid, are they apparent now.

Instead, we are graced with the sudden appearance of a plump, steel gray coyote. Either unaware or uncaring that two humans are sitting within easy shooting range of her—for some reason, I believe it's a female—the bemused dog goes happily about its business, nose to the damp ground, sniffing at a fast trot toward the little copse of conifers just below us and disappearing forthwith therein.

A couple of minutes later, a second coyote materializes at the edge of the willows. This beast, which I take to be the other's mate, is noticeably larger and looks as old and raggedy as I sometimes feel, enjoying perhaps his last golden summer on this heavenly earth. More cautious than his partner, the wise old mutt raises his scruffy face, peers up at us, twitches his nose in disdainful recognition, then turns and melts back into the marsh thicket.

After a while, having picked out our route, we ease down the abrupt slope into the head of the gulch, skirting the sprawling sedge and willow marsh as best we can.

The sun falls warm on our faces, and the cool air carries the mixed perfume of wildflowers: ubiquitous dandelions, bashful little striped geraniums, alpine bistort like cotton balls on sticks, purple monkshoods and fringed gentians and sticky asters, plus a fortune of anonymous others scattered like living jewels across the park. Along the soggy marsh edges and frequent snowmelt trickles grow lavender shooting stars, big white-trimmed blue columbines (the Colorado state flower and a pretty good choice), delicate cushions of pinkish moss campion, and white-flowered watercress by the hundreds.

We reach the eastern lip of the cirque, one of hundreds such glacier-carved bowls throughout the San Juans, and halt to confer on a search strategy. Ernie allows as how he'll walk in the open a few yards out from the trees, looking for familiar scenery and bits of bone he hopes may still be lying about even after so very long. I propose to keep just inside the undulant tree line, looking for the log remains of the cubby, which I suspect are more likely than bone to have survived forty-two alpine winters. Ernie shrugs, as if to say he considers this ploy a waste of time, but says nothing. We start slowly down the park.

The quarry proves elusive. No bone, no rotting V of logs, no nothing except sublime alpine scenery, the cleanest air and water in the world, and, in my head, a mildly troubling confusion of feelings about being here.

After half an hour of snooping down the park edge, four eyes glued to the ground, Ernie asks if I'm about ready to break for lunch. I follow him to a glacial erratic, a VW-sized boulder stranded a hundred yards out in the meadow, onto whose sun-warmed, lichen-stained antiquity we climb. Perched thus, like a couple of overgrown marmots, we dig out our brown bags and eat.

Offering the ingenuous smile that by now I've learned indicates a modest self-embarrassment at what is about to be said, Ernie takes me entirely off guard by suddenly announcing, "There's no point in you searching for a cubby, because there ain't one here; never was."

"But I thought you built a pen and stuffed a dead sheep in and set a trap, and that's how you took the grizzly."

"I never said any such thing. That was your assumption when you came to interview me; probably read it somewhere. I just let you keep believing that way, just like I've let everybody else believe all these years. I'm telling you now, though, that it didn't happen like that. I've always worried that if some do-good journalist ever got hold of the truth, he'd try to twist it around to make it sound worse than it really was. But I know that this Colorado grizzly thing, getting the story right, is important to you, so I'm going to tell you something I've never told anybody else but Meg: I didn't trap that grizzly."

Ernest Wilkinson looks off toward the trees, seeing things I never will.

"I killed it with a coyote-getter . . . a cyanide set gun. There was no law back then against using them on national forests, and I didn't have much other choice. I only had one trap left by the time I got up here, and the way it worked out I needed two."

Ernie falls into quiet reflection, and I recall how, when I'd interviewed him at his shop and asked if he'd used a cubby and what kind of trap it had been, he'd hesitated, then dropped into a second-person narrative of how catching a bear was usually done, and how he generally preferred the No. 5 Victor—but he never actually said he'd used a cubby or a leghold trap here in Starvation. Nor had he denied it. The sly old fox.

But now Ernie owns up, explaining that by the time he got up here, the herder had moved his sheep across the park and up onto the flank of Indian Ridge, trying to get away from the marauding bear. Ernie placed his last steel trap over there.

Knowing bears as he did, Ernie figured the bandit might return to where he'd already killed sheep to clean up the leftovers. To cover this angle, he decided to set out the only other weapon he had left in his depleted arsenal, a coyote-getter. He found a sheep carcass that had plenty of smelly meat still on it, hitched it to his horse with a rope, and dragged it over to where the bear's trail emerged from the trees. That done, he set the coyote-getter next to the ripe bait and coated its bait bulb with honey.

"In order to use a second bear trap," Ernie explains now, "it would have meant most of a day's ride down to the Rio Grande where my vehicle was parked, then a ninety-mile round-trip to the warehouse in Monte Vista to get another bear trap, and then back up to Starvation. A few weeks before, a black bear had killed thirty-four sheep in one night before I got him, and I figured the best way to avoid another such carnage was to use the coyote-getter baited with a dab of honey from my grub sack.

"That bear was dead within a few seconds of biting the bait," Ernie assures me. "Didn't make it but a few yards before he went down. Probably happened the first night. That's why he was already bloated and stinking by the time I got back here three days later. If he'd been caught in a leghold trap, he'd probably have stayed alive and maybe suffered all that time. There was nothing illegal about it, nothing cruel. A blast of cyanide down the throat's the fastest and most humane way I know of to kill a large animal. Still, I've always worried about admitting it . . . I'm trusting you to tell it right."

I promise to do my best. Ernie nods, looks away, and slices open a pink grapefruit.

From back in the woods comes a chorus of birdlike chirps—elk cows talking with their calves. They've heard us, or smelled us, probably both, but apparently don't feel sufficiently threatened to stampede away. A shadow slides along the ground in front of us. I glance up and see a pair of what I make to be prairie falcons, hanging against the azure vastness like hand-painted kites. They circle twice, then sail away, surfing gracefully down the upslope breeze.

We stash our lunch trash in our packs and resume our hunt.

Ernie has decided that the place we're looking for must be near the avalanche chute where the elk disappeared this morning, just below us now. We stroll on down, and it takes only seconds for my guide to pronounce that this is in fact the place. He knows for sure, he says, because here's the shell of an old salt log—a foot-diameter log maybe fifteen feet long with a channel axed along the length of its top, creating a shallow trough into which old Amarante Roybal would have poured rock salt to encourage his sheep to stay in the area, much as salt blocks are used by stockmen today.

We are standing just below the tip of a stringer of evergreens extending a few yards out into the park, the little trees paralleling a shallow drainage running down from the avalanche chute. Following the chute up into the woods is a deeply incised game trail freshly pocked with the tracks of many elk; their funky scent lingers in the air like the perfume trail of a mysterious woman. Major game runways such as this can be hundreds of years old, and I reflect sadly that it could be the selfsame path the young grizzly had followed to extinction on or about September 3, 1951.

We mill around for an hour or so, looking for bone fragments but finding none, taking pictures, talking little, thinking each our own thoughts.

We are not always of like mind, Ernie and I. He is of the old-line western rural school of thought that enthusiastically endorses "multiple use" of public lands—grazing in particular—and resents the intervention of "metropolitan people who have messed up their own environments and now are attempting to tell us rural folks how to manage our public lands, which mostly are still in good shape."

My own eyes and experiences, to the contrary, have led me to believe that too many years of too little regulation have led too many western ranchers to view public lands as exclusively theirs, and, together with sympathetic Forest Service managers, to interpret "multiple use" to mean commodities production above maintaining a healthy and natural ecology.

The newly appointed chief of the U.S. Forest Service, Jack Ward Thomas, is an ethical, intelligent, far-thinking man who will do much good if not bullied to his knees, or out of office, by western special interests, as was Bureau of Land Management (BLM) chief Jim Baca, a man too honest for politics. Thomas has summed up the philosophical dichotomy separating Ernie and me thus:

> Some tend to be anthropocentric and take a utilitarian view of land—that is, land exists for people and is to be managed to satisfy people's needs. Others are mainly biocentric in their philosophy, view humans as part of nature, and are concerned with organic wholeness.

Ernie is clearly in the former camp; I'm staunchly in the latter. Even so, I like and respect Mr. Wilkinson and believe he is big enough to grant a similar tolerance to me. "Honest men," as an old friend once counseled, "have a right to disagree."

"I just remembered something else," Ernie says as we're preparing to leave.

"When I came back up here elk hunting a couple of weeks after I'd taken the bear—that time when I looked for the skull and couldn't find it—I was riding down off Hunchback Pass there," he points, "and spotted some huge tracks crossing a patch of snow. Biggest bear tracks I've ever seen, and one that was still fairly clear was maybe a foot long by half a foot wide, but a little melted out from several days of sun so that no claw marks showed. I remember wondering if it could have been a big old sow grizzly coming down through here, the mother of the young male I'd killed, looking for him. And maybe the mother of that lookalike Blue Lake grizzly as well. Who knows? It was a really big track. Of course, that was a long time ago."

Yes, it was.

The day is running down, and after a while, though neither of us really wishes to, we turn our backs on this lovely killing field and walk away, the last grizzly slayer and me.

Awash in nostalgia for a time and a Colorado I never knew, I am haunted again by the words of A. B. Guthrie, Jr. "Progress," Bud liked to point out, "means no turning back."

5

"TORE NEARLY ALL TO PEASES"

The Wiseman Incident

Wiseman will make it. The bear won't.

—*Paul Harvey News,*
September 24, 1979

AUGUST 22, 1993: SAN JUAN MOUNTAINS

I'm driving east on U.S. 160 toward Pagosa Springs this morning. It's raining lightly, and the sanguine rise of Chimney Rock is wreathed in a swirling chemise of fog. Tourists are pulling willy-nilly off the highway for pictures, and I don't blame them; the sight is breathtaking.

As always when I pass this way, I recall that poignant diorama at the Denver Museum of Natural History—those three stuffed grizzlies standing in an autumn meadow, the bifurcate hulk of Chimney Rock in the distant background. By tonight, I'll be camped not far from where one of that glass-caged trio was killed back in 1913. But more to the point of this trip: by tonight, I'll also be camped near where the last "confirmed" Colorado grizzly lived secretly for more than two decades, only to make national headlines with the sudden violence of its death.

As I coast down the hill into the mountain bowl of Pagosa Springs, all is fog and vapor. Which is not so unusual here on chill damp mornings, given the quantities of steam venting from natural hot springs along the San Juan River's jake-legged course through town. In glorious counterpoint to all this gloom, a sunspot burns like white sulphur through the western cloud mass to glisten on the eastern horizon like a drop of quicksilver.

On a whim, I bypass the Elkhorn Cafe, my tried-and-true Pagosa breakfast stop, and pull in at a place called the Aspen. After ordering, I peruse the flip side of the Aspen's clever menu, printed on news pulp to imitate an old-style tabloid, with excerpts from nineteenth-century Pagosa papers. Amid features about a Ute hunting party passing through town and forecasts for the continued growth of Archuleta County, one clip captures my rapt attention. From the June 12, 1890, *Pagosa Springs News:*

> On Tuesday of last week Siegel Brown had quite a thrilling experience with three huge silver tip bears.
>
> Mr. Brown was riding over the range near the Blanco [River, a few miles south of Pagosa] on that day, accompanied by a small dog; the dog began to sniffle in the brush and Mr. Brown rode up to see what was the cause of the dog's alarm when three bears suddenly sprang toward him and one of them planted his claw into the horse's hip.
>
> As Mr. Brown was not armed there was nothing for him to do but to urge on his horse and race for his life, which Mr. Brown thought was then hanging on a very slender thread.
>
> While the chase was going on Mr. Brown's boot caught on some brush and he imagined that the bear was making a meal of it, but he escaped without injury except a bad scare.
>
> Siegel now declares that he who says the bears in this region do not fight is a falsifier. Willet Brown shot one of the bears this week and estimates his weight at 500 pounds.

Certainly, as Siegel Brown declared, grizzlies—in the San Juans as elsewhere—indeed will fight. The unasked question is: Under what provocation?

In all likelihood, Mr. Brown's three bears had been a sow—the large grizzly later killed by Willet Brown—and her two subadult cubs. And most probably, had Brown's dog not gone "sniffling in the brush" to disturb the bears, Brown would have ridden right on past without ever suspecting their presence. But startled at close range as she was, the sow's protective instincts would have demanded that she give chase.

Similarly, the circumstances under which a healthy adult female grizzly of some four hundred pounds was killed in hand-to-claw combat with outfitter Ed Wiseman as he bowhunted for elk one September evening in 1979 remain not only a mystery but a source of lively local debate.

The heart of the debate is who attacked whom. Most people who recall reading about the incident and the lengthy federal investigation that followed remain convinced that Wiseman or his hunter-client from Kansas, Michael Niederee, illegally bow-shot the bear as it napped in its daybed, prompting the attack. The outfitter counters that he inflicted the fatal wound with a handheld arrow while pinned beneath the attacking grizzly.

Studying the U.S. Fish and Wildlife Service's inch-thick investigation file only deepens the mystery.

Figuring prominently in the FWS investigation was a necropsy performed on the putrefied corpse of the Wiseman bear—which the Division's Bob Rouse, who was there, tells me was already reduced to "little more than a gut pile" after only the first few of several days it spent lying naked under a high-altitude sun. Eventually, the gut pile was helicoptered out of the mountains, trucked to the nearby La Jara state fish hatchery and frozen, then trucked on to Denver (thawing en route), transferred to another vehicle, and hauled to Colorado State University at Fort Collins. There, on October 2, it was finally necropsied—ten days of spoilage, rough handling, freezing, thawing, and decomposition after the fact.

The necropsy discovered two wounds. The first, to the lower throat area, was determined to have been made by a four-bladed weapon; it was superficial and was judged not to have been fatal. The second wound was to the chest and appeared to have been inflicted by a flat instrument, like a knife blade, penetrating the right lung and heart and severing the aortic arch. The examiner estimated that after receiving such a wound, the bear could have lived no longer than five minutes.

From this information, the investigators presumed that two different instruments—probably two distinct types of hunting broadheads—had been used to inflict the two wounds. Furthermore, said official reports, the position and depth of the wound channel in the chest fairly ruled out its having been made with a handheld arrow, as Wiseman claims to have done. In fact, the nature of this injury led the investigators to surmise that the bear had been shot with an arrow fired from a bow *before* the animal attacked Wiseman.

It was with those damning presumptions lodged firmly under their skins that Division and FWS officials, primarily the latter, opened the investigation mandated by the Endangered Species Act. Ed Wiseman and Mike Niederee—because they were the only humans known to be in the immediate area at the time of the incident—were the sole suspects.

While Wiseman lay in the hospital recovering from his near-fatal mauling, and after conducting initial interviews with him and Niederee, the feds turned their focus on the Kansan. Following a thorough grilling at his home and a lie detector test, Mike Niederee was cleared. From that point on, the full force of the investigation and its attendant media circus was directed at Wiseman.

Six months after it began, Wiseman's doctor finally cleared him to take a lie detector test. He passed, and the investigation was dropped. But even then, it appears that at least the feds, clinging doggedly to the belief that the fatal chest wound could not have been inflicted by a handheld arrow, still felt that someone, probably Wiseman, had shot the bear. The case was closed, it seems, not because the investigators had determined to their satisfaction that Wiseman was telling the truth, but rather and only because the government lacked sufficient evidence to prosecute.

Before I invested nearly two years in exploring the so-called Wiseman incident, I too felt sure that *somebody* must have illegally shot that poor bear. But even before I phoned Wiseman and asked him to guide me to the attack site and tell me the whole story in situ, I'd had second thoughts about his guilt. Aspects of the investigation, especially the handling, interpretation, and final disposal of physical evidence, comprised a sad little comedy of errors including repeated helicopter crashes, inexplicable delays, lost bear body parts, inadequate fieldwork (the FWS never even bothered to visit the attack site), and tenuous deductive leaps.

The most potentially incriminating piece of "evidence" against Wiseman was the necropsy report suggesting that two different types of broadheads had been used on the grizzly and that the fatal chest wound could not have been inflicted by a handheld arrow. On the other side of the ledger, Wiseman has told the same "two stabs in self-defense" story from day one, corroborated by the bear's tanned hide, which contains only two arrow holes. Moreover, all of Wiseman's arrows were tipped with Bear Razorheads—a popular broadhead consisting of a wedge-shaped main blade with a razor-thin "bleeder" blade inserted perpendicularly to form a four-bladed, or + pattern.

So? So, as a bowhunter of some three decades, I used Bear Razorheads for years—and more than once cut a hand while butchering a deer or elk in whose tissue the insert blade had lodged, having separated on impact from the main blade. This could easily account for the fact that the throat wound in the grizzly carcass showed a four-winged pattern, while the chest wound—the second to be inflicted according to Wiseman's account—showed a flat, single-bladed pattern. Had the examiners known what to look for and had they looked for it, they might have found the bleeder blade still in the bear's neck.

Another possible explanation is that Mike Niederee shot the bear before it attacked Wiseman. The young elk hunter had in fact admitted to seeing a large sleeping bruin that fit the grizzly's description—undoubtedly the same animal—prior to the attack, but testified that he backed quietly away without disturbing the snoring beast. And Niederee's arrows were tipped with three-bladed broadheads, matching neither of the wounds.

Concerning the theory that a man could not have struck the bear hard enough with a handheld arrow to achieve a penetration of six to ten inches—the depth of the chest wound channel—Wiseman's widespread reputation for exceptional strength back in those days must be considered; those who knew him well weren't the least surprised at this feat.

Also perhaps facilitating Wiseman's narrow victory was the grizzly's advanced age and physical disabilities, which may well have weakened her attack. My examination of the skull at the Denver Museum of Natural History confirms reports that both upper canines were horribly abscessed, with the right "fang" worn down to a dull, useless nub and abscessed all the way into the nasal passages. These handicaps, together with an old and imperfectly healed jaw injury, may well have inhibited the bear's biting and crushing powers. Further, virtually every joint in the old lady's skeleton—paws, limbs, vertebra—is covered with a gnarly "lipping," an unnatural bone growth indicative of acute and keenly painful arthritis. Had this been a younger, more vital grizzly with sharper teeth and better mobility, the fight might well have ended differently.

Finally, addressing the arrow-penetration enigma—whether the fatal heart wound was more likely to have been inflicted by a handheld arrow, as Wiseman maintains, or by a bow-shot missile, as the investigators suspected—a friend of Wiseman's took it upon himself to collect twenty-one affidavits from archers who had killed bears and shot completely through in the doing. And these "pass-through" shots were frequently accomplished with fairly lightweight bows. According to the necropsy report, the fatal wound penetrated the right side of the grizzly's chest but failed to enter the left, or far, side, yet did not strike any bone that would have stopped the arrow. To an experienced archer, Wiseman argues, this simply doesn't wash.

"I shoot a seventy-pound compound bow," Ed told me during our initial conversation. "If I'd shot that bear, the arrow would almost certainly have passed completely through. A bear, even a big one, is the easiest big game animal I know of to penetrate—unless you hit bone, arrows just sail right on through.

"Just examine the physical facts, and the story tells itself: only two strikes according to my recollection, only two wounds according to the necropsy report, only two arrow holes in the hide, and the fatal chest wound is only an inch and a half from the centerline of the chest . . . where do you go from there?"

Where I went from there was back to the Denver Museum of Natural History to examine the tanned hide of the Wiseman grizzly. Sure enough, there were only two arrow holes—one in the lower throat and the other down in the midchest area, very near the centerline.

Owing to the "gut pile" condition of the carcass by the time it was necropsied, the examiners, it seems clear to me, reckoned the chest wound to be far higher on the animal's side than it actually was. Even allowing for the loose skin of a bear, which conceivably could "travel" some distance—say, if the animal had its right leg raised—no way could a hole that close to the center of the chest have been inflicted by an arrow entering midway up the side of the bear. Nor would such a bow shot even be possible unless the animal was lying on its side with its upper legs raised and the bottom of its chest thus exposed (like a dog begging to have its tummy rubbed). The chest hole is, however, exactly where you'd expect it to be had a man lying prone stabbed upward with an arrow held in his left hand as the bear stood over him—exactly as Wiseman claims was the case.

By relying on a rotted carcass—which easily could and obviously did lie to them—rather than on the positions of the two arrow holes in the hide, the investigators got things bass-ackwards, or so it seems to me.

And there's the matter of the suspect's reputation. Everyone I talked to about Wiseman—clients and employees, fellow outfitters, friends, business associates, and Division personnel—spoke of him as an honest and ethical man who demands that his guides and hunters follow the very letter of the law, and who has always done exactly that himself.

"Ed and I attended the same college at the same time," says retired district wildlife manager Dick Weldon, the first official to arrive at the scene of the attack. "I was game warden for the district where Ed has always hunted and outfitted, and I can't count the times I've dropped in on his camp by surprise, or come up on him in the field, and all those years I never once had to write him a ticket. I'm sure he didn't shoot that bear. It was a classic case of being in the wrong place at the wrong time."

And the bottom line: Wiseman passed a polygraph test.

Yet even in the face of abundant evidence to the contrary, the public's suspicions remain largely intact. "I don't think I'll ever live it down," Ed told me. "Some people just flat don't like the fact—like Paul Harvey said on the noon news the day after the fight—that Wiseman made it, but the bear didn't."

In 1983 the Denver Museum of Natural History put the Wiseman grizzly's hide and skull, the fatal arrow, and a bronze sculpture depicting the fight on display in the Dalton Bear Hall. The museum had planned to leave the materials out for only a month or so, but the display proved so popular that it enjoyed a run of three years. According to Wiseman's conversations with museum personnel at the time the display was being shown, the question most often asked by viewers had to do with Ed's guilt or innocence. Even though the media had been remarkably kind to "the suspect" throughout the lengthy ordeal, a substantial portion of the public, perhaps a majority, was somehow left with the impression that here was a guilty man.

Driving up through the San Juan National Forest, I pass old logging clear-cuts and the huge scar of Wolf Creek ski area. Next comes the "Scenic Pull-off" at the apogee of the pass at 10,857 feet (clogged, as usual, with overheated motor homes). Over the top and down the eastern slope through the Rio Grande National Forest toward South Fork. Right away, the clouds begin to thin and fall behind—this is a West Slope storm—and soon I'm blessed with sunshine and a sky as blue and deep as the South Pacific.

On the bumper of a ragged old VW bus in front of me, pasted just to the left of a California license plate, is a sticker proclaiming "God is coming, and She is pissed!" No doubt.

The recently improved highway up the west side of Wolf Creek Pass is four lanes wide and fast, but the lower stretch of the eastern descent remains a narrow two-lane roller-coaster ride above a vertical plunge of fifty to a hundred feet to the creek. Overtaking and passing slow traffic here with my lame little four-banger pickup is all but impossible, even on the downhill run. I resign myself to plodding along amid a tedious march of eastbound semis and motor homes.

Eventually, Park Creek campground appears ahead, with Park Creek road just beyond. I steer right and leave the human highway behind. After a handful of miles, pretty little Park Creek, which the dirt Forest Service road follows closely, climbs out of its tight lower canyon and into marshy meadows. A few tents and pickup campers are scattered here and there between road and creek, but no motor homes or monster trailers, and little traffic on the bumpy road.

At Elwood Pass, I take the right fork down the mountain. The distant view, toward Red Mountain, is immaculate. Over the pass and down a ways, however, cattle appear and the proximate scenery instantly and literally goes to shit. Sadly, the Forest Service, ignoring long and loud protests from concerned individuals and environmental groups, has recently approved a major old-growth logging operation in the Red Mountain area. This means more new roads, less ancient forest; it also means more erosion and fewer unpolluted streams, ugly scars, less natural beauty, and easier access for road-cruising wildlife poachers. (Justice William O. Douglas said it best: "A road is a dagger placed in the heart of a wilderness.")

From here the road falls down past the nineteenth-century mining camp of Stunner, now a Forest Service campground, to the formerly pristine Alamosa River, now shamed by skull-and-crossbones signs warning campers that the water is chemically polluted and unfit for consumption. What the signs don't say is that the seventeen-mile course of the Alamosa River through verdant Alamosa Canyon is not merely poisoned, it is sterilized. Life left the river when cyanide leaked from the 170-

million-gallon tailings ponds of a recently defunct gold mining operation atop the local watershed.

Having committed its brutal rape, killed a river, and trucked away
the wealth, the Summitville Consolidated Mining Company declared
bankruptcy to avoid cleaning up its mess, which you and I are now
financing through the toxic waste Superfund—a $120 million burden
that may prevent further damage but will never undo the harm already
done. One of the most scenic and life-giving watercourses in the San
Juans is gone forever. Yet Colorado's antiquated Mined Land Reclamation Act, manipulated by a powerful mining lobby, can be relied on to
ensure similar disasters in the future. The voices in defense of the land
are loud, but without political power.

Not too many years ago, while walking along the Alamosa River
near here, a summer resident found what he and Ernie Wilkinson believe
is a fairly recent grizzly skull. Division experts say that since the skull is
minus its molars and premolars, it's impossible to say for sure. And
they're right.

On to the little log-cabin mining camp of Platoro, quaint as a movie
set, where I stop at the Skyline Lodge for lunch. I stroll through the log
foyer, dark and cavelike with a huge open fireplace smelling of tangy
evergreen smoke, and on into the little café. I take my favorite table—
directly under the mounted head of the 1951 Blue Lake bear. For a
grizzly, it's quite small; there's a black bear on a wall at the Division
office in Durango that could swallow this adolescent whole. Still, it's one
of the last confirmed Colorado grizzlies and a shrine to the vanishing
freedom and greatness of America.

Half an hour later, with my cholesterol level happily restored, I hit
the road again.

After one hour and one flat tire, I park under a shade tree, check my
gear, then reread favorite sections of Richard Nelson's compelling *The
Island Within* while waiting for my ride to show.

Two chapters farther along, a string of eight horses and mules comes
slogging down the muddy trail, led by a tall, silver-bearded man I recognize, from photos and descriptions, as Ed Wiseman.

Wiseman rides over to an old pickup with an even older horse hauler
attached, where he and the two wranglers behind him dismount and
commence tying their animals at intervals around the trailer. I walk over
and introduce myself.

Ed looks about six-one and 190 pounds, with broad shoulders, gigantic meaty paws, silver-white chin beard (no mustache), and thinning hair above a heavy brow and cool gray eyes. We shake hands and talk briefly, then Ed introduces me to the others: David, scruffy in his mid-forties; and Frank, handsome, clean-cut, early twenties. The trio haul cardboard boxes of food and camp supplies from the storage compartment of the horse trailer and transfer everything to the canvas panniers that were trailed in empty. I watch with interest.

These three men, plus a fourth back in camp, have already been here two nights, making a trip a day out to the trailhead to pack in supplies. The archery elk season opens in a week, followed by four rifle seasons, and there's work to be done before the first batch of clients arrives.

Since Ed's camp lies within designated wilderness, no permanent structures—corrals, frames for wall tents, tables, or similar et ceteras—can be erected, and no power equipment such as chain saws or ATVs can be used. Every last pound of gear has to be packed in on horseback. Likewise, every stick of firewood must be cut with ax and handsaw. And when Ed abandons his camp at season's end, the site must look as natural as it did when he arrived. Which is all exactly as it should be in those places we want to call wilderness. In under an hour, we're packed and ready to ride.

I've been assigned a gigantic mare named Tiny, an Appaloosa-Percheron mix—half Indian charger, half plow puller. Tiny proves well mannered and as powerful as she looks; her flowing blond tail sweeps the ground as she walks.

Ed, riding just ahead, sits hunch shouldered and loose in the saddle, his upper body swaying in rhythm with his horse's stride. Watching him bob along reminds me of descriptions I've read of the mounted posture of Old Bill Williams, a legendary Colorado mountain man who was ultimately put out of business by Ute warriors near the headwaters of the Rio Grande, not far from here as the arrow flies.

On his feet, Ed walks with a decided limp—a nagging reminder of his wrestling match with a grizzly. In the space of little over a minute, Wiseman's right leg from ankle to knee was literally pulverized. The left leg, right hand, and both arms were injured, and his right shoulder was bitten completely through. Seventy-seven is the number of the scars he wears today.

Our trail meanders up a wide valley, shaped and gentled millennia ago by the inchmeal grind of glaciation. The river looks more like a creek, averaging a dozen feet wide and rarely more than a foot deep, but has frequent rills and pools to keep the trout happy.

This trail is a picnic compared to most in the San Juans—not too steep and no switchbacks. And this time of year—too late for most vacationers, too early for hunters—there are blessed few people; in two hours of riding we see just one backpack camp and no other horse people. It would be an exceptionally beautiful valley were it not for the ubiquitous sign of a recent excessive bovine presence: close-cropped grass and the stubs of what used to be wildflowers, thistle, and other noxious weeds indicative of overgrazing, stream banks trampled, mushy green cow pies everywhere. Flies.

I ask Ed about his outfit's name, Toneda. He turns in his saddle and explains that it's a contraction of his name sandwiched between those of his first two hired hands, long since departed: Tony-Ed-Dave. Toneda's camp gear and tack are well used—the pommel of Tiny's saddle, for a handy example, is worn leatherless and down to bare shiny metal—but everything is clean, well mended, and functional.

As is the camp, which we reach by early evening. Its primary structures are three canvas wall tents—two to bunk guides and clients, the third for cooking and eating. Additionally, Ed has erected a cozy nylon dome tent for himself and his wife, Judy, who'll be riding in the day I ride out—two suns hence—to serve as camp boss and chef.

It's an ideal campsite, hunting or otherwise. The elevation is a comfortable 10,500 feet (accustomed to eight grand at my cabin, I feel at home up to about eleven) smack in the middle of the subalpine life zone. Slopes green with conifers rear up sharply on either side of the valley, capped with stark sedimentary cliffs. The Continental Divide runs along the top of the ridge to our back, or south, eleven hundred feet above camp. A deeply notched alpine pass establishes the western horizon. At the valley's head sits a huge cirque still partially buried under last winter's snow. A lively creek, one of three branches forming the river, slides along just below camp, fed by frequent rills flowing directly from shaded patches of late-melting snow. From it we will draw our drinking water directly, without filtration.

No cots or chairs here, just log rounds for stools and the lumpy ground for beds. I toss my duffel into one of the floorless bunk tents, then mosey around getting acquainted with the crew.

David, I learn, is a Vietnam combat vet with a Purple Heart to prove it, and a man of diverse enterprise. When not up here in the San Juans working for Ed—where his chosen uniform includes a military web belt from which appends a .45 automatic, extra ammo clips, and a foot of dangling knife—David makes his home in Houston, where he programs computers by day, plays drums in a country-rock band at night, and operates a home recording studio.

Frank seems a little uneasy with his career as a flight attendant for a major airline, mentioning his fiancée often and quietly boasting that he can find elk and follow them anywhere. Young and green, strong and confident, contagiously enthusiastic.

Wiseman's third guide this year—it's a notoriously transient profession—is Don, a likable, slow-talking turkey-calling champion fresh out of Georgia. Hunting elk, Don observes, is a lot like hunting wild turkeys. He's right.

In all, it's a cheery, energetic, and appropriately motley crew, with each member professing a deep respect for "the boss."

A rain comes up, sudden and cold, and we retreat to the cook tent, where Ed is preparing ground elk steak, fresh boiled potatoes, canned green beans, bread, and coffee. After dinner, we talk briefly before calling it a day. Sometime during the night I wake long enough to realize the rain has stopped and the temperature has plunged, promising a bright good day for the morrow's exploration: up through those seemingly impenetrable cliffs, over the Divide, and down into the Navajo headwaters to the spot where, fourteen years ago, Ed Wiseman took his place alongside the legendary Hugh Glass, who fought first a grizzly, then a hostile environment, and survived both.

On the evening of August 23, 1823, trapper Hugh Glass left his dozen companions to search for "wild fruit" along the Grand River in what is now South Dakota. In a berry thicket, Glass surprised "a large grissly Bear" with two big cubs. The trapper got off one shot with his muzzle-loading rifle as the sow charged, wounding but not killing her. Two years later, after interviewing Glass and some of his companions, James Hall, in his "Letters from the West," described the scene:

[Glass] was seized by the throat, and raised from the ground. Casting him again upon the earth, his grim adversary tore out a mouthful of the cannibal food which had excited her appetite and retired to submit the sample to her yearling cubs, which were near at hand. The sufferer now made an effort to escape, but the bear immediately returned . . . and seized him again at the shoulder; she also lacerated his left arm very much, and inflicted a severe wound on the back of his head.

Notwithstanding the "cannibal flesh" embroidery, Hall's account generally agrees with others. Down and nearly out, Glass—like Wiseman, a bull of a man—attempted to drive off the bear by stabbing it repeatedly with his skinning knife, shouting for help all the while. His companions came running, killing one of the big cubs and finishing off the sow, which collapsed either on or near the prostrate Glass.

Glass's mates, under the command of Major Andrew Henry, did what they could to bind up his "not less than fifteen . . . ghastly wounds." In inflicting the worst of these, the grizzly had achieved the "baring of flesh and bones of the shoulder and thigh." But perhaps most worrisome was a throat wound that burbled blood with Glass's every breath. Indeed, as chronicler Daniel Potts so colorfully phrased it, Hugh Glass had been "tore nearly all to peases."

To make a long and riveting survival story conveniently short, the grievously wounded man was lugged along on a "bier" for several days, then left with two "death watch" guards who, growing ever more fearful of Indian attack, eventually deserted their charge under the assumption that he was bound to die soon, and they needn't stay and die with him.

Glass survived. The bear didn't.

I stir at first light, reluctantly unzip my nylon womb, and drag on boots and garb gone stiff with the night's cold. Outside, I'm greeted by a scene as white as any January. Still August and already it's winter in the high San Juans. But the sky is a faultless unmarked blue, with steam rising in wisps and columns where the warming sun is vaporizing the night's frost.

I make my way over to the mess tent, where Ed is already on the job, cooking up appropriately huge quantities of bacon, fresh sliced spuds, and eggs fried to order with toast, creek-water Tang, and a bottomless pot of coffee. As we eat, the boss details the chores he expects his hands to accomplish in his absence today—including the digging of a proper latrine. I wash the dishes while Ed saddles our horses.

Riding back down the river canyon, back-trailing yesterday's route in, I can see no possible way up through what appears to be a solid wall of cliff. In silent reply, Ed guides his balky horse off the trail and up an avalanche chute cluttered with boulders, high brush, and sapling snags like giant pungi stakes. Several times I think we're stuck, but Ed leads confidently on, having ridden this shortcut scores of times over the years, frequently in the dark. Eventually, we break out on top.

The ridge here is narrow, and the trace of a trail along its spine shows no recent tracks of men or their horses. We follow the ridge east for a while—Tiny's left-side hooves clomping along in Rio Grande National Forest, her right in the San Juan—then plunge off the far side and down into the cloistered upper Navajo basin. I'd never attempt to hike in here burdened with a backpack. And even if I did, I might have trouble finding the place again, even though this is my second time up here in less than a year.

In early October 1992, Pagosa Springs district wildlife manager Glen Eyre and I checked the weather and decided to risk a three-day ride of some fifty miles up what we'll call the Trout Creek trail into the Navajo headwaters. Armed with an X marked on a topo map and oral directions, we would be looking for the site of the Wiseman grizzly fight.

Glen Eyre (rhymes with fire) has been a Colorado game warden for half of his forty-five years, working the Pagosa district since 1977. Like most (although not all) Division employees I've come to know, Glen is eminently qualified for his job: energetic, intelligent, a degree in wildlife management, a skilled woodsman and horseman. Eyre is slight but wiry and used to command, having led an armored combat platoon in Vietnam. And he does not suffer fools or wildlife criminals, gladly or otherwise.

Along the lower portion of that October ride with Glen, the forest was alive with the whispering of crisp autumn aspens. Wet areas were still spotted green with corn lilies and elk sedge. Above timberline,

islands of dwarf willow floated on a rolling sea of fall-sere graminoids.
Out on the tundra, glacial gravel made rocky going for our four horses.

Trout Lake, the mother of Trout Creek, is a deep tarn perched at
almost twelve thousand feet in a wind-blasted ice chest of an alpine
scarp. It's a long, wearying climb—two brutal days of backpacking or
most of one on horseback.

An hour above Trout Lake, we found an ideal campsite on a high
bench sheltered in spruce and fir, not far above a creek I'll call September. A lovely, peaceful place it was, but not overly welcoming so late in
the year. The air up there that October day, I remember, smelled like
winter.

We ate steaks grilled on an open fire that night, sipped George
Dickel sweetened with cold September Creek water, and talked, mostly
about Vietnam and bears. Although he's never seen a bruin he took to be
a grizzly in his fifteen years of patrolling the south San Juans, Glen, like
so many of his peers, offered the opinion that a scant few silvertips,
talented at avoiding man, are probably still lurking about.

Come morning, we rode out in search of the site of the Wiseman
grizzly fight. Two hours later, in a copse of trees above a tiny waterfall,
we tied our horses and explored on foot down along the upper Navajo
River canyon. Finally, we settled on a stringer of timber that looked
good according to the information we had. Moreover, it *felt* right—wild
and primitive and inexplicably somber.

Not long after dropping off the far side of the Divide, Ed and I cut the
faint damp trace of what he says is the ultimate wellhead of the Navajo
River. We follow this seep down through a checkerboard of timbered
bulges punctuating marshy parks—not the same fingers and parks Glen
Eyre and I rode through ten months ago, but close in both proximity and
appearance—past a shallow tarn ringed with the skeletal remains of giant
cow parsnips. Exiting the tarn, the creek becomes larger, and the earth
puckers into the beginnings of a canyon.

As we ride, leaning back in our saddles and sometimes almost standing in our stirrups to accommodate the steep downhill, Ed, who's been
silent all morning, opens the narrative I've come all this way to hear.

Right there, he says—stopping and pointing to a few charred pieces
of wood scattered around a low-limbed Christmas tree on the edge of a

talus of glacial gravel—right here is where he had spent what was almost his last night in this world.

A little farther along and Ed stops again, pointing across a park the size of a baseball field to an isolated snag gone silver with age. It was there, he says, right beside that snag, that he got a brief preview of the grizzly with whom he would soon become so bloody intimate. It was early September, about two weeks before the attack, and he and a client were out looking for elk. As they rode out of the timber and entered the park, exactly where we now sit, a big bear ran from the trees across the way, moving left to right, and stopped by that silvery snag, where it haunch-sat and glared at the intruders.

It didn't occur to either of the men that they were exchanging stares with a grizzly. "And why should it?" says Ed now. He's right, of course. Grizzlies, after all, had been officially extinct in Colorado for nearly thirty years. As Ed recalls, the bear had long brownish fur and dark legs with light guard hairs grizzled across the back, and was "big and fat and more low-slung than you'd expect for a black bear. For years, I'd heard rumors of five-hundred-pound black bears up here. I thought I was finally seeing one. It was a big, odd-looking bear, but I only realized after the fact that it was the grizzly I fought with."

The fall bear-hunting season was on, but neither man had a bear license or any desire to pursue the bruin. Ed had killed a black bear some years before that still ranks in the top ten of the Pope and Young Club bowhunting record book; satisfied with that, he says, he gave up hunting bears himself, though he continued to guide other hunters. This client, however, was interested only in elk, so after a while the men urged their horses on, and the "big, odd-looking bear" fled back into the sheltering trees.

We ride across the park, stop for a moment by the silver-tipped snag, then move on through alternating grassy meadows and hillocks of fir and spruce. In the moist cool shade beneath the trees, I note, thrives a rich understory of whortleberry and sweet cicely (bear foods). Gray jays dive-bomb us repeatedly, cursing, it would seem, our very existence.

Now Ed announces that we're as near to "the place" as we can get on horseback. We dismount, tie our mounts, and plop down in a luxury of green to eat our lunches. The frosty winter morning has warmed to a springlike afternoon, complete with flies buzzing my sandwich and a tiny pastel blue butterfly looping drunkenly about. Done eating, I take a tepid swig from my canteen and ask Ed if he wants a drink before we begin our hike. He declines, saying he's got all the water he needs.

And so he does. We start walking and come straightaway to a trickle of snowmelt clear as vodka. Ed drops to his knees and drinks. Still thirsty, I follow suit, putting my lips to the water and slurping like an elk. The mineral-heavy liquid is cold and deeply satisfying.

Below us, the brook diffuses and the soil becomes marshy, thick with coneflowers and skunk cabbage. Without a sound, a quarter-ton cow elk rises from her cud bed amid the waist-high greenery, not twenty feet ahead, and slips away.

Just before we enter a patch of woods and lose the sky to the dense evergreen overstory, I spot a lone bald eagle coasting on an invisible thermal far out over the canyon of the Navajo. I mumble something about thinking of balds as fishing eagles, expecting to see them cruising above rivers or perched in riparian cottonwoods at fairly low elevations; it seems strange to meet one up so high. Ed says yes, it's sure enough hard to figure, yet not an uncommon sight hereabouts.

Beneath the trees the air is cool and fragrant. The flowering season has passed within this deep chilling shade, but an understory of whortle-berry, geranium, bluebell, and clover grows in patches among a dun-colored duff of decomposing conifer needles, while fuzzy green mosses and scaly orange lichens paint weird polychrome patterns on rocks and rotting logs. As Ed leads through the trees, I ask if it feels at all strange to return to this place where he was almost killed in a manner most bloody and anachronistic by a beast that was not supposed even to exist.

"Only the first time," he says. "It was nine months before I'd mended enough to get back up here, and I happened to be alone. I wasn't really scared, but I was definitely apprehensive; I kept looking behind me to make sure there wasn't something there. But I've been back almost every year since, guiding elk hunters, so while this spot will always hold some pretty intense memories for me, I don't consider its ambience foreboding."

"Ambience foreboding," he says. Ed Wiseman, I am reminded, is a college-educated mountain man—just as Hugh Glass was schooled well beyond the norm for his time and profession. After dinner last night, I asked Ed for the ten-cent autobiography. He told me he was born in 1933 in Pueblo, Colorado, and has been outfitting and guiding in the San Juans part- or full-time for thirty years. Following college and a year of graduate school, he spent 1957 through 1959 in the military. After being honorably discharged, he went to work for the Division and spent the next three years as ranch manager at an experimental wildlife station. In 1962, he quit the Division and moved to the San Luis Valley, where he started a "poultry and hog operation" and began guiding and outfitting on the side. In 1973 he traded herding pigs and chickens for herding hunters full-time. He works construction in the winter off-seasons, and recently built a huge, ornate log house for Judy and himself.

My guide stops and points, then strides up to a misshapen fir, its waist-thick trunk growing almost parallel to the ground for the length of a man, then bending upright to its proper orientation, like the neck of a giant swan.

"This is it," he says. "Right here. This bent tree makes it easy to find. I was hunting along this game trail," he points, "standing right in front of this bent tree. The bear came charging out from over by the cliffs. It saw me and swerved in my direction. Next thing I know the two of us are tumbling backward over a log. Right there where you're standing is where the fight took place."

We drop our packs and stroll around, surveying the area. The game trail wanders over close to the lip of a thousand-foot drop, maybe thirty yards to the east of the bent tree. The canyon below is steep sided and heavily timbered all the way to its narrow bottom, through which slips the infant Navajo. Twenty yards north of the attack site rises an undulant wall of head-high boulders. Thirty feet west of the bent tree, Ed points to the broken log upon which the fatally wounded grizzly slumped and quietly died.

Looking about, I'm pleased to see that the spot warden Eyre and I settled on last October is a scant hundred yards southwest of here.

It doesn't take long to circumambulate the scene of the action: a tiny glen at the heart of a stringer of mature scaly-barked Engelmann spruce and blistery gray subalpine fir. The trees here, one and all, are too fat to shinny up, even had there been time to try, which Ed has made clear there wasn't. And the lowest limbs are well above even a tall man's jumping reach.

Ed believes the bear attacked him because it felt trapped. "Mike Niederee had come upon the bear as it slept in its nest, watched it for a few seconds, then backed silently away and circled on down the canyon. His scent would have floated up from below and spooked the bear. The cliff is right there. That rock wall behind us forms a third barrier, and here I came, blocking the only remaining escape route. Most any animal will attack if it feels cornered."

True. Especially if that animal is feeling grumpy because of a couple of abscessed teeth, various old injuries, acute arthritis, and a lifetime of instinct-insulting running and hiding.

We return to the bent tree, against which Ed takes a seat. I flop down on the duff right where the fight took place and produce notebook, camera, and cheap tape recorder, the tools with which I hope to capture Ed's "pretty intense memories."

A small plane passes over us and circles low a couple of times, buzzing annoyingly and reminding me how small these places we call wilderness really are.

We begin.

Ed calls on a metaphor to describe his hit-or-miss memories of the attack and subsequent events. "In normal circumstances," he explains, "the mind works like a movie camera, recording a constant flow of events —unlike a still camera, which can only record one frame at a time and misses a lot of action between. During the attack, my mind switched to the still-camera mode, leaving me with some very sharp snapshots, but lots of blank frames in between.

"My first memory is seeing the bear running toward me from about thirty yards, and realizing it was charging. I hollered 'No! No!' I was carrying my bow in my right hand, and I thrust it out in front of me like a shield. The bear never broke its run, never got up off all fours, and in a flash it was on me, slapping the bow out of my hand. Whether I stepped back and tripped over that log, or the bear knocked me back over it when it hit, I can't say for sure.

"In any event, I wound up on the ground with my head facing away from the bear's. It had my lower right leg in its mouth and was shaking me like a puppy would a rag. I distinctly remember feeling the skin of my leg get real tight, then hearing the flesh rip as it gave way, but I don't recall any pain. Nor any smells—if the bear or its breath stank, I didn't notice it. I'm not sure about sounds; I don't really remember the bear making any vocal sounds at all, but Mike Niederee said he could hear the bear growling and me hollering from his location several hundred yards down-canyon.

"After a while, the bear dropped my leg, turned to face me, and grabbed my right shoulder. This whole time I was lying on my left side, curled up and trying to protect my vitals, like the experts say to do. Then I spotted one of the arrows that had been knocked out of my bow quiver, lying there on the ground real close, the broadhead pointing toward the bear. It's hard to stay still for long with a grizzly gnawing on you, and the way things were going, I was afraid that if I kept playing dead much longer, I'd *be* dead. So I reached out and grabbed the arrow with my left hand, rolled over on my back, and stabbed upward."

Ed simulates the gesture, thrusting with a swift underhand motion, thumb up.

"That first jab hit somewhere in the lower throat area. The bear's only reaction was to let go of my shoulder and go back to chewing on my right leg.

"The next thing I remember, I've got the front half of a broken arrow in my left hand. I can't remember pulling it out of the bear's neck, and I can't remember breaking it, but I do remember having the business end of it in my hand and planning to stab the bear a second time. At the same time, while I can't say how it got there, my right hand was in the bear's mouth.

"And that's all the memories I have of the fight. I can't recall actually stabbing the bear the second time—the motion itself—but I remember fixing to, then knowing I had, then the bear grabbing my left leg for the first time. Within seconds, though, she dropped the leg and stood over me, blood spurting from the wound in her neck and onto my chest —a stream as thick as my thumb. My intent wasn't to kill her, but just to get her off me, to drive her away—like 'Go away! Leave me alone!'

"My next memory is of the bear walking away." Ed points to the broken log. "She just walked over there and laid down, turned her head to the left, put her left front paw up on the log and rested her chin on the paw. I've seen bears die, and I knew she was gone.

"Putting it all together later, and taking into account how long Mike thought he'd heard the bear growling and me yelling, the attack probably lasted no more than a minute and a half.

"Somehow, I was able to get to my feet. I looked around and saw my cap and bow lying on the ground and arrows scattered all around. Blood everywhere. I was shaking with an overdose of adrenaline and knew I'd better get out of the woods and into the open if I wanted to have any chance of being found; at that point I had no idea where Mike was or if he'd heard the attack, but I'd made it only a hundred yards or so before I heard him holler.

"Later, Mike told me that when he came running back up here, at first he saw only my bow and arrows and the blood—more blood, he said, than a slaughterhouse. He didn't see me or the bear at first, and assumed I'd been killed and dragged off.

"When Mike spotted the bear lying there, he hollered 'Ed!' I answered 'Help!' Then he yelled 'Are you all right?' and I said 'No.' He came over to where I was, and I sent him up the hill to bring the horses down. When he returned, Mike's mount, Buckshot, got spooked from the blood and bear smells, pulled free from where he was tied, and ran off a ways; didn't go far, but Mike wasn't able to catch him. By talking quietly to Freckles, my Appaloosa mare, I was able to get her calmed down. Mike was twenty-five years old and strong, and with his help and a couple of tries, between which I blacked out for a moment, I was finally able to get into the saddle. With Mike walking and leading Freckles, I rode a mile or more, back up to the meadow where the horses had been tied.

"At that point, I told Mike I was having trouble staying in the saddle. I was getting extremely sick, couldn't think straight, felt on the verge of passing out. I was riding slumped over the saddle and hanging onto Freckles's neck, and she was trembling like a willow leaf. I'd always thought of Freckles as skittish and unpredictable, but in those minutes she earned a home for life.

"Anyhow, I told Mike I was getting off. He said, 'Please Ed, don't. I'll never get you back on.' I told him I had no intention of getting back on, that I wanted him to ride back to camp and have someone ride out and call for a helicopter to pick me up.

"When I got laid down on the ground, my head cleared a little and I had Mike gather some firewood—it was about seven in the evening and getting dark and cold—then I gave him instructions for getting back to camp. He was brand-new to this country, to the mountains, it was the dark of the moon, we'd come in the long way, and I wanted him to take a shortcut back to camp—the way you and I rode in this morning. He must have been scared to death. I told him to ride Freckles and if he got lost, just give her free rein and she'd get him back to camp.

"Based on how long it would take *me* to make the ride to camp and back, I figured Mike would return with help by ten o'clock or so. Even though I was torn up pretty badly and soaked from head to toe in blood, I took encouragement from the knowledge that I wasn't hurt in the guts; just my legs and right shoulder and arms and right hand. We'd wrapped up the worst wounds as best we could with strips of a long-sleeved undershirt, and the bleeding had slowed some but not stopped. I kept telling myself that if I could just hold on until help came, I'd be OK.

"But ten o'clock came and went. The fire was about out, and I had no more wood to feed it. And no help in sight. I was dressed about like we are now—a long-sleeved flannel shirt over a short-sleeved cotton T-shirt, jeans, a hat—plus I had my saddle slicker to cover up with. I stayed right up close to the dying coals to get every degree of warmth I could from them. My last stick of fuel was the top of a tree that was still a little green. I remember trying to light it in three different places, but couldn't get it going.

"About the time the fire went out, a wind came up and I started shaking. In desperation, I crawled twenty feet or so over to a big log and tried to get it burning with my Bic lighter . . . getting a little delirious by then, I guess. Without fire, my best bet was a windbreak, so I crawled over and scooted up under the low limbs of that little Christmas tree I pointed out when we rode in this morning. They tell me it got down to fifteen or twenty degrees that night.

"When midnight came and help still hadn't shown up, I figured it would be daylight before they made it. I knew it was up to me to keep going until then. I was an EMT and knew the most important thing was to avoid shock, so I didn't let myself go to sleep and did what isometric exercises I could in an effort to keep warm.

"Turns out that Mike had gotten all twisted around and didn't find camp until after nine. My cook, Al Brandenburg—three fourths hippie but a super good kid—rode at a fast gallop, in the dark, all the way down to the trailhead, then drove to Platoro to call for help. I hate to think how fast and reckless that trip was; he risked his life for me.

"Within minutes after Mike finally found camp, he, my guide Ace Calloway, and Mike's father, who was a surgeon, rode out looking for me. It was four in the morning when I finally saw someone walking down the hill toward me. It was Mike with a flashlight in each hand; at first I thought it was two people. The horse he'd ridden back had fought coming over the Divide in the dark. When it finally balked and wouldn't go any farther, Mike walked the rest of the way. Seems they'd spent a lot of time milling around in those meadows up on top, then decided to split up to increase the chances of finding me, and Mike was the one who got here first. If Mike had ridden Freckles back, tired as she was, she'd have led them straight here and they'd have found me hours earlier. As it was, I spent eight hours alone.

"But I'm not criticizing. They all made the best judgments they could under extremely difficult circumstances, and I owe my life to them, especially Mike. Try to imagine how shook up he must have been after hearing all that growling and yelling and seeing all that blood everywhere, then finding me lying there torn up and with night coming on and him new to the mountains and my life almost entirely in his hands.

"So Mike rebuilt the fire to warm me and to signal the others. With Mike back, I guess I relaxed a little because I began to slip. I remember being so dehydrated that I tried to chew a stick of gum and it just crumbled into pieces in my mouth; I had no saliva whatsoever. I asked for water, but Mike had no canteen or container. Thinking fast, he dumped the batteries out of one of his flashlights and ran down to the creek and filled the case with water, and that's how I finally got a drink.

"When Ace and Doc Niederee eventually found us—that was about five in the morning and still dark—they told me that all of Doc's medical supplies and the sleeping bag they'd brought for me had been on a horse that had slid down onto a steep talus slope where they couldn't reach it to retrieve the gear . . . later that morning, the stranded horse fell over a two-hundred-foot cliff and was killed. So all Doc had to work with was his knowledge. He was wearing canvas chaps, and took them off and laid them over me for warmth. Next they elongated the fire so that I had heat the full length of my body.

"Daylight finally came, and maybe thirty minutes later we heard the rescue chopper approaching. Mike and Ace had built a second fire for signaling, and they smudged it to make smoke and laid out my yellow slicker to mark our location. The chopper made one pass and landed.

"The rescue didn't begin on a real positive note. The pilot was a Vietnam vet who'd seen a lot of bad injuries, and when he saw me lying there covered in blood, he told the others it was too late, that I was too torn up, had lost too much blood—Doc Niederee guessed it at three pints—and was too hypothermic to make it. My body temperature was down to ninety-five.

"One of the first things the chopper crew did was to unwrap the strips of shirt from my right leg to see how bad the damage was. When they did that, one of the medics lost his stomach and was put out of action for the duration; it was not a pretty piece of hamburger, I guess.

"Anyhow, they rebandaged the leg and started an IV in my left arm, which made me even colder, then flew me over the mountains to Alamosa Community Hospital. My next clear memory is of a friend who worked in the emergency room there joking with me about not wearing any underwear. I always wear a T-shirt and underpants, but there was so much dried blood—mine and the grizzly's—that when they cut off my outer clothing, the inner layers came off too, all as one piece fused together with blood. It took them three or four washings to get the blood out of my hair. And four days later, I dug a clot of dried blood the size of a small marble out of my navel.

"After that, it was just a matter of slow healing and dealing with the investigation."

Other than the "big, odd-looking bear" that he hadn't recognized for what it was, had Ed had any suspicions prior to the attack that a grizzly might be lurking about?

"Yeah, I suppose so, though it didn't come together for me until afterward, and I can't be positive about any of it even today. A couple of times I had clients—experienced hunters who'd seen grizzlies up close in Alaska—tell me they'd spotted a grizzly up here. I remember one of them saying, 'This old bear's head wouldn't fit in a five-gallon bucket.' I just laughed it off.

"And, too, in the early 1970s, a bear had torn up my camp when nobody was around. We found some seven-inch-wide tracks, but I just chalked it up to a real big black bear.

"Then, in the fall of 1978, I had a couple of clients from Chicago. The lady wanted to hunt bear over a bait while her husband hunted elk. So I walked in an old sick Shetland stallion and put him down not far from where camp is now. A couple of nights later, a bear came in and picked that stallion up by the withers and carried it up an extremely steep slope—the grade is at least thirty and maybe as much as forty degrees—for more than a hundred yards to the base of those cliffs we came up through this morning, and devoured it there. There were no drag marks except for the hooves—the horse, which would have weighed four or five hundred pounds, had been carried bodily up that hill. I've guided black bear hunts for decades, and I'd never seen anything like that before. Or since."

Does Ed believe he killed the last grizzly bear in Colorado?

"It would be presumptuous for anyone to say flatly there are no grizzlies left in the San Juans—it's big country with lots of wrinkles and folds, some of them inaccessible to humans. But it sort of looks that way to me, at least here in this area I know so well. If you study the history of grizzlies and men, and the habits and habitat requirements of grizzlies, then superimpose those requirements and that history on Colorado to-day . . . for grizzlies to exist here peacefully, without coming into con-flict with people . . . there just isn't enough real wilderness left to allow it."

The day is winding down; we've been sitting here talking for almost four hours. Knowing I may never have the opportunity to return to this special place again—the fewer people who come here, the better—I hand Ed my camera and walk the dozen paces over to where the last known Colorado silvertip laid down and passed into the realm of legend.

As Ed fiddles with the focus, I recall retired Division employee Bob Rouse's photos of the great bear lying slumped on the very spot now occupied by my butt and boots, one paw up on the log, her head resting in eternal slumber on that paw. It's a mirror image, I realize, of the way my beloved old yellow lab Lacy died not long ago—one paw resting on my leg as I knelt beside her, her big lovely head sinking slowly onto that paw, never to rise again. I hear the click of the camera and hope it hasn't caught the glint of water in my eyes.

6

"LOTS OF BLACK BEARS
BUT NO GRIZZLIES"

The Beck Study

> *The hardest thing of all to see is what is really there.*
>
> —J. A. Baker

"A grizzly bear—listed as an endangered species in Colorado—was recently trapped, radio-tagged, and released by biologists from the Colorado Division of Wildlife in the rugged San Juan Mountains of southwestern Colorado.

"The bear was captured during the week of _____ through the use of a spring-activated snare, and was subsequently immobilized with a tranquilizing drug, tattooed, ear-tagged, and collared with a radio transmitter that should provide data on the bear's seasonal range as well as aid in locating any other grizzlies that may still be lingering in the remote forests of the San Juans. . . .

"This particular animal, a ____ pound ____, is the first confirmed report of a grizzly bear in Colorado since 1979, when private outfitter Ed Wiseman was mauled while killing an approximately 16 year old grizzly sow near Platoro Reservoir in LaPlata [*sic,* Conejos] County.

"The Division, working in conjunction with the USFS [U.S. Forest Service], the U.S. Fish and Wildlife Service, and the Colorado Cooperative Wildlife Research Unit in Fort Collins, has been searching for signs of the grizzly for the past two years in the south San Juans. . . .

"Although these bears once ranged fairly extensively throughout Colorado—and were even reported on the eastern slope of the state within the last century—they were assumed to be extinct in Colorado after a government trapper killed one in Hinsdale County at the head of the Los Pinos River in 1952.

"Prior to the Wiseman incident, which gained national media attention, it was believed that these bears had been extirpated from the state. A 1956 grizzly bear search by the Division—which involved baiting thousands of acres of the San Juan National Forest with carrion—turned up hundreds of black bears but no grizzlies, and a study conducted from 1970 to 1973 by the Division, the USFS, and the USFWS came up with the same conclusion—lots of black bears but no grizzlies."

As things turned out, the only part of the above "Grizzly Contingency Article" the Colorado Division of Wildlife's public information office need have written was the bottom line—"lots of black bears but no grizzlies." It was a conclusion that reassured some and frustrated others.

Among those in the know, the South San Juan Mountains Grizzly Bear Survey is generally referred to as the Beck study, after its leader, Colorado's widely respected black bear biologist Thomas D. I. Beck. With the Division since 1976, Beck has seven years of college and eighteen years as a bear researcher to his credit.

When Ed Wiseman met his grizzly in late September of 1979, Tom Beck was incommunicado somewhere in the Black Mesa area of west-central Colorado, in the midst of the first season of a monumental seven-year study that would establish him as the leading authority on black bears in the West. Thus Beck was not available to visit the scene of the Wiseman incident before the physical evidence was removed. Nor did he take part in the ensuing investigation. But when it became apparent that a search for more San Juan grizzlies was in order, Tom Beck got the job.

Throughout the summers of 1981 and 1982, Beck would keep two teams of two men each in the field—running snare lines, combing the woods for tracks, dens, digs, and other potential grizzly spoor . . . and watching, always watching.

The epicenter of the surveyed area was to be the upper Navajo River, where the Wiseman grizzly had died. From there, Beck's crews would fan out to explore and set traplines along dozens of local streams, big and small, ranging from Wolf Creek Pass on the north almost to the New Mexico state line in the south, and about fifteen miles either side of the Continental Divide—in effect, the entire South San Juan Wilderness plus much of the fifty-eight-thousand-acre Banded Peak Ranch in the Tierra Amarilla de facto wilderness.

In his "South San Juan Mountains Grizzly Bear Survey, Environmental Assessment" of 1980, Beck justified the project after the following fashion: "Prior to making major management commitments to preserve Colorado grizzly bears, both state and federal agencies want to be assured that indeed a population does exist. . . . The grizzly poses management problems that are often controversial and evoke emotional responses. Thus it is understandable that agencies want to know that a population does exist. The primary purpose of this work is to document such a population by capturing one or more grizzly bears."

Beck went on to discuss the hands-on techniques he planned to employ: "It would be very difficult to develop management plans to accommodate grizzly bears and multiple-use philosophy on public lands without basic data on seasonal ranges and habitat selection as well as the current distribution of the bears in the San Juan Mountains. Therefore, all grizzly bears caught . . . will be instrumented with a radio-transmitter collar. Subsequent tracking will provide much of the basic data needed for critical habitat designation and development of management plans."

In his "Discussion of Alternatives," Beck discouraged adopting an alternative that would mandate the Division to "conduct a survey that does not involve capturing bears but only recording sign and/or sightings," arguing that "[grizzlies] in this area have long been persecuted by man and may have responded by adopting extreme aversion behavior. It is probable that more bears can be caught than seen with the same manpower."

Beck's consultants for the project included representatives from the Forest Service, Fish and Wildlife Service endangered species experts, Charles Jonkel of the University of Montana's Border Grizzly Project, Dick Knight of the Interagency Grizzly Bear Study Team, and "a multitude of other biologists and administrators involved with grizzly bear research and management." Beck's lack of hands-on experience with grizzlies—which critics of the study frequently call attention to—was amply compensated for, Beck felt, by the strength and breadth of his consultants.

Beck's "Environmental Assessment" passed muster, with the resulting project agreement stipulating three primary "Segment Objectives":

1. Capture as many grizzly bears as possible.
2. Investigate distribution and seasonal habitat use of grizzly bears.
3. Document causes of mortality to grizzly bears in the south San Juan Mountains.

Presaging that final objective, Beck had noted in his environmental assessment that "it is possible that illegal killing of grizzly bears by livestock people and/or black bear hunters has kept the population down. . . . Only by identifying the causes for failure to increase can we implement management plans designed to enhance the grizzly bear population."

Along the same trail, under "Procedures," the project agreement specified that "frequent walking trips in the vicinity of domestic sheep flocks will be made to look for evidence of dead bears."

The cost for the proposed three-year study was estimated at $21,000 —a cheap date even in 1981–82.

The field talent Beck recruited for the opening season included Rick Mace, Mark Jandreau, Roger Smith, and Tim Thier, all veterans of the Montana Border Grizzly Project with extensive experience in live-trapping and handling grizzlies, as well as identifying grizzly spoor.

During the spring of 1981, these four concentrated their efforts on "relatively lower elevation areas where potential grizzly bears were present. . . . Riparian areas, avalanche chutes, seeps, and aspen stands . . . were frequently searched. . . . A number of spring snowshoe trips were made to high elevation areas to search for tracks and den sites."

Come summer, the search literally escalated, following the seasonal green-up—as, Beck logically assumed, would any grizzlies in the area— concentrating on "isolated drainage heads, upland riparian zones, shrub-fields and open, alpine areas. The upper main branch of the Navajo River, where the grizzly bear was killed in 1979, was monitored almost daily."

Complicating the study was a dearth of information on the natural history of Colorado grizzlies. Without an established knowledge base, the best Beck's team could do was to assume southern Rockies grizzlies would behave like northern Rockies grizzlies—searching out the same food sources at the same times of year, using similar sites for dens, and so on. In retrospect, this was an assumption Beck has since come to question. (After many years of fieldwork, he is now convinced that the differences between northern and southern Rocky Mountain bear habitats are far greater than the species differences between black bear and grizzly bear usage of those habitats; in other words, Colorado grizzlies, Beck feels, probably behave more like Colorado black bears than like northern grizzlies.)

Further muddying the picture was the team's anomalous discovery that San Juan black bears sometimes dig for plant roots, at least those in the carrot/parsley family (Umbelliferae); specifically, sweet cicely *(Osmorhiza)*. "This feeding behavior," Beck reported, "was thought to be a trait restricted to grizzly bears, at least in the Rocky Mountain region. Until this [black bear digging] was documented, it was presumed that all bear digs found in Colorado were . . . grizzly. This overlap in habitat use and feeding behavior obviously complicated verifying grizzly bear sign."

In summarizing what *was* found, Beck reported that "no recent, positive grizzly bear sign was found in the study area in 1981. However, a number of older sites were found and labeled as possible grizzly bear sign."

Specifically: "A possible grizzly den was located in the upper Navajo River, directly above the site of the 1979 grizzly killing. This excavated den was located in an open-timbered, spruce-fir stringer between two avalanche chutes. . . . This possible grizzly den showed remarkable similarities to those located via radio-instrumented grizzlies in Montana, Wyoming, and British Columbia in terms of site and den characteristics. No bedding material or hair was found in the den. It is possible that the den was excavated and then abandoned prior to the onset of denning.

"A possible grizzly feeding site was located [on the Tierra Amarilla] in an open-timbered sidehill park. . . . A substantial portion of the area was pock-marked with small digs. . . . It is believed the bear(s) had been digging for the roots of loveroot *(Ligusticum)*. . . . A number of old daybeds were found beneath nearby spruce trees. In these beds were scats that contained roots. The estimated age of the feeding site was 3–5 years."

(Here the report is unclear: Did the daybeds containing root-filled scats correspond in age with the three- to five-year-old dig, or were the beds more recent?)

"A second possible grizzly bear feeding site was located [also on the Tierra Amarilla]. In this instance, the roots of biscuitroot *(Lomatium)* were dug. A total of 6 digs were found. . . . The age of this site was estimated at between 3 and 5 years. . . .

"On 19 June a large dig was located . . . on the Rio Grande National Forest. The dig was on a steep slope in the alpine . . . and appeared to be a case where a marmot had been dug from its den. The skull of a marmot was located within a few feet of the 2m × 1.3m × .5m excavated area. A portion of the marmot's burrow was still visible at the bottom of the excavation. . . . Judging from the appearance of the marmot skull and the vegetation beginning to reoccupy the site, this probable grizzly dig was from 1 to 3 years old."

Given that the Wiseman bear had died two years prior to this find, and considering the assessment that the marmot dig could have been excavated as recently as 1980, the presence of a living grizzly was an inescapable, albeit unverifiable, possibility, making this the most encouraging discovery of the summer.

During the winter of 1993, I discussed the marmot dig with 1981 searcher Tim Thier, who still traps and studies grizzlies for a living, now in the employ of the FWS in Montana. Tim sent me several 35mm slides of the dig, and after examining these projected on a screen, I felt compelled to argue that the relatively fresh appearance of the excavated soil along with the sparsity of revegetation in the disturbed area suggested that the dig could hardly be as old as three years.

Tim responded thus: "All I can say is that I feel comfortable [that the dig was] not made in the summer of 1981. There were still patches of snow present near the site, indicating the vegetation didn't have much of a chance to recover from the previous winter. Also, the marmot skull was bleached with no evidence of tissue remaining. Had the marmot been killed in 1981, surely there would have been something. The dig did not appear real old, but we could not say for sure that it was less than two years old."

In other words, Thier does not directly dispute my contention that the dig was less than three years old—nor, thus, the implication that this grizzly dig could not have been made by the Wiseman bear. In the end, all Tim is sure of is that this "confident" grizzly dig was not made the same summer he and Mark Jandreau found it.

The abstract of Tom Beck's summary "Job Progress Report" for the first season reads: "No grizzly bears were captured in 1981, nor was any verifiable recent evidence of grizzly bear activity found. Several instances of possible grizzly bear activity were located. Eighteen black bears were captured and tagged."

The significant words there are "verifiable recent evidence." Problem was, any potential grizzly spoor—dens, digs, or what have you—that could not be taken with confidence to have been made since 1979, had to be considered possibly relics of the Wiseman bear's tenure.

Beck's crew for the 1982 field season included two veterans from '81, Roger Smith and Mark Jandreau, plus Coloradans John Broderick and John Trupkiewicz. The '82 search area was essentially an expansion of the areas surveyed the previous summer, except that "no work was done east of the Continental Divide in 1982, based on the dearth of bear sign seen [there] during 1981."

Not coincidentally, as Tim Thier pointed out, domestic sheep were scarce on the west, or San Juan, side of the Divide, while the east, or Rio Grande, side was heavily grazed. Additionally, said Thier, all the herders he encountered "were armed and would undoubtedly shoot anything that threatened their sheep." Thus a dearth of bears.

Another change for the second summer was that more time was spent searching for bear sign than running snare lines, which, in 1981, had produced just blackies.

The only potential grizzly spoor discovered in '82 was "a large bear dig similar to grizzly bear digs in Montana," found near timberline on national forest land just north of the New Mexico border. However, "analysis of the scat and extensive diagnosis of the dig site provided no evidence as to the specie of bear responsible." Based on circumstantial evidence—no claw marks visible in the turned earth and three black bears captured in the vicinity—it was presumed that this dig, grizzlylike as it appeared, was most probably the work of black bears.

The abstract for the 1982 "Job Final Report" reads: "No grizzly bears were captured in 1982, nor was any verifiable evidence of grizzly bear activity found. Nine black bears were captured and tagged."

The study had been intended to span three years, but after two summers without trapping a grizzly or finding any verifiably recent grizzly sign, and having covered the entire intended search area and more, Tom Beck came reluctantly to feel that other state endangered species projects could better benefit from the limited "nongame" funds, and called it quits.

The last page of Beck's final report includes the following conclusions and recommendations: "Failure to catch a grizzly bear does not mean definite absence of bears. Therefore, land management plans should attempt to maintain conditions which minimize human disturbance to the region in case a few grizzly bears do remain.

"All livestock owners and herders in the south San Juan Mountains should be advised of the possible presence of grizzly bears and their protected status.

"Efforts should be made to advise all bear hunters in southern Colorado of the possible presence of grizzly bears and the difficulty involved in accurately identifying bear species in the field."

Reminiscent of the Wiseman incident, the inconclusive Beck study left the door open to critical speculation by those who felt that the search was in some way—well, *rigged*. For a long while, I was among that suspicious number.

Adding fuel to this speculative fire is Tim Thier's uneasy feeling that the trapping effort had been intentionally crippled by "someone in the Division higher than Tom Beck, who mandated that we had to follow the same baiting regulations imposed on black bear hunters, restricting us to using primarily sucker fish for bait."

In a recent conversation, Tim told me that "we tried baiting grizzlies with fish a few times in Montana, using salmon and steelhead, both of which are native species that grizzlies sometimes feed on, but had very poor success. In a place like the San Juans, where grizzlies are unlikely ever to come into contact with fish, it strikes me as a very poor bait, especially with a tiny population of bears as man-shy as any surviving San Juan grizzlies no doubt are. I believe Tom wanted very much to catch a grizzly, but I've often wondered if somebody higher up failed to share that enthusiasm. Our job was to catch a grizzly, yet we were not allowed to use the most important tool—good bait.

"Other than that, I had no complaints. We were essentially given free rein to go wherever we wanted within the designated study area.

"My gut feeling at the conclusion of the search was that there may be a few grizzlies left in the south San Juans. But if so, they've got big problems. For one thing, it may not be a genetically viable population. But the thing that concerned me most was the large number of sheep in the high country. And every flock was tended by a couple of fellows who appeared to be Mexican illegals; we'd try to talk to them, and they all claimed not to speak any English. They all carried rifles, and we were left with the impression that their instructions were, 'If anything messes with the sheep, you shoot it.' These guys knew nothing about distinguishing between black and grizzly bears, and there was no way to explain to them that it was a serious crime to kill grizzly bears, even to protect livestock. When sheep are allowed to graze in grizzly country, it all too often leads to conflict. In the end, the bears always lose.

"I certainly hope there are a few grizzlies left down there. And if there are, I hope we'll do all we can to help them recover—if possible, without augmentation, in order to preserve their genetic uniqueness."

NOVEMBER 1993: DOLORES, COLORADO

It's taken several months, but I've finally been granted an audience with Tom Beck. It's not that he's aloof; rather, he's rarely home and harried when he is. Even his fellow Division employees joke about how hard it is to track Tom down and get his undivided attention for any length of time. Across the past half-dozen years, I've spoken briefly with the elusive bruin biologist a few times—in person at public meetings and on the phone—but that's it.

I would put Tom Beck in his early forties, about five-nine with a mesomorphic build, a neatly trimmed beard, dark hair thinning on top (though not nearly so thin as my own), and chameleon eyes that segue from brown to gray to green with changes in the ambient light. I suspect that he's a bit of a workaholic, and he's obviously happier squeezing into an occupied bear den or standing in icy water working with an endangered river otter or even speaking in public than he is sitting in his windowless home office faced with an erupting volcano of paperwork and a phone, he says, that never quits ringing.

Beck's passion for fieldwork is no doubt a big part of what has made him one of the leading black bear experts in the world; he is no mere data-based, desk-bound biologist. So broad and deep is his influence within the Division—based on respect for his extensive knowledge, proven judgment, and a courageous willingness to speak his mind—that he could single-handedly (it has been suggested by others than himself) make or break any proposed future grizzly programs in Colorado.

Tom lives with his wife, Sandy, in a comfortable but unpretentious

house on a few acres of piñon and juniper with a striking view of the La
Plata Range of the San Juans rising blue-white in the east. As I coast
down the long dirt drive leading from a graveled county road to the Beck
house, horses graze lazily in a front-yard pasture. Iridescent magpies
explore the abundant equine pies, pecking for squirming treats. ("Mag-
pie," one etymological theory holds, derives from "maggot pie.")

When I park my truck and climb out, a plump yellow lab shuffles up
to greet me with a wet touch of nose and a wag of tail. Tom emerges
from his garage office and tells me the dog's name is Chunky. Right on.
My host offers a solid handshake and invites me into his home.

The interior of the Beck abode is decorated in what I'll call "nature abstract," with paintings and photos of deer, bear, elk, mountain
goats, birds, and montane scenery everywhere, but nary a hide, antler,
bone, feather, or other palpable portion of any actual wild animal in
sight. Scattered about on various tables are well-thumbed copies of
*Backpacker, Amicus Journal, Audubon, Defenders, Natural History, Na-
tional Geographic,* and suchlike others. Bookcases contain works by Leopold, an almost complete set of Abbey, the regional classic *Wildlife in
Peril: The Endangered Mammals of Colorado* by our mutual friend John
Murray, Lopez's *Of Wolves and Men,* Maclean's *A River Runs Through It,*
the nature writings of John Janovy and Archie Carr, and scores more
of similar import, plus such pseudoscientific esoterica as *Racks: The
Natural History of Antlers and the Animals That Wear Them* by some local hack. I compliment Tom on his taste in literature, agreeing as it
does so well with my own.

"This is all light reading," he jokes. "Out in my office I have one of
the best black bear libraries in the world."

As I set up my cheap tape recorder on the dining room table, Tom
takes the phone off the hook, a courtesy I appreciate given its reputation
for continual ringing.

Employing my usual journalistic tact, I open by remarking that a lot
of people believe the Division doesn't want grizzlies in Colorado, and
hold that the Beck study's failure to trap a silvertip was preordained. The
directness of Beck's reply surprises me.

"Concerning the Division not wanting grizzlies . . . as an agency
position, I think that's accurate; most of the administrators in the Division don't want grizzlies here. Nor did they want any to be found in the
early '80s. But even so, there was no official interference with the search,

and if you had suggested to my field team that you thought their effort was fixed to fail, they'd have shot you right where you stood. They—I, we—*wanted* to find grizzlies. Of course, we didn't succeed, but I think we all believed at the end that three, four, five bears could still be out there and had simply eluded us."

Pushing the question of official interference, I ask about Tim Thier's concern that some anonymous higher-up may have tied the searchers' hands by proscribing the use of road-killed deer and elk for bait—the sort of indigenous carrion that grizzlies would find familiar and feel comfortable approaching.

"I understand Tim's concern," Tom grants. "But there was no directive from above saying what baits we could and couldn't use. We simply followed the Division's standard bear-baiting policy. Hunters were forbidden to use wild game to bait black bears. There was already considerable strain between the Division and bear hunters, and we didn't want to worsen things by using deer or elk carcasses in our studies while telling hunters they couldn't do the same. My black bear survey overlapped the grizzly study, and both efforts followed exactly the same trapping rules —no wild mammal baits. If there had been any overt attempt to tie our hands, I'd have known about it and I'd have fought it to the death. There wasn't.

"Regarding fish as a bait, I believe that successful baits act on a bear's curiosity, not necessarily prior feeding experience. I know that fish works well for black bears in some parts of the northern Rockies but not in others. I think the extrapolations are more critical by region than by species."

I mention that some folks within the grizzly community have suggested that "Beck's mistake" was employing traditional black bear snaring techniques to try and catch a grizzly; they say the acutely cautious San Juan griz is too clever to be taken in a leg snare. Again, Tom rises calmly to the challenge.

"Four of my six field men were experienced grizzly trappers out of the Montana Border Grizzly Project. That's why I hired them; essentially, I high-graded Chuck Jonkel's best men. They knew what they were doing, and I'm sure they'd agree with me that while the behavior of grizzlies and black bears is quite different, the techniques used to trap them are essentially identical.

"When you're dealing with a bear that's extremely wary, a survivor, he's going to be a damn hard bear to trick, grizzly or black, no matter the technique or bait employed. That's why the Wiseman grizzly was able to survive for twenty-some years in secret in an area that's swarming with livestock and heavily hunted. In the eighty years since grizzlies were fairly plentiful in the San Juans, human pressures have acted to focus intense natural selection in favor of clever shyness. The bold bear that wandered out into a meadow got shot. The bear that showed itself near sheep or cattle got shot. The dumb bear that came to a bait got shot or was poisoned. There was a *tremendous* effort by the livestock community to exterminate grizzlies during the first half of this century. And only since the mid-1950s has that effort not been officially sanctioned and federally aided. Sadly, illegal killing of grizzlies may continue even today at some level in the San Juans; who knows?

"But my point is this: the animal that survives that kind of persecution—like the bacteria that survives penicillin—he's beaten the best you've been able to throw at him, and he's going to be one tough booger to get a collar on."

What about spoor?

"Interpreting a bear's species from sign gave us a tough time. Spoor is rarely unambiguous. And due to the political ramifications attached to the grizzly in Colorado, we need unambiguous evidence, clear and simple proof that grizzlies still exist here, before we say they do. There's so much distrust on all sides these days that almost any evidence short of a bear in hand is going to be stringently challenged. Both figuratively and literally, we need proof that can stand up in court.

"Certainly, as critics have pointed out, the survey wasn't exhaustive —that country is huge and tough and time-consuming, and we had to leave a lot of its most inaccessible nooks and crannies unexplored. We were chasing ghosts with a limited budget and minimal manpower. Even so, I had the best talent available, we used the best technology and techniques known to provide unambiguous evidence, and we made an honest effort."

Having recently walked and ridden many of the same miles of the radically corrugated south San Juans and Tierra Amarilla that had been covered by the Beck team, I understand Tom's pride in how much of it they *did* manage to scour in just two summers.

• • •

In retrospect, the Beck study may have ended with "lots of black bears but no grizzlies" because in fact no grizzlies are left in the San Juans. Or possibly, as Tim had worried, because San Juan grizzlies weren't attracted to the unfamiliar smell of rough fish. More likely, Beck's men failed to snare a great bear because, as Division biologist Hal Burdick had suggested in his final report on a San Juan grizzly survey conducted a decade prior to the Beck study, there were so many bold and uncautious black bears in the area that they filled every last snare, over and over; hypercautious grizzlies didn't have a ghost of a chance.

But—and of this I have become absolutely convinced—the Beck study did not fail to trap a San Juan grizzly because it was a game fixed for the losing.

7

"SOME MIGHTY BIG
BLACK BEARS"

The Schutz Sighting

> *Perhaps certain things about the world are best*
> *discovered by engaging the senses completely and*
> *leaving the analytical mind at rest.*
>
> —Richard Nelson

On November 1, 1990, Pagosa Springs district wildlife manager Glen
Eyre submitted the following report to the Colorado Division of Wildlife's nongame/endangered species office in Denver:

> On October 28, 1990, I received a call from Dennis Schutz, who was
> working on the Banded Peak Ranch near Chromo, Colorado. [A few
> days] before, he observed four bears in a remote drainage on the
> ranch, and he thought they might be grizzlies [and that they had
> left] some tracks with definite claw marks. He first saw three cubs in
> a meadow near a group of trees. He thought they were all adult bears
> because they were so big. Then what apparently was the sow came
> out and she was huge, [at which point] he decided the others were
> her cubs. He watched them for about 20 minutes while they played
> and dug around under some old logs. Then they left with the sow in
> the lead and the other three following her. The three cubs were all
> the same color, which was light brown with even lighter tips on the
> hair. He said that the sow's back was "steeper" than on any black
> bears he has seen, but he wasn't sure you could call it a hump.
>
> On October 31, 1990, Dennis and I hiked into the area. . . . We
> found several tracks in the snow near where the bears had crossed the
> creek. Most of them were melted out. However, there was one pretty
> good front track and one pretty good back track. . . . It is defi-

nitely an interesting track; however, I think it is not [sufficiently conclusive] to call it grizzly. We don't know whether the tracks are from the big bear or the cubs.

Because the tracks were in snow and even the "pretty good" prints had melted somewhat, Eyre attempted to estimate the approximate original size. The front track taped five inches wide and six inches from heel to middle claw, with the toe impressions too indistinct to measure. The hind track was four inches wide and nine inches from heel to middle claw; again, the toe prints were indistinct. Finally, there was "no wedge apparent in the instep" of the hind print.

Eyre took a Polaroid photo of the hind track, which was the clearer of the two, but because of the glare of the snow and lack of contrast, plus the limitations of the camera—a fixed-focus lens, no fill flash, and, especially limiting, no polarizing filter—all you can really say after viewing the print is what Glen said in his report: "It's definitely an interesting track."

In a note accompanying his sketches of the tracks, warden Eyre wrote that "it was $2^3/4''$ from the front of the [front paw] pad to the tip of the claws."

Go figure. By subtracting the $2^3/4$-inch gap between pad and middle claw, we get pad dimensions of 5 inches wide by $3^1/4$ inches long. Let's assume for the moment that this print was made by the largest of the four bears, the sow. In "Black Bears of West-Central Colorado," Tom Beck reports the largest known front pad measurement for an adult female Colorado black bear at about $4^3/4$ inches wide by just over 3 inches long—a quarter inch both narrower and shorter than the Schutz track.

From that same report, we know that an *average* female Colorado black bear's front pad measures about $4^1/4$ inches wide by $2^1/2$ inches long. Finally, an average female Yellowstone grizzly's front pad measures around $5^1/8$ inches wide by $2^5/8$ inches long.

By squaring all these pad sizes and comparing, it appears that if the Schutz tracks were made by the biggest of the four bears, she was either a humongous blackie—a full two square inches larger than the state record —or a slightly (two-plus square inches) larger grizzly than the Yellowstone norm.

According to Bergmann's rule, San Juan grizzlies should average somewhat smaller than Yellowstone grizzlies, in that body size for a species tends to increase with distance from the equator. But then, a century ago, west-central Colorado produced the half-ton monster Old Mose. Moreover, Tom Beck believes San Juan bears, blacks and grizzlies, defy Bergmann's rule and are slightly *larger* than northern Rockies bruins due to habitat superiority. "Bergmann's rule," says Beck, "isn't a real good rule."

But what if, as Dennis Schutz believes, the tracks Glen Eyre measured and photographed were not from the big female but from one of her three subadult cubs? Since it is impossible to average track sizes for a category as broad and blurry as "subadult," we have no standards to measure against.

But we do have the dimensions of the right front paw of the 1951 Starvation Gulch grizzly, which Ernie Wilkinson estimated to have been approximately thirty months old and to weigh about three hundred pounds at the time of death. This subadult male likely had been estranged from his mother only weeks earlier. The Wilkinson grizzly's front pad measures just under 4 inches wide by 3 long, compared to the Schutz track's approximate 5 by $3^{1}/_{4}$ inches.

Viewed in this light, and assuming—based on their size and the fact that they were still with their mother—that the Schutz subadults, like the Wilkinson male, were about thirty months old, maybe younger but probably not older, the Schutz tracks should just about fill the subadult grizzly bill while seriously stretching the limits of credibility for a black bear cub, even a male, still young enough to be with its mother.

Unfortunately, the report fails to note the distance from pad to middle claw of the hind track, so we have no way to deduce rear pad length. The track's 4-inch width, however, falls slightly short of the largest known female Colorado black bear hind pad width—$4^{3}/_{16}$ inches—while slightly exceeding that for the average female black bear: about $3^{7}/_{8}$ inches. Meanwhile, the average width for female Yellowstone grizzly hind pads is about $4^{3}/_{4}$ inches.

In the end, all we can determine from these measurements alone, allowing for the many indefinites they embody—the front and hind prints could even have been laid down by two different bears—is that the Schutz tracks were made either by a new state-record black bear sow or by a slightly larger than (the Yellowstone) average female grizzly . . . or, as Schutz believes, by a jumbo male grizzly cub.

But there's more. Glen Eyre's notes accompanying his sketches of the tracks include the statements that "no wedge was apparent in instep" of the hind pad, and "I believe that if a line was drawn across the front pad, the last toe would be below the line, but it was hard to say for sure." The "wedge" to which Glen refers is a distinct notch in the instep characteristic of black bears. Thus the absence of a wedge in the rear Schutz track is strongly suggestive of a grizzly. But since the track was made in snow, which is not an ideal tracking surface, this evidence, too, is inconclusive.

Eyre's mention of an imaginary line drawn across the front pad refers to a feature that, in a perfectly clear track, is generally considered a foolproof distinction between grizzly and black bear. As Canadian grizzly biologist Stephen Herrero explains in his hair-raising *Bear Attacks:* "The toes of a black bear arc more, whereas the grizzly's are more in a straight line. This characteristic can be tested on clear tracks by placing a straightedge at the base of the big-toe track and lining up along the top of the pad. If the line passes below the middle of the small toe, this indicates a grizzly bear . . . above the middle of the small toe, it is probably the track of a black bear."

If Eyre's guesstimate was correct, that "the last toe would be below the line," we are probably looking at the print of an exceptionally large female black bear. However, considering Herrero's restrictive "on clear tracks," which these weren't—the toe pads were too indistinct even to measure—we are forced to rule out this estimation as credible evidence . . . just as we would be if Glen had thought the line would have fallen above the middle of the last toe. And finally, *deep* tracks, made in soft mud and snow, defeat the whole toe-line scale; I have a plaster cast of a deep grizzly mud track in which the entire little toe falls well below the toe line.

The bears' coloration, while consistent with known Colorado grizzly pelts, still offers nothing definitive, since both species can be almost any color from black to blond. And though Schutz's description of the sow's back being " 'steeper' than on any black bears he has seen" is again suggestive of grizzly, it, too, is inconclusive.

On a "Grizzly Sighting" form appended to his written report, in answer to the question, "Any other characteristics which indicate grizzly bear rather than black bear?" Eyre noted that Schutz had reported the biggest of the four bears as having a dished face. This provides perhaps the most pregnant piece of information to come from this highly promising yet ultimately inconclusive sighting.

JULY 1993: TIERRA AMARILLA, COLORADO

The fifty-eight-thousand-acre high-country paradise designated on Colorado maps as Tierra Amarilla (Yellow Earth) is but a fragment of an 1832 Mexican land grant that originally included much of what is now southern Colorado and northern New Mexico. Today, Colorado's crudely phallus-shaped T.A. remnant rises south to north from above the back-road speck of Chromo, with the crest of the Chalk Mountains marking its western boundary, the Continental Divide roughly tracing the eastern border and the little Navajo River burbling down the middle.

Ecologically disruptive enterprises such as livestock grazing, energy exploration, logging and its attendant road building have all been minimal over the past century. That blessing and the natural ruggedness of the land have allowed the T.A. backcountry to remain among the truest wilderness areas left in Colorado. Additionally, its private status provides insulation from ecological abuses such as ATVs, unlimited hunting and camping pressure, free-roaming poachers, firewood cutting, and snowmobiles and skiers in winter.

Not long ago, I had the pleasure of chatting at length with Dusty Hughes, the widow of Charley Hughes, one of three brothers who owned the T.A. for most of the twentieth century, calling it the Banded Peak Ranch. Dusty says the land was purchased around the turn of the century by William E. Hughes, a Texas cattleman and Civil War vet known to most as "the Colonel." Local rumors that the ranch was won in a card game or traded for a remuda of horses, says Dusty, are patently false. Even so, the purchase price was "a steal."

From the Colonel, who never came up from Texas to see the place, the T.A. was willed to Lafayette "Fet" Hughes, who in due course passed it along to his three sons—Bill, Charley, and Fet Jr. These gents drew lines on a map dividing the substantial property into three roughly equal parcels of about nineteen thousand acres each, stacked one atop the other along the valley of the upper Navajo River. The brothers then numbered slips of paper 1, 2, and 3, tossed them in a hat, and drew to see who got what. Bill wound up with the lower third, Charley drew the middle ranch, and Fet Jr. became owner of the upper property. Even thus divided, the estate continued to be known under the single name Banded Peak Ranch.

Bill Hughes, now an octogenarian, still owns the lower ranch. The upper property is operated by Rick and Holly Lapin, Holly being a descendant of Fet Jr. Charley Hughes died in 1987, and after searching long and hard for a buyer who would "treat the place with the respect it deserves," Dusty Hughes sold the middle ranch to the people for whom Dennis Schutz now works.

Presently, Bill Hughes leases a small river-bottom portion of his property to a local woman for small-scale cattle grazing, but the bulk is left to the abundant deer, elk, bears, and cougars. Bill's ranch also contains a small, decades-old oil-drilling operation known as Gramp's Field, a popular wintering ground for elk. Hopeful rumor has it that Bill plans to put the place in a land trust so that it can never be subdivided or further developed after his death; God bless him if he does.

The Lapin property sees no grazing and has no oil fields, but is leased each fall to a commercial outfitter who brings in a total of fifteen elk hunters, and is being actively logged—many say brutally, though Rick Lapin uses the adverb "prudently."

The middle ranch, Schutz's baby, is the most pristine of the three, in essence a wilderness preserve, with no logging, grazing, or commercial activity of any stripe, save for four elk hunters Dennis personally guides each fall.

In the early days, all three slices of the Banded Peak pie saw some limited logging, but two seedlings were planted for every tree removed, the old logging roads are mostly overgrown today (except for those the Lapins have reopened), and in all, the place has come down to the present owners, and the present wildlife occupants, in near immaculate condition.

And today I'm getting my first close look at this likely grizzly sanctum sanctorum. Rubbernecking the scenery as I cruise along the rutted gravel road paralleling the river, I'm reminded of Round River biologist Dennis Sizemore's observation that the San Juans are "another Yellowstone waiting for permission to happen." Here in the valley of the Navajo, that's more than a metaphor; here you feel as if you *are* in Yellowstone. Not the same scenery, of course, but the same magical time-warp atmosphere . . . Tierra Amarilla . . . Yellow Earth . . . Yellow Stone.

Looking out across the broad valley, giant ancient cottonwoods mark the course of the Navajo and border the lower edges of broad pastures sloping gently up to huge pure stands of quaking aspens along the lower reaches of the mountain slopes on east and west. Higher up, the aspens intermingle with, then give way to, dense mountainside forests of spruce and fir and, finally, alpine tundra and butt-naked sedimentary cliffs, the latter often sculpted by erosion into the weirdest shapes imaginable: hoodoos, spires, pinnacles . . . gray conglomerate shades of Utah's Canyonlands, dissected, labyrinthine, and foreboding.

The entire valley is generously watered, and wildlife is visibly abundant. Mule deer loaf within the flickering shade of cottonwoods along the river and its tributary creeks, or browse confidently in the open near the road. And after dark, I've heard, it's not unusual to have to brake and wait while long lines of wapiti cross in front of you.

And the birds: this is, to borrow a phrase from Terry Tempest Williams, a feathered landscape. On my drive in this morning I've spotted a mature bald eagle, aloof in his winged majesty; a hunting pair of red-tailed hawks; a remarkably fleet-winged falcon moving far too fast for identification; nervous, flighty flocks of bluebirds; more flickers than you could flick a Bic at—the place is quite literally alive.

After a while, I steer onto a side road marked "Dead End," pass through a heavy pipe gate guarding the boundary of the Banded Peak Ranch, and continue on for several miles more, frequently consulting the full page of directions dictated to me by Dennis, veering onto progressively fainter two-tracks.

Finally, I round a curve going up a steep wooded hill and am looking at ranch headquarters, a modern utilitarian building lacking any hint of rustic charm but tucked away politely out of sight. It does, however, offer a pulse-pounding view of the valley below and the mountains across the way, the latter striped vertically with avalanche chutes still white with last winter's snow.

As I crawl out of my truck, I'm challenged by a low-slung vociferous Aussie shepherd/heeler mix—the archetypical western ranch dog—who hushes her excited barking and becomes immediately chummy when I bribe her with a dog biscuit from the bagful I keep handy for just that purpose.

"That's Belle," says Schutz, appearing in the open doorway of a double garage cluttered with tools, feed bags, tack, and other ranch staples. On hearing her name, the dog runs happily to her boss.

My host, I observe—this is only the second time I've seen him, and it's been two years since our brief introduction at Peacock's 1991 Pagosa camp meeting—could be actor Sam Elliott's brother. Schutz is in his early forties, stands probably three inches over six feet, is athletically slim and amply mustached, and has a headful of salt-and-pepper hair. Even so, he's almost shy, at least around folks he doesn't know well. Like me. In all, a handsome, soft-spoken, likable gent.

We shake and exchange howdies but have a long day scheduled so waste little time on small talk. After stuffing our day packs with sandwiches, fruit, and other trekking necessities—no canteens needed, says Dennis, explaining that "the water up there is as pure as a mother's love"—the three of us hop into a topless antique Willy's Jeep and bump out across a big grassy pasture, passing close by a mirrored lake where trout leap for joy, rolling into a shady grove of mature white-barked quakies and, twenty minutes later, up as close as wheels can take us to the base of a towering cliff along the timbered flank of the mountains. I check my topo map and put the elevation here at about nine grand, well within the luxurious upper montane life zone.

We shoulder our packs and start walking—Dennis in the lead, I following a few paces behind, and Belle everywhere at once.

Southwestern Colorado has been essentially rainless all summer, and the sere and wilted San Juans show it. But not here in this well-watered valley. The exceptional richness of the flora here would be evident even to a blind person, who could smell its heavy fragrance and would brush against its palpable presence with every step.

We hike through a dense aspen forest with a tropical understory comprising grasses and sedges and meadow rue and sweet cicely and sweet vetch (with its erotically feminine ivory flowers) and bluebells and red something-or-others and frisky violets (in shades of blue and white) and golden mule's ears and my little geranium friends and knee-high primordial ferns and homely skunk cabbages and giant cow parsnips and hat-high western monkshoods (in glorious florid purple), with lucent little streams to hop across every few hundred yards. Heaven.

"Somebody," I quip to Dennis, testing his mettle, "needs to log off all these damned big old trees, open the place up to the sun, cut up all this sprawling scenery with some good old bob-war, run a bunch of cattle and sheep in here to clear out all this clutter of vegetation and muddy up the streams, get some shit happening, turn this place into proper western ranchland."

"Not while I'm here," he says, smiling. "And I hope to be here for a long time."

We make no effort to walk quietly and now and again disturb a lone young bull elk or a cow-calf pair bedded in grassy enclaves among the trees. The big ungulates rise reluctantly and trot away, though never very far, summer-fat and slow and obviously happy.

Dennis Schutz is obviously happy here as well. But he is neither fat nor slow as he lopes long-legged up the unrelenting thirty-degree slope. Even at six-three, Dennis tells me, he's "Shorty" to his brothers, all of whom are taller; the youngest is six-eight. You can guess the Schutz family sport.

We mostly follow a webwork of elk trails prudently switchbacking up the mountain, decreasing the grade as effectively as any Forest Service engineer. But now and again the game trails go angling off in the wrong direction, at which times Dennis takes us straight up the middle, occasionally scrambling on all fours.

Thankfully, my guide proves not to be one of those eat-my-dust macho hikers but stops every few minutes, depending on the difficulty of the terrain, and pretends to look around, as if he's getting his bearings or enjoying the scenery, thus allowing me a precious minute or so to catch up and find my misplaced breath without making an issue of it. I'm onto his tricks.

During one such halt, Dennis picks up a small perfect silver-gray feather dropped by some local nuthatch, holds it up to the sky and admires it, then sticks it in his camouflage cap. I find myself liking this big man more by the minute.

Onward.

The aspen-spruce-fir overstory is so dense that we're walking in shade most of the time, a blessing on this warm July midday. And we've seen no bloody skeeters so far. An unending obstacle course of blowdown enhances the physical challenge, though the elk trails dodge around the worst of it. We come to yet another little creek and this time stop and kneel for a long drink, cold and delicious. Belle splashes in and laps her share of the lambent liquid a few yards downstream from us; a well-mannered mutt, or well-trained.

Another few minutes and we break out of the forest and into a big open avalanche chute where resilient patches of last winter's snow still lie knee-deep. We cross the chute and duck back into the timber, where we pick up another elk trail paralleling the slide route up toward timberline. This shady path leads us circuitously around and behind what from below had appeared to be a solid wall of cliff. Before long we're strolling out across a timbered ridge connecting the protruding cliff to the main body of the mountains. Dennis informs me that this is the apogee of our hike; I check the map and put us at a modest 10,600 feet—about sixteen hundred feet above the Willy's and that far again below the crest.

Now—uphill from the game trail we're following and barely visible among the thick understory of ferns and forbs—Dennis spots the tines of a large elk antler projecting from the duff. We scramble up to investigate and in the next few minutes unearth the moss-stained antlers and skull and most of the rest of the skeleton of the biggest and deadest bull elk I've ever seen. The main antler beams, grasped about halfway up, are so thick that I miss by a good inch being able to wrap my ample paw around and touch thumb to middle finger. I have "a thing" about antlers, all antlers: there is more mystery, drama, and heroism written in these intricate, improbable sculptures than we can ever imagine, much less comprehend. Dennis shares my enthusiasm.

As we study the remains, we wonder how the big bull came to his final rest here on this steep hillside, and why his skeletal remains, after what appears to be quite a long time, are still essentially all of a piece.

The animal obviously had not been fed upon by bears or other large scavengers, else the bones would be scattered far and wide. This suggests a winter death, when the bears were snoring and the coyotes and cougars had followed their prey to lower elevations. Winterkill. The biggest bulls usually come down last, and this one may have stayed high too long and gotten trapped by a sudden deep snowfall. From the size and condition of his antlers, I'd say he was terminally old; his time had simply come.

"Could be," Dennis concurs. "Or maybe he was wounded by a hunter over on the national forest and made it this far before giving up the ghost."

"Could be," I concur.

I photograph Dennis with the antlers, then we restore them and the other bones to their places in the duff of eternity, there to continue their gradual reunion with mother earth.

It's mostly downhill now. We descend back into the aspens and in due time cut another avalanche chute. Ahead, Dennis halts, signals me to join him, then whispers, "This is it."

I check my watch: a little after noon. It hasn't taken all that long to get here: a couple of hours of fast hard hiking. Yet the chute is supremely secluded and utterly invisible from the valley below. And with no real trails in and so much blowdown, it's impassable to horses.

It's hard to find a catchall name to describe this place. Dennis calls it "a hidden hanging *vallecito,*" or little valley, and that sums it up as good as any. It is hidden, it is suspended halfway up a mountainside, and it can be viewed as a little valley. Even so, it's a place of many parts. It's obviously an avalanche chute in winter, as evidenced by the absence of trees marking its precipitous down-mountain course and the snowpack still lining its bottom in July. But the trough the avalanche course follows was obviously carved by the small swift stream—I'll dub it Willow Creek—that flashes like a ribbon of mercury down its breast.

At its widest point, from forest edge to forest edge, the valley is maybe eighty yards across. A ways below here, Dennis tells me, Willow Creek doglegs and the valley narrows into a walled canyon and gets brushy and deep and damn hard to beat your way through, even going downhill. My map says we're standing at about 10,200 feet. As I look up the mountain, the swath of open green clinging to either side of Willow Creek is visible all the way to the jagged spine of cliffs topping out at a dozen grand.

Our side of the *vallecito,* the northeast, rises moderately into the mixed forest of spruce-fir-aspen we just hiked through. The far, or southwest, slope ascends much more abruptly, near the top almost vertically, through a dense "dog-hair" (skinny and thick as hair on a dog . . .) woods of spruce and fir to open tundra and finally bare rock, nippling out at last against an azure firmament.

After standing for a while just inside the tree line, talking little and whispering when we do, eyeballing the scene carefully to make sure we won't spook any creatures who may have beat us here—Dennis has registered his concern that we not barge in and "blow out" his bears should they happen to be here again—we step from the woods about where the bruins had first appeared, at a point where a stringer of small evergreens girdles the chute to less than half its width above or below.

The first thing I notice is that something has recently been digging in the soft damp soil here; an area about a foot wide by two feet long and several inches deep has been excavated into the tunnel network of a pocket gopher. Certainly, it *looks* like the work of a bear—but there are no big clawsome tracks, no big dirt clods, no huge piles of bear scat or anything else to suggest grizzly. Except, of course, the dig itself, which could also be the work of skunk, raccoon, coyote, or wolverine.

Grass grows deep and green in Schutz's *vallecito,* peppered with a full complement of subalpine wildflowers, including especially vetch and wild carrot—grizzly favorites, both—plus lots of skunk cabbage. Domestic sheep, which millennia ago had all their natural caution bred out of them, eat hell out of these leafy greens, then give birth to two-headed lambs. Wild creatures, meanwhile, have the God-given sense to eschew skunk cabbage; a most discerning and benevolent plant.

Dynamite bear habitat, this, and balm to the eyes to boot.

After a few minutes spent nosing around the area where, nearly three years ago, Schutz's mysterious bears had played and dug and fed, we stroll down the chute a paced-off seventy-eight yards to where Dennis had been sitting when the bruins materialized. We take seats exactly where Dennis had rested that quiet autumn afternoon, and as we eat our lunches I produce my cheap tape recorder and open my interview with Mr. Schutz by requesting a brief biography.

His look suggests he's not real comfortable talking about himself, but I persist and learn that Dennis is a lifelong San Juan local, having been born on the family ranch just north of Chromo in 1951, graduating from Pagosa Springs high school in the late 1960s, and, following a tour of military duty, taking a degree in physical education at Fort Lewis College in Durango. Over the years, he's earned his keep by ranching, teaching, coaching basketball, ranching, shoeing horses, ranching, guiding hunters, ranching, driving a snowplow on Wolf Creek Pass, plus a little occasional ranching. Schutz's primary duty as foreman here at Banded Peak is patrolling for trespassers and poachers.

That in the bag, I ask about the bears.

It was the second rifle elk season (of three annually), Dennis tells me, and he'd decided that day to patrol up along the boundary between the ranch and the South San Juan Wilderness, looking for hunters who might have inadvertently, or advertently, strayed over the line. On this day, as usual during the fall hunting time, Schutz, who always goes unarmed, was accompanied by an off-duty sheriff's deputy with the authority to ticket or, if necessary, arrest miscreants.

But less than a mile after their hike began—following the same steep path we took up this morning—the rent-a-warden "began experiencing some difficulty with the altitude" and turned back. Dennis continued on alone, all the way to the top, where he hiked a good ways along the convoluted ridge. By midafternoon, he figured he'd best head down in order to beat darkness back to his vehicle. But rather than retrace his route up, he decided to bushwhack down through a steep patch of mountainside he'd never before visited, thus extending his day's patrol while also enjoying some new country.

"I wasn't exactly sure how I was going to get down from there," Dennis recalls. "It would be easy to get cliffed-up. But on that side ridge back up there, near where we found that big bull's skeleton, I jumped a bunch of elk that took off down the mountain toward the valley. I figured they'd know a safe route down through the cliffs, so I followed them."

The wapiti's trail led Dennis down through the dark timber into the aspens and, eventually, to this hidden *vallecito*. Typical for late October at this altitude, it had already snowed, and though most of the white had quickly melted, broad patches up to a foot deep remained along the creek.

Dennis had been humping it hard most of the day, so when he stumbled into this restful scene, feeling confident that he could make it out before dark, he decided to take a break. With an apple in one hand and binoculars in the other, he found a comfortable seat at the forest's edge, using the same aspen for a backrest that he's propped against now.

"I don't think I'd been here for more than five minutes," he recalls, "when the first bear came out, right up the hill there where we were checking out that gopher dig." The bear appeared from the timber, walked out into the center of the chute, and started digging. Dennis was wearing a camouflage jacket and cap and sitting quietly. There was no noticeable breeze, and the bear ignored him.

"My first thought," he remembers, "was, 'Boy, that's a mighty big black bear!' "

After a minute or so, a second bruin appeared from the same little clump of trees, dashed into the meadow, and pounced on the first bear. The ensuing tussle looked, to Dennis, more like play than a serious fight. "I couldn't understand," he says, "why two full-grown *big* bears, weighing maybe three hundred pounds each, were behaving like cubs."

Now appeared a third animal, which immediately joined the fray. The trio "played and bawled and slapped and rolled around in the grass and dug and fed for twenty or thirty minutes" while Dennis watched through binoculars at a range we had just paced off at less than eighty yards. And throughout, he kept thinking the same thought, "Man, those are *some mighty big black bears!*"

Then, up from the creek gully behind the three playmates appeared a fourth bear. When it joined the others, Dennis was awestruck by its size. "This one was twice as big as the others. If they weighed three hundred pounds each, she weighed five or six hundred. It's hard to estimate a bear's weight, but I've seen lots of black bears and some really big ones, and this animal was entirely out of that category. As soon as I saw her, I got goose bumps all over and the hair on my neck stood up— literally. I could hardly believe my eyes, but I got a good close look through binoculars and after a while it dawned on me that I was looking at a family of grizzly bears."

Without moving, Schutz glanced around at the nearby trees, "looking for something climbable in case the sow spotted me and charged. But as you can see, it's just these spindly spruce and quakies here, with no low limbs to grab onto and pull myself up. So rather than attempting to crawl away unnoticed, I decided just to sit still and watch and hope for the best."

Schutz describes the three young bears as being a uniform light brown. The sow's thick pelage was "tri-toned," with a light brown torso, dark legs, and "light-tipped guard hairs across the back."

I ask if he saw a hump on the big bear. "The best I can answer is that there was something different about the profile of her back than I've seen on any black bear; it sloped down steeply from shoulders to hips, while blackies usually appear slightly higher at the hips."

As so often happens in close encounters with big bears, Dennis didn't think to look for details like the size and coloration of the front claws. "In retrospect," he says, "there's a whole lot I wish I'd have looked for that I didn't. But with the four biggest bears I'd ever seen only a few yards away, it just didn't occur to me to try and memorize every little detail. If I'd had a camera along that day, all of this would be a whole lot easier.

"It seemed to me that the sow knew something was wrong from the moment she appeared. Maybe she'd spotted or scented me, I don't know, but I definitely felt she knew I was here. Maybe, because the air was so still, it had taken awhile for my scent to drift up to her, and when it did, that's when she came up out of the gully to check things out."

Although Dennis didn't hear the sow make any vocalizations when she appeared from the depression in which she'd apparently been feeding or resting all the while, the cubs immediately ceased their play. The sow sniffed and peered in Schutz's direction, hesitated, then abruptly turned and walked away, crossing the creek and heading up the snow-packed chute, moving briskly, her three outsized cubs trailing behind in single file.

"Once," Dennis smiles, "one of the cubs broke out of line and attempted to dart past Momma and into the lead. That old sow reached out and swatted him a good one, and he fell right back in line and stayed there. After that, there was no nonsense, no playing; they just got the hell out of Dodge. But three times before they disappeared into the trees several hundred yards up the chute, the big bear stopped and turned and raised up on her haunches—not standing erect, but with her front feet off the ground—and looked right at me. Through binoculars, it felt like she was staring me straight in the eyes."

Dennis remained motionless for several minutes after the bears disappeared, concerned that the sow could be watching from the trees and that if he stood up and revealed himself, she might come charging back down the hill. When it felt safe, he walked up to inspect the area where the cubs had played, finding the grass and wildflowers matted down and the earth torn up. He then started out on the bears' trail, hoping for another glimpse, but quickly thought better of it, reversed course, and left.

"I was so pumped with adrenaline by then," he admits, "that I don't even remember hiking out, and some of it was steep talus and tricky going.

"At home that night, I studied bear photos in books, which confirmed my conviction that the bears were grizzlies. The next day I phoned the Division, but it was hunting season and Glen [Eyre] was busy; it was a week before he could come back up here with me. During that time some elk had come down the trail the bears had followed up the creek, blotting out most of their tracks. We finally found a couple of prints that hadn't been trampled, and Glen measured and photographed them. I don't think they were put down by the sow, because the three cubs were walking in a straight line behind her—that's twelve paws hitting the ground pretty much right on top of her tracks; the only clear prints, it seems to me, would have been those of the last bear in line. And too, even as big as those tracks were, she was a lot bigger."

Because it was late October with cool days, a low-riding sun that found its way into the bottom of the valley only briefly each midday, and a hard freeze every night, and since the two "pretty good" tracks Glen measured and photographed had been further shaded by vegetation, Dennis doesn't think they were significantly enlarged by melting.

We stash our lunch trash in our packs and stroll back up the chute for one more look around where the bears had been and a drink from the creek from which they would have drunk. We invest another half hour in taking pictures, then head for the Willy's, where four icy beers (*not* brewed with bogus "pure Rocky Mountain spring water") wait in a cooler.

We may never know for sure if Dennis Schutz in fact met a family of four Colorado ghost grizzlies in the south San Juans in October of 1990, or if he was—as so very many before and since have been—merely dazed, dazzled, and confused by having "some mighty big black bears" practically in his lap. But having come to know him, I consider Dennis to be a cautious and precise observer and reporter, and a man as good as his word. I believe he saw exactly what he thinks he saw.

Nor am I the only optimist here. Schutz's report figured heavily in prompting grizzly champion Doug Peacock, bear biologist Dennis Sizemore, and local environmental attorney Bruce Baizel to launch the San Juan Grizzly Project—not an effort to be undertaken solely on the basis of specious evidence and blind hope.

According to "A Guide to Judging Grizzly Bear Reports" published by the FWS for use by agency personnel in the northern Rockies, there are three "Judgment Criteria for Observations":

1. amount and kind of physical characteristics described for the observed bear;

2. distance from which bear was observed, length of time, weather, and;

3. subjective evaluation of interviewer about observer's reliability.

By my reading of the considerable fine print contained in these guidelines, the Schutz sighting qualifies as a Class 2A grizzly report . . . this on a scale ranging from 1A (irrefutable) to 3D (totally useless).

Ultimately, like so much else pointing to the existence of San Juan ghost grizzlies, the Schutz sighting is inconclusive. Yet . . .

"Down there in the T.A.," Glen Eyre will tell you, "anything is possible."

8

THE SNOWSLIDE CANYON
GRIZZLY EXPEDITION

A Silvertip for the Weminuche?

You can't always get what you want.
—Traditional

Here on the southwestern edge of the Weminuche Wilderness, the summer's drought shows. Many riparian areas have gone dry, desiccating thousands of acres of wildlife forage. Grass is sparse and brown. Wildflowers are withered and dying; others never bothered to bloom at all. The leaves of deciduous trees and brush are relinquishing their color long before their time. Puffs of dust rise under the hooves of our horses as they labor up the parched Pine River trail.

At 492,418 acres, the Weminuche is the largest and highest of Colorado's official wilderness areas. The bulk of it lies within the San Juan National Forest, whose 1,869,931 acres fairly blanket the West Slope of the Rockies in southwestern Colorado; the remainder spills east over the Continental Divide onto the San Juan's sister forest, the 1,831,207-acre Rio Grande. (On a map of Colorado, look for the Weminuche within an area loosely bounded by the towns of Silverton on the northwest, South Fork on the northeast, Pagosa Springs on the southeast, and Durango on the southwest. Pronounced *Wem'-in-ooch,* the name honors a local Ute Indian band that hunted and explored these rugged mountains centuries ago and blazed many of the trails still in use today.)

My friend and guide Cary Carron and I are embarked on a four-day journey into the Weminuche heartland, to a place called Snowslide Canyon—up the Pine River trail, then down the Vallecito Creek drainage, seventy-some eyeball-popping miles.

It's good to be in the saddle at last. There's a lot of prep work to this cowboy business: assemble and load the hundred pounds or so of grain and tack required for each horse—the latter including saddles, bridles, harness, and various equine et ceteras—hook up horse trailer and drive to horse pasture, catch grain and bridle horses, lead horses to trailer and load, drive to trailhead—in this case, the Pine River campground behind Vallecito Reservoir between Durango and Bayfield—unload horses, gear, and tack, hoist up and cinch down riding and pack saddles, load, weigh, and balance panniers, hang panniers from packsaddle ears, top-load duffels and other light gear, tarp and tie loads with squaw or diamond hitch, mount up—curse, dismount, take that leak—mount up and ride.

Consequently, even with a daybreak start, it's midmorning by the time we're on our way.

Cary leads two rude pack horses; the beasts behave as if they were raised in barns, farting continually, lifting long tails to drop haybiscuits, blowing off their recent soft days in pasture.

The sidehill trail we're following parallels along above its namesake river, Los Pinos, and penetrates a dense upper-montane forest of Gambel's oak, quaking aspen, ponderosa pine, spruce, and fir. The drive from my cabin to the Pine trailhead takes only about half an hour, and the trail is famous for its moderate grade and immoderate scenery. The fishing in the azure pools and shallow white-water races of Los Pinos, a small river, is always good. Wapiti, mule deer, black bear, blue grouse, bighorn sheep, and ptarmigan abound. Even so, this is my first trip up the river. Many's the time I've thought about it, but I've always delayed and inevitably deferred—precisely *because* the trailhead is so accessible, the hiking so easy, the scenery so sublime, the fishing and hunting so rewarding. I don't like my wilderness crowded.

Not long into the ride, I spot a shiny green black bear scat lying like a redolent gift alongside the trail. "Good omen," I announce, pointing out the pile to Cary. He turns and looks, grunts, turns back away. I take no umbrage, not really expecting others to share my nose for wildlife scatology.

A few minutes more and the long summer's drought begins to end, exactly as forecast—not by any weather professional but by one of Cary's fellow game wardens. "Where Carron goes," he warned me, "clouds follow. We call him the Rain Man."

Warden Carron is in his late thirties, about six-two, 190 pounds, with arms that bulge the sleeves of his gray uniform shirt and a big bushy Wyatt Earp of a mustache; he sits his Appaloosa like an Old West movie marshal. Steady, competent, confident, courteous, Cary honors his profession. With a degree in wildlife biology under his belt and a heavy handgun on it, Carron is a man for the job.

As our horses clomp along, Cary and I discuss the sad fact that owing to the drought and consequent shortage of native vegetation, bears are being forced out of their preferred backcountry haunts and wandering into "settled" areas—campgrounds, rural subdivisions, and the like—searching for sustenance, delighting some people and scaring others, but causing little real trouble. Except, that is, for a couple of the boldest among them, who've been terrorizing campers along this very trail for the past few weeks.

At first, attracted like flies to sheep shit by the aroma of garbage and food left out, the shy bruins would slink into camps while the occupants were absent, root around and devour unsecured edibles, lick the bacon grease from unwashed skillets—then retreat unseen back into the sheltering woods. But as the summer progressed and the drought worsened, the bears have grown ever more desperate, to the point of strolling into occupied camps when the irresistible smells of cooking permeate the valley, taking what they want from under the very noses of horrified campers.

Just a few days ago, one of these bandit bears burglarized the Granite Peak Guard Station—our goal for tonight—smashing a window and weaseling in. Tore hell out of things in the little log shack, Cary hears tell, had a good feed, and left. The Forest Service backcountry ranger who normally occupies the cabin—this summer it's a young woman from somewhere back East, unarmed and inexperienced with bears—was away at the time.

Three hours above the trailhead, we come to a fork. The left path leads north up to Emerald Lake—lovely, remote, fishy, popular. We bear right, keeping to the trail less traveled.

Or maybe not. Here come three backpackers—wet, mud-splattered, and smiling bravely—followed a few minutes later by a long somber line of stiff-in-the-saddle dudes led by a young wrangler dressed like a Hollywood gun-and-gallop bad guy, black hat and all. Headed down and out, all of them. The San Juan side of the Weminuche, to offer the example closest to hand, receives an average of 170,000 "recreation visitor days" —agency bureaucratese for "one person for twelve hours"—each year. Still, for those not afraid to step off the trails, there's plenty of room to be alone.

Four hours' ride above the trailhead, we break out of the sodden forest and into foggy Willow Park, a long narrow mountain meadow set about with a few trees, quite a few glacial erratics, bogs, and willow thickets—moose country. And Los Pinos runs through it all, with bright little cutthroat trout idling in its cold dark eddies, blunt noses pointed upstream, meeting the current of life teeth-first. We break for lunch.

A pale blue hole opens in the clouds, and a cold sun leaks through, spotlighting a distant waterfall fluttering like a chrome ribbon at the head of a far-off canyon high on the opposite slope of the valley. From here, that place looks immutably impenetrable. I ask Cary if he's ever been up there.

"No. And neither has anyone else I know of. No trail in, trees as thick as hair on a bear, blowdowns everywhere, cliffs all around. That up there belongs to the elk."

"And the bears."

"No doubt."

The sun fades back out. The rain resumes. We eat and run.

Near the upper end of the park we pass a camp consisting of two tents, a folding table and chairs, other junk. One gray horse is tied to a tree nearby; he snorts and stamps nervously as we ride past. Buck, my Colorado quarter horse (one-quarter horse, three-quarters mule), returns the greeting with a long, arrogant fart. The door flaps of both tents are tied open; no one home. On the table sit a carton of milk, a tub of butter, a loaf of bread, a jar of jelly, and other inadvertent bear baits.

No wonder they're having bruin trouble hereabouts.

It takes our little pack train half an hour to transit Willow Park and begin a slow, tortuous hump up a narrow, gravelly trail weaving between boulders big as trucks. Hard going for the horses, their iron shoes striking sparks on the rocky path.

When the switchbacks are finally behind us, we come to another cutoff, this one trailing up along Flint Creek to Barebottom Park—an intriguing name, that. We hold northeast, as ever, passing close beneath the Pope's Nose. "Holy shit," I observe with appropriate reverence, peering up at the enormous granitic proboscis.

"It's nothing to sneeze at," Cary fires back. Touché.

Farther and higher into the Weminuche, fording Pope Creek, edging up into the subalpine life zone, aspens disappearing, blue spruce giving way to Engelmann, snow-patched tundra capping alpine peaks all around. Here again the valley of Los Pinos broadens, opening into another linear mountain park.

From a finger of trees along the river a quarter mile ahead rises the slow heavy smoke of a damp-wood fire. The pointed tip of a gigantic tepee shines wet above the trees. A remuda of horses grazes along the silver slip of stream. Suddenly, déjà vu strikes, and I experience an almost sensual stirring in my gut. At this moment I *know* what it felt like to be a Ute hunter returning to camp on a rainy evening in the absolute genuine unsullied wilderness of this place a century and a half ago.

At least I think I do.

Linguistic evidence—about all there is to go on—suggests that the Utes arrived in southern Colorado some eight hundred years ago. Embodying elements of the Plains, Woodlands, and Desert cultures that surrounded them, the Utes took to mountain living and became the premier native exploiters of the San Juans' natural resources, hunting and exploring even unto the most remote mountain corners—evidence of their presence has been found as high as thirteen thousand feet. Come winter, local Utes retreated to large encampments down in the sheltered foothills and sunny mesas south and west of the mountains. Nominal tributes to the significance of these early native mountaineers are ubiquitous across the San Juans today, with Ute lakes and Ute creeks and Ute peaks and Ute parks in abundance.

Most often, small roving bands of Ute hunters would bivouac in crude shelters called *wickiups,* constructed by leaning saplings and tree limbs together to form a conical skeleton, then covering the frame with slabs of bark, evergreen boughs, or leafy brush. For larger, longer-term summer mountain encampments, they enjoyed the relative comfort of honest-to-goodness hide tepees that looked not unlike the canvas imitation peeking at us from ahead even now.

We leave the trail and angle down the hill, splash across the shallow river, and ride into a sprawling camp of half a dozen tents in addition to the big tepee. Cary introduces me to the outfitter who owns all this gear and all those horses yanking up wildflowers down along the river, and who has a permit from the Forest Service, in accordance with that agency's policy of multiple abuse, that allows him to pack way too many dudes up here, with way too many horses, for fishing, camping, and general recreating. The friendly outfitter offers me a speckled tin cup of steaming black watery camp coffee, which I accept without hesitation. Cary jaws for a minute with the old cowboy, then checks the fishing licenses of a half-dozen well-fed doctor dudes from Mississippi.

On we ride, into a dismal dusk.

At the far end of the big park looms a unique double-peaked mountain, standing heads above all visible others. That would be Granite Peak on the left, with a slightly lower unnamed rise to its right and a grassy saddle between. The Forest Service guard station of the same name must be somewhere twixt hither and yon, with Granite Lake and Snowslide Canyon—the purported grizzly bear capital of the Weminuche—beyond.

By the time my coffee buzz fades, a log fence appears alongside the trail, boxing in several open riverside acres as a pasture. Four gray-speckled horses snort and whinny and come prancing up to greet us. On the locked log gate hangs a sign warning off trespassers with GOVERNMENT PROPERTY. PLEASE KEEP THE HELL OUT OR ELSE. Or words to that effect.

"Cuts down on vandalism a little," Cary explains.

We dismount and lead the tired horses a final muddy quarter mile through the pasture, into a dark copse of evergreens, and up to the covered porch of the one-room guard station.

The door stands open; nobody home. As we're unsaddling and unloading, a young woman—college aged, short red hair, freckles, cheeks flushed with exertion—comes straining up the steep hill from behind the cabin, a five-gallon water bucket sloshing in each hand. My gentlemanly instincts prompt me to offer assistance, but she seems to have things under control; she doesn't know me from Arnie, and I don't want to be unintentionally insulting. (Being a gentleman is risky business these days.)

The young woman sloshes past us and into the cabin with her two-fisted liquid load, which she deposits on the floor at the back near a big cast-iron cookstove.

A moment later, a man in his early thirties comes chugging up the hill with two more buckets brimming with spring water. Cary introduces him as Steve, trail maintenance boss for these parts. We shake, and Steve introduces us both to Kelly.

With the four of us and our gear crammed into the cozy little cabin —no more than about sixteen by twenty feet—I wonder aloud how we'll ever find room to set up four cots. I volunteer to sleep outside on the covered porch, but Steve says that won't be necessary. "We've fit five, six in here before. Just don't eat beans for supper."

Darkness comes, and we fire up two ancient Coleman lanterns hanging from the cabin's exposed rafters, brightening the room and revealing a muddy smear of bear tracks on one wall, around and below a shattered and boarded-up window. "Broke in a few days ago and ate everything but the mouse poison," says Steve, sounding almost proud, as if it had been his own personal bear.

"Glad I wasn't here," says Kelly.

"Wish I had been," says some old gray-bearded blowhard.

After dinner (no beans), we sip whisky and pure Rocky Mountain bucket water and pass the evening talking quietly while the woodstove crackles, the lanterns hiss, and the rain pisses without surcease on the rusty tin roof.

I wander over to examine the dozen or so cryptic notes scribbled by previous tenants on the inside of the door frame; built early in the century, this little cabin has some stories to tell. Most of the notes simply cite the date the guard station was closed for the winter, along with the number of elk killed by local hunters and the snow depth: "October 10, 1956—5 elk down, 3 ft. snow on ground and snowing hard."

It snows hard throughout the San Juans, winter after winter. At a modest 6,512 feet on the southwestern flank of the mountains, Durango (real estate inflation capital of the West and proud of it) gets only about eighty inches of snow in an average winter. But up along the Divide, at double Durango's elevation, annual snowfall increases to several hundred inches. Any surviving local grizzlies would most likely den at or near timberline on steep slopes, selecting avalanche chutes or other microclimates that ensure a deep insulating snow cover.

Someone's digital wristwatch beeps irritatingly, signifying ten o'clock, and we agree to call it a night. We stand and push the little table aside, stack the chairs on top, and drag four bundled army cots down from the rafters. Too tired and wired to sleep immediately, I lie pop-eyed, staring into the dark, envious of Cary's instant snoring slumber, mentally previewing tomorrow's twelve-mile-loop ride—up through Snowslide Canyon, over the Divide, and down the North Fork of Los Pinos to Weminuche Pass, then back here for a second night in this little log den with the bear tracks on the walls.

I first learned of the Weminuche grizzly sighting back in early February, in conversation with Bruce Baizel, local rep for the San Juan Grizzly Project. Bruce had recently picked up an "official rumor" that an anonymous informant had reported seeing a mature grizzly in the Weminuche and had submitted a clump of hair to prove it. The sighting had occurred in July 1990, somewhere between a local landmark peak called the Rio Grande Pyramid and Rio Grande Reservoir—not all that far from Starvation Gulch.

"The Division is taking this one seriously," Bruce told me. "There's even talk of a press release sometime soon."

"Sometime soon" indeed: it appeared in the very next day's edition of the *Rocky Mountain News:*

Lab Report Backs Grizzly Sighting in San Juans

by Gary Gerhardt

A laboratory report from the Wyoming Game and Fish Department indicates a 75% to 80% chance that hairs recovered in the Weminuche Wilderness area of the San Juan National Forest are from a grizzly bear.

Rick Kahn, a biologist with the Colorado Division of Wildlife, said he was given the hair by a man who claims he came upon the animal two summers ago as it was digging before it caught his scent and hurried away.

"He said he was on horseback in a remote area south of Rio Grande Reservoir when he pulled up above timberline and saw the bear actively digging about 300 to 400 yards away," Kahn said. "He watched it for 20 to 30 seconds, then dismounted and made his way through a gully and came up within 50 yards of the bear."

Within four or five seconds, the bear realized the man was nearby and ran to the crest of a hill, looked back, then disappeared.

"Everything he described was in line with a grizzly," Kahn said. "He said it had a dish face, hump on the back, looked to be about 300 pounds and, with the sun low . . . he really noticed the golden color of its fur."

A couple of weeks after the Division went public with the sighting, I snagged a copy of the Wyoming Game and Fish Department hair analysis, signed by senior forensic analyst Tom Moore—the same widely respected expert who had scrutinized the hairs collected by the San Juan Grizzly Project in 1991 and pronounced them probable grizzly. Based on his study of several "hairs from the leg area of an animal," sent to him by Colorado's senior big game biologist, Rick Kahn, Moore concluded that "comparison of hair characteristics [from the sample] to the hairs in the standard collection at the Wyoming Game and Fish Department laboratory show the hairs to be most similar to an animal in the Ursidae Family, bears, most probably Grizzly bear."

For a second opinion, the Division sent three unidentified hair samples to the Montana Department of Fish, Wildlife, and Parks lab at Sun River. Sample 1 was black bear, sample 2 was from the Wiseman grizzly, and sample 3 was the Weminuche hair. The Division asked Montana to identify all three.

In a report signed by chief analyst Keith Aune, the following conclusions were noted: "We determined sample 1 to be hairs from a black bear. Samples 2 and 3 were more similar to each other but were not clearly identified as bear hairs . . . they were not consistent with the known characteristics of bear hair and the samples did not compare well with known samples in our collection. One major difficulty we faced was that the samples did not include the entire shaft of hairs. In addition we observed that at least some of samples 2 and 3 appear to have been cut when collected.

"Additionally, we looked at samples from tanned hides of grizzly bears and feel that the process of tanning may have impacts on the condition of the medulla which is a key character in identification. The medulla characteristics from samples 2 and 3 and from some tanned bear hides were inconsistent with those described in the keys."

I found the Montana report intriguing on several counts.

First, by commenting on the similarities between sample 2, the known grizzly hair, and the Weminuche sample, Dr. Aune indirectly bolstered Tom Moore's conclusion that the Snowslide hair was "most likely grizzly."

Second, Aune's concern with the missing roots of samples 2 and 3 hairs raised my eyebrows. The known grizzly hair, sample 2, lacked roots because it had been scissored from the hide of the 1979 Wiseman grizzly. But what of sample 3? Why did "at least some" of the hairs in the Weminuche sample also appear to have been clipped above the roots?

Along the same suspicious line of thought, the Montana report noted that both samples 2 and 3, in common with hairs from *tanned* grizzly hides, "were inconsistent with those [untanned bear hairs] described in the keys." Since the sample 2 hairs were in fact from a tanned hide, the question arises: Had the mystery hairs—which, like sample 2, "appear to have been cut when collected"—also been sheared from a tanned hide?

Searching for answers, I phoned Rick Kahn at the Division's Denver headquarters. By this time I'd learned that the sighting had taken place at the head of an alpine canyon called Snowslide, high in the Weminuche. The Division's press-release description had been plenty close enough for media work.

Kahn impressed me as open and honest. In an hourlong conversation, he told me, I believe, everything he could in good conscience tell.

Kahn said he'd first met "the gentleman in question" in the fall of 1990 at a public meeting. During his presentation, Kahn had mentioned that enough evidence exists to suggest that a few native grizzly bears may still roam the San Juans. After the meeting, a man from the audience took Kahn aside and asked him several grizzly questions.

Kahn didn't think much of it that first time. But over the next several months, as the series of meetings continued, the questions continued as well, and Kahn began to suspect that "there was something going on."

"I was beginning to worry," he told me, "that this guy had killed a bear he thought could be a grizzly."

Not until a year later, during the fall of 1991, did the man admit to Kahn that yes, "something had happened." After getting a guarantee of anonymity, the man invited Rick to his home and recounted the following events:

On July 1, 1990, he had horse-packed alone into the Weminuche. The plan had been to meet some friends at the trailhead and ride up with them, but he had arrived late and found that the others had gone on ahead. Riding alone up "an old cutoff trail between the North Fork of the Pine and Snowslide Canyon," the man stopped to let his horse blow. As he gazed idly around, he noticed, way off in the distance, some odd activity that looked "like a man digging a well." He could see dirt flying in the air.

The man rode down through a swale and to the top of the next little swell, closing the distance between him and the well digger to about three hundred yards. "This was just at timberline," Kahn explained, "with fingers of timber coming out onto the tundra." Through his binoculars, the man could see now that the digger was a bear.

The man rode back down into the swale, tied his horse, and stalked forward on foot. When next he peeked up, the digger was only fifty yards away. The bear didn't notice him at first, but when the man raised his binoculars, the animal stopped digging and turned to stare. After a few tense seconds, the bear seemed to reach a decision and "moved away quickly."

When it reached a stringer of trees at the top of a rise, the beast stopped suddenly and swung around for a last brief look before disappearing.

While relating all of this, Kahn said, the man "had hit on a lot of the characteristics considered to be typical of grizzlies: blond coloration, humped shoulder, dished face. The only thing he didn't mention was the front claws; he never focused on the claws. And in my experience, that's fairly common; when you look at a bear, you tend to focus on the animal's upper body and head, not its feet. What he noticed most was the hair color. The sun was low, backlighting the animal, and he described its fur as having 'a beautiful golden sheen.' "

When he was sure the bear was gone, the man went over to examine the dig. The tundra near the base of a rocky talus was "pretty dug up, maybe a hundred square feet."

Lacking a ruler, the man compared the length of a clear hind print with his hand, later measuring it at eight inches or a little better—though whether this measurement included the toe pads, he didn't say. Assuming toes were included, eight inches is just right for a medium-sized grizzly but by no means out of bounds for a big black bear. According to Colorado bear biologist Tom Beck, the largest known rear pad measurements (not including toes or claws) for a Colorado blackie are about 5½ inches wide by 7½ long. Anything bigger is definitely within the realm of grizzly likelihood, in which species adult male hind pads average about 5½ inches wide by 7½ long.

The informant explained to Kahn that he'd seen a lot of bears up close, including grizzlies in Yellowstone and Alberta, had hunted and killed black bears, and felt he was competent to distinguish the two species and make an educated guess at live weight. He estimated this bruin at 300 to 350 pounds. Like the track measurement, this falls within a zone of possibility overlapping both medium-sized grizzlies (the mature grizzly sow killed in 1979 in the south San Juans weighed an estimated 400 pounds) and very large black bears. The man was convinced he'd seen a grizzly.

"Initially, I considered him to be highly credible," Kahn told me. "It seemed he had nothing to gain by making a false report. As a former game warden, I've got a pretty good bullshooter alarm, and it didn't go off with this guy. Part of it was his insistence on remaining anonymous, even within the Division; I was to reveal his identity to no one. That rules out ego and a desire for publicity as motivations for lying."

I asked Rick why the man had taken so long to come forward. "He was scared of the U.S. Fish and Wildlife Service, afraid that if grizzlies were found in the San Juans, 'the feds might close things down'—referring to hunting, grazing, outfitting, logging, mining, and other traditional multiple-use activities. Over the months we talked, I guess he came to trust me."

From this scant information, I surmised that Mr. Mystery must be a rancher or an outfitter, who understandably wouldn't want his peers to hold him responsible for "closing things down."

Kahn told the man he'd like to release the sighting to the press, but the informant implored him not to, and that was that.

Until December of 1992, two and a half years after the sighting, when Kahn received an envelope in the mail containing a clump of animal hair. There was no letter, not even a return address, but Rick had a hunch who had sent it. "I phoned him and asked what was going on. 'Well,' he says, 'I forgot to tell you part of the story. When the bear stopped and turned to look at me as it was leaving, some hair rubbed off on a tree.'"

Where before, the sighting report had fallen into place for Kahn, with the arrival of the hair it began to fall apart. "Frankly," he explained,

"I had trouble accepting that 'I forgot' business. If you look through the files, there have been several credible grizzly sightings in the San Juans over the years, both before and after the death of the Wiseman bear in 1979. I was convinced this was another. But when that hair arrived, it soured the deal for me. I believe that if my informant had the hair when I talked with him at his home—even if he didn't want to tell me about it for some reason—he would have slipped and made some reference to it."

I told Rick of my suspicion, based on the Montana lab report, that the hair might have been sheared from a hide.

"Could be," he agreed. "But it's also entirely possible that it's a clump of shed fur. The first of July is still springtime up that high, and bears are still shedding their winter pelage. Underfur as well as guard [outer] hair frequently rubs off in big wads or gets snagged on trees and brush. Tommy [Moore] in Wyoming looked at it and said he'd seen hair clumps like that before, but it was strange that the sample contained no guard hairs. So I don't know."

The location of the sighting also raised some doubts in Denver. Grizzly sighting reports from down in the south San Juans are easier to believe, Kahn feels, "because a grizzly died down there recently, and it's much more remote country; a bear could hide in any number of places there, and nobody would ever bother it. But Snowslide Canyon gets so much traffic . . . it just doesn't seem like a viable grizzly refugium. If there are grizzlies up there, given the number of people who pass through every summer, why haven't there been other sightings? And where do the bears go in the fall, when the place is swarming with hunters?

"Of course," the biologist equivocated, "if we were to assume that grizzlies still exist down south, one of them could walk that far in a couple of days. It would have to cross U.S. 160 at Wolf Creek Pass, but that's no real barrier."

Day two dawns, just barely. We rise, eat, and ride out.

After a couple of miles, we veer off the trail and make several crossings of shallow feeder creeks before picking up a side trail leading into a steep-walled canyon.

"Snowslide," Cary announces.

Within the V of the canyon, the trail snakes northeast, close along booming little Snowslide Creek. Water-logged alder, evergreen, and willow limbs salute us with wet slaps as we pass.

I can see few symptoms of drought here. In places open enough for the sun to find the soil, grasses and sedges *(Carex)* stand green and tall; no cattle or stinking swarms of woollybuggers up here to preempt them. Purple harebells by the hundreds hang droopy-headed under their own wet weight.

Snowslide: an apt name, considering that the canyon's steep eastern wall is guttered vertically every quarter mile or so with brushy, boulder-strewn avalanche chutes—favorite feeding grounds for bears and elk. Even now Cary spies a cluster of wapiti in the first of the big chutes; a dozen fat white bums glowing softly against the dark green distance.

Ahead, a sodden marsh hawk squats atop an isolate boulder that sparkles pink, black, and white with feldspar, mica, and quartz. With its feathers fluffed for airing, the hawk looks as big as an eagle.

Since this place is the goal of what has been a long and occasionally painful ride, we don't rush it but stop frequently to glass the avalanche chutes and brushy slopes opposite, looking for bears but seeing only elk. Even in the light rain, the scenery is dazzling; an hour passes with the easy feel of minutes.

Deep into the canyon, we round a bend and come face-to-jowl with a bull moose. The horse-sized deer stands just across the creek, maybe eighty yards away, a soggy bouquet of dandelion greens protruding from his elongate muzzle. This is a young Shiras, or Wyoming moose. His smallish antlers, three feet or so across, age him at three to four years. Homely as a blind date, gangly as a teenager, yet ineffably beautiful.

This is my first encounter with a San Juan moose, and I am jazzed. Cary, though not one to show emotion, must be equally pleased. After all, he worked hard the past couple of winters, along with other local Division wildlife managers, to capture more than a hundred moose—in Utah, Wyoming, and northern Colorado—and transport them here. The forced immigrants were released at several locations along the Slumgullion Pass stretch of the upper Rio Grande. But moose being moose, the animals quickly dispersed into prime habitat throughout the Rio Grande and San Juan National Forests. The Division hopes the population will increase naturally within the next several years to a forestwide carrying capacity of "several hundred." After that, excess animals will be culled through scientifically calculated and closely regulated annual hunts.

The San Juan moose project was in the works for more than five years. It took that long to conduct necessary habitat studies, file required paperwork, arrange an exchange of Colorado bighorn sheep for Wyoming and Utah moose, and convince a cadre of concerned local ranchers that a few hundred moose spread across several thousand acres of mostly public land wouldn't gobble up all of "their" livestock forage.

They won't. Moose are browsers, preferring twigs and brush to the grasses, sedges, and forbs so loved by grazing domestics. Moose also wade for aquatic greens that cattle and sheep don't even know exist. And unlike elk, moose don't band together in winter herds of hundreds and descend to lower elevations to trample grain fields and golf courses and collide on dark icy highways with speeding traffic. Rather, moose keep mostly to the high country, where they winter alone or in small groups.

What intrigues me most about the San Juan moose project is that moose are not native to Colorado; some experts believe that Cheyenne and Sioux hunters halted the animals' southern drift before the far-ranging deer could infiltrate Colorado and Utah. Even so, I'm glad they're here, and I'll bet they are too. This proud young stud, at least, looks content, at ease. So at ease; in fact, he dismisses us after a brief stare and resumes feeding.

I dismount, dig out my camera, attempt to jump the raging snowmelt creek, fall in, get real wet real fast, scramble up the far bank, ease forward through the willows, and sneak a few too-close pictures. The moose finally sees or scents me and retreats into the trees. I recross the creek, and we ride on.

As we ride, we kick around the politics of wildlife management in Colorado. I confess that it strikes me as odd that the Division—remembering that it takes its direction from the Colorado Wildlife Commission—was eager and financially able to establish the nonnative moose, while carnivorous extirpated, endangered, and threatened *native* species go begging. Why?

"Because," says Cary, "before this decade is out, we'll be hunting moose here. And it's hunters who pay the tab for Colorado wildlife. Besides, moose don't eat cows or sheep. Moose are not perceived as dangerous. In short, moose are popular with hunters, popular with the nonhunting public, and they don't raise the hackles of stockmen."

In friendly rebuttal, I suggest that moose can be damned dangerous. The late A. B. Guthrie, Jr., had dozens of moose horror stories told to him over the years by Montana hunters and guides: of cowboys getting chased on horseback by nearsighted bulls apparently bent on romancing their mares (or worse), of campers treed and held at bay all freezing night. Some Montana woodsmen, said Guthrie, have had so many bad experiences with bull moose in rut that they consider them more dangerous than grizzlies.

And regarding the perception that grizzlies are a serious threat to livestock: certainly, it happens, especially with sheep, which the great bears seem to detest as much as most everyone else. Yet *verified* grizzly predation on livestock is statistically insignificant. In fact, throughout the entire sprawling Northern Continental Divide Ecosystem—the grizzliest area in the lower forty-eight—less than 1 percent of domestic livestock fall victim to grizzly bears each year. The ranching community's perception of the threat of grizzlies, and for that matter wolves, is vastly inflated.

Several years ago, the Great Bear Foundation, a Montana nonprofit, established a fund to reimburse Montana and Wyoming ranchers for verified grizzly losses—so long as said ranchers had done nothing blatantly stupid to bring bear trouble on themselves, which is often the case. The annual payout averages a paltry $3,500. Were the San Juans ever to get a few new grizzlies, GBF has offered to help us set up our own rancher reimbursement program.

But there's more to it than money. Limited livestock "depredation" (I hate that fabricated word, which assigns to natural predation on unnatural prey the human value of "plunder") by black bears, cougars, and feral dogs is a resented but accepted fact of ranching. But should even one sheep or cow be killed by a grizzly, widespread panic ensues. It's the *idea* of "grizzly bear" that excites emotions and incites hatred, more than the reality.

Concerning the grizzly as a direct threat to humans: given the swarms of people who infest the backcountry of Yellowstone and Glacier National Parks annually and the incredibly ignorant, often suicidal stunts they pull as a matter of course, grizzly maulings are mercifully rare.

To wit: Glacier National Park boasts the highest number of grizzlies per square mile of any area its size south of Canada; every year an average of two million visitors troop through, many of them hiking and camping in prime backcountry grizzly habitat. Consequently, Glacier has the highest number of grizzly-caused human deaths in the lower forty-eight —nine since the park opened in 1913. That puts grizzly deaths statistically dead last behind a litany of such mundane park killers as falls, heart attacks, drownings, and auto crashes—which incidents together have accounted for more than two hundred deaths in the same eighty-one years.

For a nonpark paradigm, Montana's gigantic Bob Marshall Wilderness—"the Bob," as it is known locally—has always had grizzlies, as many per square mile as any nonpark federal holding in the lower forty-eight. And heavy human visitation as well. There are occasional grizzly "incidents" there, usually involving a bear or bears entering a sloppy camp and rooting around for food. Yet in the Bob's fifty-five-year recorded history, just one person has suffered a grizzly death.

The few grizzlies we might ever have down here in the San Juans—assuming even a best-case restoration scenario—would never pose a significant threat to human life or property. The statistical probability of another Wiseman incident in Colorado is nil.

Contrary to what the ranching community wishes the world to believe and may believe themselves, livestock would not be unduly threatened either. Especially not if public-lands stockmen, wool growers in particular, are compelled to take a few commonsense precautions.

It's noon and still raining when Cary and I finally attain upper Snowslide Canyon, which sits right at timberline. The scene is exactly as Rick Kahn described it: open, verdant, lots of little snowmelt brooks, with bogs and shallow sumps bordered around by dwarf willow, and shaggy stringers and isolated clumps of small spruce and fir punctuating the tundra. From the standpoint of the Big Four of wildlife habitat—food, water, cover, and room to move—I can't imagine any better grizzly range. My shortness of breath tells me that we're at least eleven thousand feet up.

Although past their prime now, wildflowers enliven such tundra country as this by the millions during the brief snow-free summers, having adapted to the mean environment by staying small and close to the ground, thus ducking under the worst of the near-constant winds and gaining a modicum of relief in the slightly warmer ground-level microclimate. Where not grazed off by domestic sheep (it's too high and rugged up here for cattle), grasses and sedges join the wildflowers and other forbs to provide a paradise for Rocky Mountain bighorn sheep (Cary says there should be some about today, but we haven't seen them), mountain goats (over in the adjoining Needles), wapiti, and, at least by natural design, grizzly bears.

We find a scenic aerie on which to picnic and let our eyeballs do the walking as we eat, searching for the telltale meadow digs that indicate grizzly—averaging maybe ten square feet in roughly oval diameter, several inches deep, with large overturned clods of earth throughout.

Virtually everything that distinguishes the grizzly from the black bear can be attributed to the former's evolutionary adaptations to serious digging: the longer, heavier, straighter front claws; the more massive hump of shoulder muscle; the more heavily muscled jaws and elongate molars designed for masticating tough roots.

Even the fierce aggressiveness of *Ursus arctos horribilis* is thought to be a product of having evolved on treeless tundra and plains, where its favored root-plants are most numerous. While *Ursus americanus,* with its short, curved, tree-climbing claws, had the evolutionary option of fleeing danger to hide within its preferred forest habitat, the tundra-prone grizzly had little choice but to stand and fight to protect itself and its young. Those individual grizzlies best equipped, physically and behaviorally, to fight (or bluff) and win were more likely to live and reproduce and raise more grizzlies exactly like themselves. Natural selection.

After half an hour of visual searching, the morning's persistent light rain suddenly intensifies to a downpour that fogs our binoculars and chases us off our sandstone balcony. And we have seen nothing resembling a bear dig, much less the elusive golden beast itself.

But then, we didn't come here expecting to invest a few casual hours and find anything of significant import. Were we to hike up and peer off the far side of any of the dozens of other local vistas, our view would be entirely different. What's more, with three turns of the seasons having passed since the 1990 sighting, a shallow bear dig would have been thoroughly camouflaged by vegetation.

Throughout the summer of 1992, Dave Kenvin, a veteran Division biologist based out of Monte Vista, headed a search for wolverines, which, like the grizzly and the lynx, are thought to be either extirpated or critically endangered in Colorado. Kenvin's team spent a month here in Snowslide, using infrared-activated cameras placed on game trails.

Any animal that passed along a monitored trail, day or night, would trip the shutter, capturing itself on film. At the same time, Kenvin's crew searched on foot for evidence of wolverines, keeping a sharp eye for grizzly spoor as well. And they found . . . *nada*.

Still, it would be hubris to claim that no grizzly is here just because none has been found. Didn't the Wiseman bear survive for twenty years and more in absolute anonymity? The Weminuche is a big, wild place.

As we're walking back to the horses, I eyeball the southeast horizon, taking in the distant alpine plateaus containing the *rincons,* or "hidden corners," named Grouse and Dog. Only a hardy and adventurous few have ever scaled those tricky heights and explored those untracked redoubts. One such is my friend T. Mike Murphy, veteran hunting outfitter and card-carrying grizzly doubter. Yet Mike admits to having seen "strange digs" up there in that time-warp alpine world.

I muse aloud that if I were a grizzly, I'd be up there in one of those *rincons,* not down here on this tourist strip.

"If I were a grizzly," Cary counters, "I'd be down in the south San Juans, not up here in the Weminuche."

Just so. Until and unless Rick Kahn's mysterious and at this point suspicious informant condescends to guide the feared "authorities" up here and show them exactly where he saw what he claims he saw—and explains that inexplicable hair sample while he's about it—until then, I'm afraid I have to dismiss the Snowslide Canyon grizzly sighting as improbable.

Onward, through the fog.

Riding almost due north, we top the Divide at twelve grand, whereupon the rain turns to snow. We follow along the top for a ways, then double back to the southwest down the precipitous slash of North Fork Creek, a cheerful Pineward rill laddered with burbling little waterfalls.

By midafternoon we break free of the dense, dark, dripping forest and into a huge grassy park. This is Weminuche Pass, the headwaters of Los Pinos. Dominating the western horizon is the glacier-gouged massif of the Rio Grande Pyramid. At 13,821 feet, it's the highest, sharpest, and most awe-inspiring peak in these parts. Extending from the Pyramid's muscular left shoulder is a long naked ridge with a ship-sized rectangular bite out of its middle—the Spanish Window, so called because it served as a landmark for early Spanish explorers.

Someplace between here and there is where government trapper

Lloyd Anderson killed the purported last Colorado grizzly back in 1952. We dismount and let the horses graze free while Cary searches with his binoculars and I photograph these restful fields of Elysium.

Certainly, this place is prime time for sheep grazing, and I imagine them—the horror!—blighting this tranquil scene by the thousands, summer on summer, cropping plant life to the roots, fouling God's own drinking water with their excrement, displacing natural prey species such as elk and deer and tempting hungry predators with their insipid nonstop bleating.

Thankfully, sheep haven't been grazed up here for more than a decade now. But not because the Forest Service wisely decided it wanted them out for the good of the ecology; rather, because this place is so remote and stock access is so difficult and the wool and mutton markets are so depressed that it has become economically unfeasible. Consequently, the native flora are returning: among big bunchy grasses and the darker sedges all around us now grow a gleeful abundance of monkshood and alpine bistort. The latter *(Polygonum)* sport bulbous pink-white flower plumes atop long stalks, resembling Texas-sized Q-Tips. The thick, twisted, starchy roots of bistort are grizzly candy. Indians dug them too.

A breeze rises and stiffens, and for the first time in two days the sky blues off, allowing the sun to make a proper show. Mountain and meadow are flooded with a strange and lovely light. A pastel rainbow appears like a heavenly crown above the Pyramid, then loses faith and fades.

Likewise, our brief idyll here is ended. Cary has spotted what look to be a couple of fly fishermen, so we hit the leather and gallop dutifully down to check them. Just one of the men is fishing—they have only one pole between them—and he has no license on him: "I left it in my other pants back in camp; never expected to see a game warden way up here." (That old line.) Cary writes him a friendly citation, and we move along.

A pair of red-tailed hawks come rocketing down the wind, flying low, grappling and playing and filling the air with their wild *keee . . . keee*ing. We follow in their wake.

Dusk is upon us when again we see the pole-fenced pasture of the Granite Peak Guard Station. Home, as it were, from the hills, so to speak. These man-made structures—fence, gate, and cabin—strike me as inappropriate intrusions here. I say burn them to the ground and scatter the ashes.

Tomorrow, after we've had our night's rest therein.

After dinner (no beans), I pour socially lubricating splashes of Tennessee hooch from my dwindling quart, and we talk quietly, winding down. I ask Steve, who's spent eight summers in the Weminuche, if he's ever seen anything he thought could be the spoor of grizzly. He says no, he hasn't, and doesn't think any are about, but admits that his work keeps him tied tight to the trails.

I confess that I'm growing doubtful as well. The Weminuche, I complain, is just too slashed with trails, too overrun with hikers and riders and hunters and anglers and their dogs and camps. (Not to mention, which I don't, presumptuous Forest Service guard stations.) "There's no place left up here," I conclude, "big and wild enough to shelter a grizzly in protective anonymity."

"I wouldn't go quite that far," says Cary. I don't believe he has totally made up his mind about the presence of grizzlies in the Weminuche—he believes there may be a few left down in the south San Juans—but nonetheless he's decided this evening to take the part of an optimistic devil's advocate. "Get half a mile off most trails, and you could camp all summer and not see another person. You might hear them from a distance, but they won't see or hear you, not if you don't want them to."

That seed of possibility grows, and we fall to brainstorming about Weminuche redoubts that could, theoretically, yet shelter a grizzly or two. Cary opens with the headwaters of Willow and Porcupine Creeks. Steve contributes the Three Sisters and Blue Spruce Canyon. I suggest Grizzly Gulch. Kelly sits quietly on her cot, reading by flashlight, waiting politely and patiently for lights out.

The morning is clear, chilly, and invigorating. Get up, load up, shake hands good-bye, ride out, retracing yesterday's route up Los Pinos and past the Snowslide cutoff to the lower canyon of Rincon la Osa (Bear Valley). It's a steep hour's lug up through the narrow, forested gorge along La Osa Creek, and with old Buck cruising on autopilot this morning, I loop the reins over the pommel and scribble in my notebook as we bump along.

After about an hour, the grade gentles and opens into a spectacularly verdant *vallecito*. This little valley park is maybe two hundred yards wide and walled in tight by evergreened slopes. The creek, not yet having fallen into its boisterous charge down the canyon, meanders lazily through acres of aromatic wildflowers: Indian paintbrush, harebells by the purplish zillions, biscuitroot and yarrow, showy daisies, mule's ears, purple asters. Plus elk sedge (like black-tipped arrows), willow and alder along the creek, low-down whortleberry everywhere.

And fauna as well. In shallow eddies in the creek, petite native cutthroats, startled by the thudding vibrations of our passing hooves, dart nervously about. A yellow-bellied marmot (wolverine food, grizzer grub) bounds onto a boulder the size of a bison and pipes a shrill alarm to its unseen mates, then drops off the back for a game of peekaboo. Golden-mantled ground squirrels and Colorado chipmunks sprint recklessly across our path while a pair of gray jays dog our progress, hoping perhaps that the horses will leave them some fresh seedy pies.

Bear heaven, this. Elk heaven, too. Just plain heaven. (If the biblical version lacks rivers and *rincons,* gray jays and trout—none of which I recall hearing any preacher mention—I don't need it.) I wish we could linger here, make camp for a couple of nights, and wallow in the beauty. But, of course, we have a schedule to keep. And Cary, eyeing a pile of whipped-cream cumuli growing in the west, is thinking about 12,430-foot Gunsight Pass, the biggest lightning rod in the Weminuche, where we must cross the Divide.

So on we ride, showing our backs to this Hidden Valley of the Bear. Ahead looms Gunsight Pass.

This particular Gunsight Pass (there is also one down in the south San Juans) is a knife-edged ridge of crumbly scree barely wide enough to support a mountain goat path. It is the highest and spookiest stretch of trail I've ever sat a horse across. Cary leads the way, as usual, with the two pack animals and me in obedient tow.

We survive this minor adventure and pass through the narrow notched "gun sight" to the west; it's all downhill from here. We stop for lunch on a vantage overlooking the fantastical polished-granite glacier-scape of the Ute and Flint Lakes basins. The scene is a startling reminder that over the past million years or so, the San Juans have seen three major glaciations. The most recent, corresponding with the Wisconsin glacial period at the tail of the Pleistocene (that most lively of recent epochs), closed only about ten thousand years ago. If in fact it has closed. Up here, it's hard to say.

As has become comfortable habit, we glass as we eat our lunches, searching for movement, blotches of contrasting color, anything animate. *Nada.*

I'm about to comment on how perfectly, gloriously *deserted* this icy fantasyland is when Cary spots a long line of tiny dots moving slowly up the valley of Middle Ute Creek. Another outfitter dragging another load of dudes. This is most discouraging; you can't get away from people and their bloody commerce anywhere in this vast so-called wilderness. At least not in midsummer along major trails. In an effort to stifle my rising indignation, I remind myself that backcountry crowding, here and elsewhere, is due at least in part to the tenacious fervency with which I and legion other whoreson "nature writers" have preached the gospel of the "wilderness experience," that holy pilgrimage of misplaced moderns. We too, I fear, are accidental hypocrites, insulting the very thing we most love.

We finish our elk jerky and cookies, off-load some used water, mount up, and brake cautiously down a twisted ladder of tundra switchbacks . . . past East Ute Lake, into the timber and along the rock-strewn hell of Flint Creek "trail" to Flint Lake—11,620 feet high and only the trout know how deep—down Rock Creek to Rock Lake—a popular destination for hikers and horse people coming up the Vallecito Creek thoroughfare—where I dismount and walk the next mile or so.

It was along this stretch, somewhere between Rock and Ute Creeks, that Lloyd Anderson, back in 1967, trailed a sow grizzly and two cubs for twenty minutes while they fed peacefully. They were, boasted the erstwhile grizzly slayer, "within shooting range" the whole time.

Butt-sore (speaking for myself) and starving, we reach Vallecito Creek an hour before dark and go into camp in the pines and aspens at the base of an avalanche chute the size of Chicago, a mile or two above Sunlight Basin. It has been a twenty-four-mile day.

We unload and tend the horses (a lot of work), haul water from a nearby spring, build a fire, get rained into the tent, cook, eat, kill what's left of old friend Jack, talk awhile, then bag it for seven hours of seamless slumber.

Come morning of the fourth and final day, our whole world is a Sunlight Basin.

Homeward ride the wild-grizzly chasers, paralleling the liquid turquoise of Vallecito Creek—perhaps the most comely stream in the entire
San Juans—passing below the distant lip of Grizzly Gulch.

Lots of people out today.

Among the sweat-soaked multitudes, we meet a handsome young
backpacking couple who politely step off the muddy, horse-mucked trail
and allow us to pass. As I come abreast of the two, the young lady, a
petite, dark-skinned beauty with big brown eyes—an absolute heart-
breaker—eyes our horses, giggles, and jokes: "You guys are *lazy.*"

"Hey," I fire back, faking outrage, "this cowboy stuff is a *lot of
work!*"

Two hours more and we bottom out at Vallecito Creek campground.
The Great Snowslide Canyon Grizzly Expedition is finished, *kaput,* and
the largest mammalian predator we've seen in four long days and seventy-some miles was one timid weasel.

Regrettably, despondently, and notwithstanding Cary's "secluded
pocket" theory, I have fairly written off the poor beleaguered
Weminuche, Snowslide Canyon included, as a probable repository of
native grizzlydom.

A couple of weeks pass and I get a call from Bruce Baizel. He wants to
let me know that his two most intrepid searchers hiked into Snowslide
shortly after Cary and I were there . . . and hiked out a few days later
with two monstrous, oven-fresh bear turds. They found them, Bruce tells
me, "way back up a hidden fork above the main canyon.

"These scats," Baizel boasts, betraying his characteristic levelness of
mood, "take the prize. Biggest we've ever found. Size doesn't mean
certainty, but we're real hopeful."

Well . . .

9

A GLACIAL INTERLUDE

Digging Grizzlies in the
Northern Rockies

> *Surely the United States of America is not so poor
> we cannot afford to have these places {the last
> remnants of true wilderness}, not so rich that we
> can do without them.*
> —Margaret Murie

Most every summer for God only recalls how long, Caroline and I have
vacationed in Glacier National Park in extreme northwestern Montana.
Because the Northern Continental Divide Ecosystem, of which Glacier is
the beating heart, still shelters all of its magnificent native megafauna—
grizzlies, wolves, wolverines, moose, wapiti, bighorns, mountain goats,
ospreys, eagles—it is, by my lights, the most magical place south of
Canada. We hike, camp, fish, canoe, graze on bush-ripened berries, sometimes wander north across the border into Alberta or British Columbia,
make love among the mosses and ferns and mosquitoes, and lie awake in
wonder at the eerie night calls of loons and, on one thrilling occasion,
wolves. And we frequently manage to scare ourselves sleepless conjuring
up toothy monsters *out there* in the vast blackness just beyond the gossa-
mer walls of our tent. Thus is generated the spiritual voltage that electri-
fies the Glacier backcountry experience.

So of course we pounced on an invitation from writer, photographer,
and naturalist Rick McIntyre to spend a week at the Polebridge Ranger
Station on the North Fork Flathead River, which scribbles the western
border of the park.

McIntyre is a tall, sandy-haired Scot who has spent fifteen summers as a park ranger at Denali in Alaska, more at Glacier and elsewhere, wintering in various desert preserves. A more widely experienced national park guide you'll not find. And I enjoy his company. Rick owns a degree in forest management and admits to having been indoctrinated by his forestry professors at the University of Massachusetts as a "wise use" proponent years before the euphemism was coined. "But field experience," he says, "quickly converted me to a preservationist."

Rick knew of my Colorado grizzly search and said he'd try to arrange for us to drop in on researchers involved in radio-tracking park silvertips. And, Rick offered, maybe we could take a "grizzly hike" with former park bear manager Neal Wedum.

I've not yet had a chance to meet Wedum, but I've heard a good deal of him: native Montanan, Glacier backcountry ranger for eighteen years, bear management team leader for six. I look forward to meeting and "grizzly hiking" with this man.

But first, Rick sets us up for a day afield with Wendy Clark, a field researcher for the U.S. Fish and Wildlife Service.

The FWS, Rick tells me during our daybreak drive to Wendy's cabin, is interested in identifying grizzly "linkage zones" (the current PC euphemism for corridors) connecting Glacier Park with the Whitefish Range via the North Fork Flathead Valley, a linear patchwork of national forest and private lands. Once these invisible bear highways are mapped, the feds hope to negotiate with landowners and developers for protective covenants.

The motivation for the study is the worry that Glacier grizzlies may have become, or soon may become, genetically isolated from their Montana kin by an ever-building wall of civilization surrounding the park. Before they're finished, the researchers hope to collar and track the movements of fifteen North Fork grizzlies—a number that Doug Peacock and other critics of heavy-handed biology consider obscenely excessive; Doug, in fact, condemns the entire study as redundant. At the moment, just three North Fork grizzlies, two females and a young male, are wearing radio collars.

Wendy Clark is a tall, mesomorphic young woman in her mid-twenties. With a master's degree in ecology, Wendy has worked on research projects in Labrador and elsewhere and describes herself as a "gadabout field researcher." Today, Wendy is stuck with the mundane chore of testing various telemetry methods for relative error, searching for the most precise method of keeping tabs on her collared bears. Perhaps picking up on my disappointment that we won't actually be tracking bears, she says, "I'll keep an ear out, and maybe we'll pick one up."

As we bang along the muddy, rutted North Fork road, the old pickup's Sisyphean wipers swipe hypnotically at the persistent light rain endemic to this boreal climate. Every now and again, Wendy stops to erect a pipe antenna and do her thing. Between stops, she fiddles with the dials on her radiotelemetry receiver and talks about her favorite local bear, whom she calls JoAnne. Since being trapped and collared, this young female has been radio-located almost daily in the very yards of cabins along the North Fork yet has never gotten into trouble or even been spotted by the residents. Here is a grizzly who has learned to live peaceably among people—which, of course and sadly, means secretly. Rick and Wendy assure me there are others.

Most North Fork residents, Wendy says, though not all, are conscientious about handling garbage, pet food, and other potential bear baits. Many have gardens and keep small livestock, yet the tracking studies are revealing that JoAnne and other grizzlies utilize the valley all summer every summer without succumbing to what must be a great temptation to raid.

We stop again, and Rick and I go wandering along the muddy road, looking for berries and bear and wolf tracks and finding two of the three. Meanwhile, Wendy puts on headphones and rotates the ten-foot antenna until she gets a clear signal from one of the transmitter collars Rick hid in the surrounding woods a few days ago. When she gets a solid lock, Wendy reads the bearing with a compass and records it in a logbook. If the magic works, three such readings will pinpoint the hidden collar via triangulation.

Each stop takes about fifteen minutes, then we squeeze back into the truck and drive on. All morning, Wendy has kept her tracking receiver turned on, tuning alternately to the frequencies of her three collared bears. Now, to our mutual pleasure, comes a beeping, inaudible to Rick and me until Wendy says "Listen!" and turns up the volume. JoAnne.

We pull over, erect the antenna, and take a bearing. After a few moments Wendy announces that the grizzly is in a thicket of dog-hair lodgepole pines probably less than two hundred yards from us.

Hoping for a second fix, we grab antenna, battery pack, and receiver and strike off on foot, into the drizzling fog, hiking along a private dirt

road toward a cluster of ancient log summer cabins scattered around a
lovely little lake called Garnet. After a quarter mile or so, we come upon
a mushy-fresh bear plop stained purple with berries; Wendy takes another reading. JoAnne, she whispers, is now a mere hundred yards or so
east of us, still invisible among the pines.

It's a strange feeling, knowing a grizzly is close yet seeing neither
hide nor hair of the creature. Nor hearing or smelling it. Nor, for that
matter, fearing it. Here too, just like at home in the San Juans, there be
ghosts. Wendy echoes my unspoken delight, saying, "It's cool, this radio-tracking."

As we're leaving, one of the summer residents comes walking by
with her dog. We say hi, and Wendy advises her of the nearness of the
grizzly; the woman just smiles and shrugs. "Yeah," she says, sounding a
little frustrated, "they're around all the time, but we almost never get to
see one."

Nice neighborhood.

As we drive on, Wendy tells us about her other two grizzlies, both of
which also use the North Fork Valley in near-total anonymity, though
both, particularly the young male, are more "standoffish" than JoAnne,
staying farther back in the woods, lying low and proving harder to keep
tabs on.

All of this, of course, bodes well for the future of grizzlies in Colorado. It *is* possible for great bears and thoughtful people to coexist in
mutual respect and harmony.

About noon, Wendy stashes her equipment for the day, and we
follow the North Fork Road the final few miles to the Canadian border,
roll through the check station with a wave and a grin to the guard, and
stop a quarter mile beyond at Joe's Place.

My hosts explain that the big, log-cabin, in-home restaurant is operated during the summer months by the late Joe's daughter Arlene. After
we down big hot bowls of Arlene's homemade stew, Rick and Wendy
chat with their friend while I contemplate the wild and fierce life that
once invested the plush blond hide of a small adult grizzly killed locally
by Joe many moons ago.

Arlene is talking about her recent winter vacation to Arizona. "The
weather's great, but all those scorpions and other little creepy things that
live in the desert . . . they get into your house and your car and your
shoes and your clothes. You've got to be on the watch all the time. But

then, people who live down there come up here, and they're scared to death of grizzlies. Me, I don't mind the bears; you can *see* them. I guess it's what you're used to."

Absolutely. It's *people* that frighten me. They get into your house and your car, and you've got to be on the watch all the time.

Next morning, Caroline and I decide to hike up to the Huckleberry Mountain fire lookout. My pal Peacock spent several summers perched up there—it provided the platform from which he fell seriously in love with grizzlies and grizzly wilderness—and I've always wanted to visit the place. Ed and Clarke Abbey once made the hike, expecting to meet a grizzly around every curve in the trail; Ed described the experience to me as "thrilling."

But first, in need of junk food, ice, and cold drinks for tonight—the American park-camper's staples—we are forced to briefly join the mobs at Apgar Village. On the drive back along the North Fork road, only a few hundred yards from the Huckleberry Mountain trailhead, a big black bear lopes across in front of us, its pelage shining like polished ebony. Caroline is mentally comparing this bear to the one that shuffled through our front yard earlier in the summer, and asks what I think it might weigh. I tell her it's the biggest of the seven blacks I've seen so far this season; it could go as much as three hundred pounds. It's also the blackest black bear I've ever seen. Down in the southern Rockies, the more common ursine colors are cinnamon, blond, and infinite shades of brown.

We've only just started up the jungly lower Huckleberry trail—posted with one of those ominous orange signs reading

> WARNING
> Grizzly Frequenting Area Traversed By This Trail
> BE ALERT

—when we're overtaken and passed by a noisy family of five archetypical tourists, the heart-blood of the national park system. They're predictably in a hurry, brutally clean-cut, the children happily chirping out "Ninety-nine Bottles of Pop on the Wall" and Mom coaching them to sing even louder and Dad's tourist-shop walking staff clanging with a cheap copper bell attached to its hilt by a plastic thong.

Local wisdom: How do you tell the difference between grizzly and black bear droppings? Grizzly scats are the big ones with the bells in them.

Jangling through the boonies like some amplified Tinkerbell is anathema to my notion of a quality wilderness experience—I simply won't do it. Yet I understand the park's motivation for encouraging backcountry hikers to engage in singing, whooping, loud talking, and Tinkerbelling: a surprise run-in with a grizzly could spell disaster for all involved. Caroline and I split the difference, eschewing bells and bottles of pop on the wall, but talking a little more and a little louder than usual, staying alert, and, in places where visibility is limited and it *feels* like a good idea, offering up the occasional humbling "Hey bear!"

The first mile or so of the Huckleberry trail passes through a dense conifer forest with an understory grown up crazily in ferns and sweet cicely and giant cow parsnips and other favorite bear foods. It is shadowy and a little spooky here. Perhaps that's why, just ten minutes after they passed us, the jingle-bell family comes trooping back down the trail, every bit as fast as they went in, but tailgating now, the children no longer singing, the parents looking a little sheepish.

Why?

We don't ask and they don't say.

The trail climbs up into a brushy lodgepole forest. Lots of old moose droppings everywhere, big, woody, desiccated pellets suggesting that a Bullwinkle or two wintered hereabouts. Glacier has plenty of moose, though they're shy and rarely seen.

Three or four miles from the trailhead and maybe halfway to the lookout, while contouring along a steep hillside, we round a bend and are greeted by a thicket of low brush hung throughout with gems of purple and blue; huckleberries and serviceberries (called Juneberries down Colorado way) enrich the slope for dozens of yards below the trail. My urge is to drop my pack and start picking, but I take a minute first to scan the immediate area for fresh bear sign. I find just one modest chartreuse scat, by no means fresh.

These berries are the biggest and ripest we've ever seen; the field guides say we have blueberries and even a few huckleberries down in Colorado, but I've never been lucky enough to encounter the edible proof. And our serviceberries, chokecherries, and wild strawberries, though abundant, almost always get picked over by the critters before we can get to them. (A circumstance that Abbey would describe as "hard, but fair.")

It's incredible that this late in the season such a bountiful berry bonanza as this should have survived essentially untouched. Maybe the bears have been saving the best for last. A hungry grizzly could show up any minute now, any bloody second, and we know we should keep moving.

Which we do . . . right into the midst of the patch. Eschewing the serviceberries in favor of the larger and tastier hucks, we pluck the juicy gems with flying fingers and pop them alternately into our mouths and into a pint-sized plastic zippered freezer bag I carry in my day pack for just such happy occasions.

They say an adult grizzly will put away twenty pounds of berries a day during its fall fattening binge, but after an hour of concentrated picking, our hands, lips, and clothes are stained purple and we have less than a pound in the bag, a similar weight down our collective gullets; slow stoop labor. Still, we're having great fun, and I sense that this may be the closest I'll ever come to experiencing the quintessence of grizzly-ness.

Too late to make it to the lookout now and hike back down before dark; another time.

The big morning finally arrives, and Caroline and Rick and I rendezvous bird-early with Neal and Pam Wedum at the Apgar Visitor Center. We leave my truck under a shade tree in the parking lot there, and the five of us cruise in the relative luxury of the Wedums' van along the scenic southeastern shore of Lake McDonald to the parking area at the foot of Logan Pass on the Going-to-the-Sun road. After a short wait, we board the park's overpriced, overcrowded shuttle bus for the ride to Logan Pass, where we begin our hike out along the Garden Wall section of the Highline trail. Soon we're far above the road (which itself seems on top of the world), paralleling the Continental Divide toward Bear Valley and the Granite Park Chalet. Visibility this early September morn is greatly reduced by blowing fog, lending the precarious cliffside Garden Wall path an otherworldly ambience.

Neal is another of these physical young fellers (Jim Tolisano, Ernie Wilkinson, Ed Wiseman, Dennis Schutz) I keep tagging after into the boonies, and not an easy man to keep up with. "I've got a comfortable pace," he explains, "and it's hard to go slower." And he is saddled with a big heavy packful of medical and mountain rescue equipment that Pam says he always carries when hiking Glacier—which he's been doing for more than forty of his "on the verge of fifty" years.

Pam Wedum is an open, cheery, energetic, and intelligent woman who's fun to be with. I'm not at all surprised when she and Caroline hit it off like old pals.

As we walk, we talk, and I learn—mostly from Pam and Rick—that Neal was among the first on the scene of many of Glacier's most notorious grizzly incidents in recent decades. And several of those incidents, Neal interjects with a teaser's grin, took place on or near this very trail.

Glacier's most recent and perplexing grizzly disaster was the mauling death of John Petranyi, aged forty, killed and fed upon by a sow grizzly and her two subadult cubs.

On the morning of October 3, 1992, Petranyi was hiking alone down the Loop trail after spending the night at the Granite Park campground. He apparently surprised the bears at close range on or near the trail. The sow did what grizzly mothers are programmed to do in such instances and launched a preemptive assault on this sudden threat to her cubs.

Evidence suggests the sow broke off the attack and retreated after giving Petranyi only a light mauling—not unusual. Perhaps, had he played dead until the bruins were good and gone, he could have saved himself. But apparently Petranyi attempted to flee, perhaps calling for help as he ran, inciting the bears' instinctive prey-chase response and provoking a second attack. This time, for reasons we may never understand, the grizzlies dragged Petranyi to a nearby wooded promontory and . . .

A few days later, following multiagency consultations, it was decided the responsible bears posed too serious a threat to humans to risk merely trapping and relocating them, and they were hunted down and killed.

It's hard to keep such horrifying incidents from creeping into your thoughts and dreams when hiking and camping in Glacier. Yet when you consider the density of overlapping human and grizzly populations here, and when you factor in the unforgivable rudeness and blatant stupidity of many park visitors—stashing food and garbage in tents, hiking alone and after dark in areas known to be heavily used by grizzlies, intentionally approaching and otherwise harassing bears, and in countless other ways trolling for trouble—all such sins considered, it's a wonder, a gift in fact, that Glacier's grizzlies show the remarkable tolerance they do.

It's an easy seven-plus miles from the Logan Pass Visitor Center to the Granite Park Chalet, almost level on a well-maintained trail; Neal is hiking in sports sandals. As we lope along, Rick and Neal entertain Caroline, Pam, and me with endless lighthearted bear stories.

Like the time a few years ago when Rick was riding his bicycle along the Denali Park road, far from the nearest structure, and heard a sound "like a panting dog" and an odd rhythmic slapping close behind him and getting closer. He glanced back to see an adult grizzly giving chase and closing rapidly. Knowing better than to try and outrun the bear, Rick braked to a stop, dismounted, and turned to face his pursuer, placing his frail vehicle in front of him.

"I yelled and clapped my hands at the bear," says Rick. "It stopped, hesitated a moment, then walked away. I don't think it recognized me as a human until I did that, then it lost interest and went back to eating grass alongside the road."

In retrospect, Rick allows as how the sight of a speeding bicycle and pumping legs may provoke the same chase response in grizzlies that it does in domestic dogs. We have much left to learn about living with wild nature.

Neal rejoins with a colorful recollection of the day in 1991 when he was rangering alone along the Highline trail just above Ahern Pass and heard loud crunching noises from somewhere above him. "I glanced up," he says, "into the eyes of what looked like the world's biggest grizzly. It was lying behind a clump of brush on a little bench maybe fifty feet above the trail, its head raised, looking right at me. A big bloody chunk of meat was clamped in its jaws, saliva drooling from its muzzle. The adrenaline rush almost knocked me off my feet. My first thought was that the bear was eating a hiker, and having surprised him on his meal, I'd be dessert."

Neal kept walking, even as he slipped the safety off his canister of pepper spray. The behemoth bear didn't charge but watched intently until the interloper had passed out of sight.

When he was safely beyond the threat, Neal climbed through a finger of subalpine fir leading up the cliff to a narrow shelf, then worked across the cliff face until he was directly above the bear. "I had to know," he explains, "what, or who, was being eaten."

The carnivore's feast turned out to be a full-curl Rocky Mountain bighorn ram. "The sheep probably died in a fall, and the grizzly's nose led him to it. Bears can't catch healthy bighorns, but they can smell a dead one from miles away."

After radioing instructions that the trail be closed a safe distance either side of the danger, Neal eased back down the slope, keeping to the trees, then inched forward until he was watching the feeding grizzly from what, in retrospect, was "too damn close." Just as he was becoming almost relaxed in the presence of this six hundred pounds of teeth, claws, and muscle, and with no warning whatsoever, the bear exploded down the hill directly at him, breaking off its charge just twenty feet from one badly shaken park ranger.

"That," Neal concedes, "got my attention."

The canister of pepper spray had long since been returned to its holster, the safety clip replaced. "No matter, since I wouldn't have had time to use it even if I'd had it in my hand; it happened that fast."

The grizzly glared at the man for "a long time," then turned and shuffled back up the slope toward its meat cache . . . only to whirl around and charge again, this time getting in-your-face close before abruptly stopping.

"He was so near I could feel his breath. And the look on his face was clearly saying, 'OK pal, I've warned you twice. Now either move along, or you're lunch meat.' I moved along."

Warmed to his favorite topic, Neal goes on to recall the time a sow with two cubs of the year followed him for a long tense while, staring hard and walking parallel about fifty yards above the same stretch of krummholz trail we're on this very minute. Eventually, she lost interest and wandered away.

Such light conversation carries us quickly across the miles. ("See those scuff marks on that tree?" says a jovial Wedum as we're descending the Loop trail later in the day. "That's where a hiker going down the trail met a sow with two yearling cubs coming up the trail and tried to climb to safety. Didn't quite make it. But he was lucky; the sow let him off with only a minor thrashing.")

At a high pass called the Haystack, the terrain opens to rolling alpine tundra and the sky begins to clear. We've been seeing big billy mountain goats all morning, and now, a hundred yards ahead, we spot a bachelor band of seven bighorn rams. When it becomes obvious that they have no intention of fleeing as we continue to approach, I say I'd like to stop for a few minutes to take pictures. This leads to an impromptu lunch break, during which one brash young ram tries to move in on our sandwiches and an immature bald eagle makes a couple of fast low passes, apparently just curious. The clouds are all but gone now, but the day remains windy and cold—the usual for a place so close to heaven.

We move on, and as we approach the big native-stone Chalet, grizzly excavations become fresher and more frequent. Neal and Rick coach and correct as I attempt to decipher the purpose and approximate age of every dig we pass.

A half mile short of the Chalet and only fifty yards downhill from the trail, a couple of park rangers inspect a heap of fresh dirt below a crater so huge it looks to have been scooped out by a backhoe. "Marmot dig," says Neal. We go down for a look.

Sure enough, clear prints in the fresh-dug dirt show that a big griz and a little griz did the work, opening twin craters separated only by a slab of rock too massive and deeply anchored for even a pair of ursine backhoes to dislodge. A splotch of fresh blood at the bottom of the slightly deeper of the two pits is mute evidence that the bears' calamitous efforts were rewarded. I take several pictures, including one of six-foot McIntyre standing waist-deep in the crater, which the rangers say was not here last evening.

After this fashion, our hike becomes a field workshop. I learn that shovel-sized clumps of turf turned over in excavations several inches deep and up to a hundred square feet in area are the spoor of grizzlies digging for glacier lilies and other sweet-rooted forbs, whereas deep pits with rocks big as basketballs tossed out are evidence of grizzly probes into the tunnels of rodents.

Back in June 1992, Rick Bass and I found a fresh excavation into the tunnel system of a ground squirrel while afield with the San Juan Grizzly Project up on the "White River" down in the south San Juans. The little cave was dug level into a cutbank and measured approximately three feet wide, two feet deep, and eighteen inches high. Neither of us really knew what to make of it then, other than to suspect that *some* kind of bear had done the digging. The one picture I took shows little detail. Wish I could see that dig again now.

We finally reach our midday goal, the medieval-looking Chalet—a wilderness oxymoron writ in native stone. The impressive old building was built in 1914 and for decades offered modest but secure backcountry shelter and home-cooked meals to hikers. In 1987 it was designated a national Historic Landmark—only to be closed recently because of water, sewage, maintenance, and political problems. The structure is being renovated even now, and the park intends to reopen it as soon as possible, which will be none too soon for the Wedums. "The fresh huckleberry pies they baked here," Neal assures me, "were the best in the universe."

Half an hour of glassing the aptly named Bear Valley below the Chalet, as well as the several square miles more of alpine and subalpine slopes visible from this gusty aerie, reveals abundant fresh grizzly sign, including scores of digs, but no furry backhoes.

Even so, the day is by no means a loss. Thanks to Neal Wedum, Rick McIntyre, and the bears themselves, I'll be returning to Colorado with a solid grounding in grizzly diggery. Even now, Neal points to a long chain of meadow digs stair-stepping down a distant swale to a tiny gray tarn shimmering like a dish of molten lead under the sullen sky. "That's real common," he says, "a chain of digs like that. A bear finds a little valley, or a slope grown up in glacier lilies or some other favorite food plant, and goes right down the hill digging. When he's done, the place looks like some berserk farmer charged hit-and-miss down the mountain with his John Deere. Most of the really big digs are done at night."

After an hour atop the wind-blasted peak that contains the Granite Park Chalet and offers some of the most outrageously beautiful mountain scenery in the world, Pam mentions that we still have a four-mile hike down to the Loop parking area, and if we want to make it before dark without being rushed, we should probably start thinking about moving along.

We do, but not very far. Just below the Chalet, we encounter resident ranger Walt Tabb, who invites us into his little backcountry ranger cabin to warm up with hot cocoa.

Neal knows both Walt and the cabin well, picks up the ranger logbook, and begins reading some of the more humorous entries from his long tenure here, mostly about bears and "tourons," the bear-team term for particularly dumb tourists.

Walt remarks that he's had his share of problems with people pulling no-brainers likely to give the local grizzlies a bad name. The worst so far this summer was a churlish pair of Europeans who steadfastly refused to obey the rules for handling food and garbage at the nearby campground. After repeated warnings, Walt caught them eating sardine sandwiches in their tent, with empty sardine tins and other smelly litter tossed all around their camp spot.

"Wrote them a stiff ticket and ordered them out," he says, rubbing his beard in disgust. "But they got in the last punch, boasting that they wouldn't have to pay the fine because they were leaving the country in a couple of days."

"You couldn't pay me enough to spend a night in that campground," says Pam, referring to all the "bad karma" left there by years of sloppy campers.

The stocky little ranger cabin, I've noticed, has heavy iron grating over its few small windows and a massive wood door that can be barred from the inside. I wonder why.

We pass a pleasant half hour, thank Walt for his cocoa and hospitality, and head on down the Loop trail, one of the most heavily used byways in the park, by grizzlies as well as people. Only a hundred yards below the cabin we encounter yet another fresh dig, differing from all the others only in that it rips right across the trail.

A little farther on, we pass the site of the Petranyi tragedy, and below that the little meadow that years ago held the original Granite Park campground, now restored to the grizzly travel corridor and feeding area nature intended it to be. It was here, just after midnight on the bad night of August 13, 1967, that Julie Hegelson was dragged from her sleeping bag and fatally mauled by a grizzly. Julie's male companion was also attacked, but he survived. The sow identified as the culprit had been hanging around Granite Park for years, attracted by garbage and handouts.

Didn't park officials know, I ask Neal, that they'd located the campground on a natural bear runway? "No," he says. "They didn't worry about such things back then. There had never been a grizzly-caused death in the fifty-seven-year history of the park, and they probably assumed the bears were benign."

Incredibly, the same night, at a popular backcountry destination called Trout Lake, another young camper, Michele Koons, was killed by another "garbage grizzly." This tragic coincidence supplied the meat for Jack Olsen's adrenalizing *Night of the Grizzlies*—a book not to be read just before backpacking into Glacier.

In spite of the suicidal stupidity of many campers—such as the sardine-eating Europeans described by Ranger Walt—there have been no bear problems at the new Granite Park campground, which is wisely located atop a ridge not normally used by bears. Additionally, park officials expend considerable effort these days to eliminate the threat of human-conditioned "garbage bears." The official Glacier catchphrase is "A fed bear is a dead bear." A fed bear could also be a dead camper, but that doesn't rhyme.

Finally, with the day nearly done, the clouds lift, the fog dissipates, and the sun appears just in time to set.

As we lope down the steep Loop trail, I'm struck by the restraint shown by these Glacier bears in mugging only an average of two humans from the more than two million who overrun the park each summer, and snuffing only one every several years. Translate that to the San Juans of Colorado. There, even following a full-blown restoration effort (which, I predict, we'll never see), we'd have only a handful of grizzlies—maybe a couple dozen—spread over a huge area of undeveloped wilderness visited by only a relative dribble of people. Compare that to Glacier's record, and you get a sense of the magnitude of the potential grizzly *non*threat in Colorado.

I recall a recent encounter with an old-line Colorado rancher from over on the Rio Grande side of the Divide. An outspoken member of the citizen's advisory committee on the Weminuche Wilderness, this woman is typical of the highly opinionated, shamelessly ignorant rural view of grizzlies prevalent throughout the Rocky Mountain states. Having heard that I was researching grizzlies in the San Juans, the rancher approached me and announced, "I hope you're not going to come out in favor of grizzly reintroduction here. We worked long and hard to clean the grizzlies out of this country, and we're getting along just fine without them.

"The grizzly," she continued, waxing authoritative, "is the dominant animal in the woods; it goes along killing and eating anything it wants —wildlife, livestock, even people. I was in a sheep camp near here once, back in the '40s, where a grizzly had come in and killed thirty-four sheep in one night. And did you know that already this summer, twelve people have been killed by grizzlies in Glacier Park?"

No, I thought, holding my piece, I sure didn't know that. Nor did I bother to mention my recent conversation with the selfsame government trapper who'd killed the big brown-colored *black* bear that had offed those thirty-four sheep.

These are the attitudes, the ignorance-based prejudices, that dominate the rural West.

When we reach the Wedums' van, both Neal and Rick become profusely apologetic about not "bumping into" any grizzlies on today's twelve-mile hike through one of the most *horribilis* stretches of bear country below Canada. I tell them not to worry about it, I've had a great time, and the instructions and photos I've gotten today will qualify me as arguably the most experienced resident authority on grizzly digs in the San Juans—which, of course, implies a severe lack of such knowledge down there.

"If you *really* want to see some grizzlies," teases Neal as we part ways back at Apgar, "come on back next summer and you and I'll spend a few days backpacking. We'll see some grizzlies, guaranteed."

Thus begin nine months of nervous anticipation.

10

"BLOOD, HAIR, AND THE GROUND TORE UP"

La Tierra Amarilla: The Last Best Hope?

*As soon as you pay attention, you are at once
humbled by what you do not know.*

—Dolores LaChapelle

Within days of returning from Glacier, I got a call from Bruce Baizel of
the San Juan Grizzly Project. Bruce had just heard from Round River
ecologist Jim Tolisano in Santa Fe. Jim had been talking with an acquaintance in the local environmental community who had said he had a
friend who'd hiked through a high back corner of the Tierra Amarilla in
June 1993 and observed a sow grizzly with one cub, feeding on an open
tundra slope.

Bruce told me the name of the place, a big glacial bowl just below
timberline, in the center of which sits a deep tarn. This anonymous
observer, it was said, was a "working field biologist who knows his
bears." He also knew he was trespassing on stringently posted private
land. His fear of being chastised for that, or worse, along with concern
that if "the authorities" got wind of his sighting they would coerce him
into revealing the location and "come bulling in to mess things up,"
were his professed motives for refusing to go public with the sighting.

Just another grizzly sighting report, and fourth-hand information at
that. Even so . . .

The next day I phoned the Santa Fe man who'd let slip the information to Tolisano. He was clearly not pleased to learn how far the news had
traveled, saying that his biologist friend would never forgive him if he
found out, and refused to reveal the friend's identity or any further

information about the sighting. He did, at least, confirm what I'd heard from Bruce.

Next I went to the maps and located the tarn I'll call Grizzly Lake, way up high in the south of the T.A. The lake sits just below timberline, at the bottom of a cirque walled in on west, north, and east by raggedy cliffs and peaks like bear's teeth, and on the south by a fifty-mile slope of national forest. Hike a few minutes up from Grizzly Lake and you're onto the tundra, a little ways down and you're into the subalpine forest. And no livestock nowhere. A seemingly perfect grizzly hideout.

Moreover, the marmot dig and skull discovered by Tom Beck's 1981 searchers and confirmed as recent grizzly spoor had been found within sight of Grizzly Lake. And in 1990, district wildlife manager Dick Weldon had found an extensive marmot dig he felt sure was the work of a grizzly, and this only a fistful of miles southeast of Grizzly Lake.

Hooked, I phoned Banded Peak Ranch foreman Dennis Schutz, by now a solid friend. Yes, he said, he knew the place well and would be glad to take me up there. We could "pack light and ride hard" and be there in a day.

SEPTEMBER 28, 1993:

"GRIZZLY LAKE," TIERRA AMARILLA

After two hours of uphill riding, we enter the bottom of Heavenly Valley, a broad avalanche chute spilling from a high cirque that Dennis says is always full of wildlife. Verifying that praise, our hoof-pounding arrival sends a dozen wapiti crashing up the left side of the *vallecito* and a clot of mule deer bounding up the right. Three turkey vultures rise heavily from a copse of runted spruce beyond where the deer had been bedded, circle a couple of times for altitude, and soar indolently away. On what had these feathered morticians been feeding? We decide to break for an early lunch and watch for a spell.

After twenty minutes, the vultures still haven't returned, and our binoculars have revealed no hint of what they were scavenging, if anything. We debate strolling up the mountain to investigate—imagining a bear kill—but it's a hell of a hump, the sidehill terrain all broken and brushy, so we opt to head on to Grizzly Lake.

Breaking out of the little valley midway up its port side, we steer onto what Dennis calls "the Devil's trail." The muddy elk path quickly verifies its name, crossing a greasy-slick talus close along a bone-crushing drop-off, then winding up through crowded evergreens bristling with hat-grabbing, eye-poking, flesh-rending snag limbs. But this, too, finally passes, and the dark forest gives way to a weird and lovely purgatory of krummholz . . . back to the Pleistocene.

Out on the tundra, we ride the swales between swells, skirting wide around a tiny, marsh-moated pond called Cub Lake. We round the next little knoll above the pond, and suddenly I'm back at Granite Park in Glacier. Here in the lap of this hidden saddle, perched midway between krummholz and tundra, an entire little hillside appears to have been bear-dug.

I lever my horse to a stop—he stands to dropped reins—climb from the saddle, and drop to my knees to examine the digs. The excavations are roughly oval in shape, stair-stepping down a gentle, south-facing slope. The digs average a hundred square feet in area, are six inches to a foot deep with lots of big dirt clods still visible throughout. Complete revegetation plus weathering of the sharper features prove these excavations are not this year's work. Beyond that, it's hard to say.

Dennis rides back, curious as to why I'm crawling around on all fours grinning like a dolt. I explain that just two weeks ago I examined and photographed dozens of grizzly digs at Glacier, a great many of which were identical to these in every way—size, shape, depth, clods, the stair-stepping down a gentle slope. Looking around, I see multitudes of alpine bistort—a favorite dig-for grizzly food.

"Dennis," I say, trying to conceal my excitement, "I think these may be grizzly digs."

"How sure are you?"

Good question. I survey the geomorphology of the little saddle, ruling out water erosion as the excavator—no way; the digs are well up on the sidehill above the bottom of the swale, with no lateral run-off channels anywhere.

Nor are these choppy, vertical-edged dishes the work of gelifluction ("soil flow"). This almost-rare erosive phenomenon occurs on alpine slopes where the surface soil is composed primarily of fine-ground gravel and other glacial debris (regolith), and underlain by a permafrost substrate. In spring, when the thawed surface layer becomes saturated with snowmelt, big teardrop blops of the liquefied regolith mass will sometimes break loose and flow with glacial sluggishness downslope, leaving a dished hollow above and a lumpy lip below. But here the soil is soil, not regolith, and firmly anchored by plant roots. There is no permafrost. And finally, the sharp edges, lumpy clods, and lack of a lower lip all deny that these depressions could be slumps.

They are, I believe, grizzly digs, possibly for *Claytonia,* the spring beauties that pink the tundra as soon as the snow melts each summer, lasting into August. Grizzlies dig up and devour the little plants by the hundreds, relishing especially the delicate radishy taste of the root tubers.

The troubling bit is: How old are these digs (assuming digs they are)? Were they excavated within the past decade, or could these depressions be the work of the long-dead Wiseman bear?

I take some pictures, and we ride on, making our first crossing of the Divide for the day. The alpine bowl that reveals itself on the far side is pintoed with alga-pinked swatches of last winter's snow. Across one of these icy remnants meanders the trail of some large animal. After switchbacking down a precarious talus to the bottom of the bowl, we invest in a brief side trip to check out the tracks, but they're old and badly melted and ultimately unidentifiable.

Down, down into the "crooked wood" again, and Dennis's dog Belle, who's been running circles around us all day, suddenly lines out for a patch of dwarf willow fifty yards ahead. As she squirts into the bottom of the clump, a lanky coyote, twice as big as Belle but probably weighing less, explodes out the top. Dennis whistles once, and good, always obedient Belle returns and falls in behind, tongue-lolling proud.

For the next long while, we sail our equine ships across a rolling sea of alpine tundra, reaching Grizzly Lake in late afternoon. There we set immediately about preparing for the evening: unsaddling and brushing the horses, splitting wood for a fire, carrying water up from the lake, spreading ground cloth and bedrolls on the lumpy frost-heaved soil, and the rest of the mundane but heartily satisfying camp-chore ritual.

That done, we strike out across the tundra on an evening hike, climbing toward a low spot on the northern rim of the Divide. Dennis says he wants to show me a certain "hole" that lies just beyond, where "something strange" happened awhile back.

The elevation at Grizzly Lake is about eleven-five and up in every direction. Dennis lopes effortlessly ahead. I follow, lugging and chugging, very much affected by the altitude. What begins as a pleasant leg-stretch after a day in the saddle quickly degenerates into respiratory torture. Given a few days up here to acclimate, I'd be fine. But we don't have a few days, only two, so all I can do is keep lifting one leaden boot ahead of the other.

Onward, past twelve grand and still climbing. A predictably cold alpine wind buffets this way and that, uncaring and real. I fetch my watch cap from my day pack and pull it like a sock down over my burning ears, wishing I'd brought gloves as well.

Finally I approach the rim, tripping over scree slabs that shift and slide and clank like terra-cotta shingles under my clumsy boots. Dennis is standing on a promontory just ahead, and when I join him the world shifts beneath me, my head goes into a spin, and I have to sit down fast. Vertigo is unusual for me, having spent the best five years of my youth hanging in the sky on whirling rotors and an insincere prayer. But this is an unusually abrupt, windy, and disorienting aerie, and I'm exhausted and a little altitude-punky.

When I regain my equilibrium, I butt-scoot up to the edge of the cliff and peer down some two hundred feet into a fairy-tale *rincon,* a high hidden bowl a mile across its corrugated bottom. Unlike the tundra we've just walked over, the parklike amphitheater below is still green with grasses and forbs and glinting with silvery slivers of running water.

Across its middle, the undulant cirque is whiskered with subalpine spruce and fir. At the far end, where the bench holding the bowl cliffs off no telling how far down to who knows what, one tiny diamond of a tarn mirrors the late sun. On all sides, access to the *rincon* is hindered by steep talus slides or outright denied by cliffs. Forget horseback access. I check the map, find the place nameless, and, with the reckless power of a god or a government cartographer, dub it Schutz's Hole.

` After searching the hole for several minutes with binoculars—we see one lonely-looking cow elk and a few soaring ravens—I settle back against a slab of rock cold as a tombstone to hear about the "something strange" that took place down there not quite four years ago.

It was late September 1989, and elk season was on. Old Charley Hughes had died; the ranch was in escrow and being hunted under the supervision of a professional outfitter. Dennis had hired on as an elk guide and was shepherding a New Mexico bowhunter. Early in the after-noon, while glassing from where Dennis and I now sit, the hunters trumpeted a couple of bugles down into the cirque and were answered by two bulls. It took them a good long while to find a way down, but when they did, they were rewarded by a distant glimpse of a seven-by-seven, or "imperial," bull—a rare huge monster even by local standards. It was while maneuvering toward the big deer, circling the inner curvature of the cirque in an attempt to sneak in close above him, that the two men stumbled onto the scene of the recent "bloody slaughter" of an elk.

This was a year before his Willow Creek bear sighting, and grizzlies were the last thing on Dennis's mind. Yet, he tells me now, "the atmosphere down there reeked of violence. There had obviously been quite a battle. It was a full-grown elk—judging from the size of the hooves and bones, either a cow or a young bull that would have weighed maybe five hundred pounds—and it clearly had not died without a struggle. There was elk hair and blood all over the place, and the ground was all torn up. A blood-smeared drag trail showed where the elk had been pulled maybe fifty feet from where it died to where it was eaten. The hide had been peeled off the carcass and was ripped to shreds, bones were scattered all around, most of the ribs had been bitten off and devoured, and the skull was missing; we searched all over but never did find it; some scavenger had probably dragged it off, like they often do."

I have to chuckle, so closely does Dennis's colorful narration parallel Mark Twain's description of the scene of a ferocious dogfight, with "blood, hair, and the ground tore up."

"And three different spruce trees around the kill site," Dennis continues, "had been clawed about six feet up their trunks. The claw marks were thick and widely spaced and deep and several inches long, and real fresh. It was one more element adding to the weird feel of the place. I didn't know what had killed and eaten that elk, but it was big and it liked its meat fresh . . . the blood hadn't even turned black on the grass and bones. Night was coming on, we were unarmed except for our bows and agreed to forget about the big bull and get the hell out of there. I haven't been back since."

I ask Dennis if it appeared the elk's remains had been covered with debris, as both cougars and bears will sometimes do between feeding sessions. He says no.

I ruminate the possibilities. It could have been a mountain lion; they take even the biggest bulls sometimes, though it's usually when deep snow gives the big-footed cats a leg up on the action. And though they roam everywhere, you don't expect to see cougars at timberline as late as the tail end of September, when most deer, their primary prey, have already migrated down. And not even a female lion with yearling cubs could consume an adult elk in one go but would have covered the leftovers with debris to camouflage them from scavengers while resting nearby between feeds. And whether a 150-pound cat could drag a quarter-ton elk that far I'm not qualified to guess. As for the claw marks— assuming that whatever autographed the trees also killed the elk, of which Dennis is convinced—such high, deep, precise engravings are atypical of the catlike scratchings of pumas.

Black bear is more likely. A big blackie could certainly kill a medium-sized elk, if he could catch it. But black bears rarely try for any elk larger than a calf, unless of course the animal is injured or ill. And again, no black bear, not even a big boar or a sow with older cubs, could eat that much flesh and bone all in one go but would have covered the remains and napped near or even on top of the cache between feeds. Without seeing the claw marks, I can't even guess whether or not they were the work of a black.

Had Dennis come upon the scene of a fresh grizzly kill? The long drag of a heavy carcass, the indications that an entire elk was consumed in a brief time, and the claw-marked trees all hint at that likelihood. When a grizzly hunts elk, sometimes it's just a matter of one powerful slam-dunk and the prey goes down, spine smashed. Other times, especially when the elk is an antlered bull and the encounter takes place in the forest where the prey has trees to put between itself and its attacker, it can be a prolonged battle, though inevitably ending with the elk dead and "blood, hair, and the ground tore up." Finally, grizzlies are known to stalk and ambush rut-distracted and exhausted bulls (which the "slaughter" victim easily could have been) during September.

"I'd like to go down there tomorrow and poke around."

"Thought you might," says Dennis, grinning. "Matter of fact, I was counting on it."

The sun is about gone and the cold wind getting no warmer, so we withdraw from the edge of the abyss and trip back down the mountain to camp, home sweet atavistic home, where wait the proverbial cheery fire, chow, and sleep.

• • •

Morning. A hundred yards below camp, Grizzly Lake mirrors snowy peaks. Moby trout leap and roll, leaving rise forms that grow concentrically outward, like well-lived lives. A small group of elk feed and play on a subalpine slope across the lake, a quarter mile distant but brought detail-close by the optical magic of binoculars. After a while, the bull of the batch singles out what must be a sweet-smelling preovulatory cow and chases her round and round a little clump of spruce, never quite catching up and she obviously not quite ready. After a few turns round the Maypole, the amorous bull gives up and pretends to graze, offering a classic display of displacement behavior.

Feeling ornery, I whistle a challenge bugle out across the lake and await the antlered Romeo's reaction. And wait. If he hears me, he's not sufficiently impressed to reply; I'm far too far away, I guess, to pose a threat to his sovereignty over the little harem. After a while, the boss cow leads the group off into the forest south of the lake, there (no doubt) to bed through midday and chew contemplative cud.

We eat a quick breakfast of cold muffins and hot coffee, pack lunches of fruit and peppered buffalo jerky, saddle up, and ride out. As we're leaving, a camp robber glides in to rob our camp of any food or garbage that's been left unsecured; she'll be disappointed.

Rather than retrace our hike of last evening, which would bring us again to that windy aerie from which there is no way down but free fall, we loop around and above the lake, riding close past where the group of elk had been not so long ago. The bull's musky rut scent still perfumes the air; you can *smell* the lust in it. From the lake, we climb toward the northeastern curvature of the Divide; Dennis says he knows a way down into his namesake hole from there.

Up this high, autumn is already dying into winter, with most of the wildlife long since moved down to lower climes, the grasses and sedges gone sere, and a few aged asters and harried harebells about the only survivors of what must have been a resplendent alpine summer. Two hundred yards ahead, a big coyote works the scree like a street person checking trash bins, poking his long snoopy nose into every crevice, hunting picas, those yummy little "rock rabbits" of the alpine. Belle doesn't see him, but the picas have the coyote spotted; their shrill, piping alarm cries electrify the cold morning air.

A hundred feet above the coyote, a red-tailed hawk spirals with deadly intent, big as a young eagle and every bit as beautiful, with a gleam of what I imagine to be hopeful anticipation flashing in anthracite eyes, looking to pick off a coyote-distracted pica. I tip my hat and wish all of them equal good luck. They'll need it.

The wind is in full fury when we reach the rim, and I'm amazed to see an occasional bright yellow aspen or cottonwood leaf floating by *above* us, sylvan butterflies carried up two thousand vertical feet. One at a time, the adventurous leaves sail over the Divide, where they abruptly lose their lift and flutter down the far side, many to be snagged by the webwork boughs of altitude-stunted conifers, lending the blue-green little trees the festive look of Christmas.

From this remarkable vantage, we sit in our saddles for a while, watching coyote, hawk, and picas and inspecting our back trail, glassing the tundra slopes that funnel up and out from the lake, looking for bears and seeing nothing of the sort. But my steady mount Lurch is enjoying the break, munching bunchgrass the color of old gold, one long stem sticking a foot out the right side of his mouth, wobbling up and down as he chews, giving him the look of a contemplative country bumpkin.

An hour or so out of camp, we drop down off the wind-blasted hogback Divide and onto a narrow shelf above the east rim of Schutz's Hole. Here Dennis leads into a wind-sheltered alcove among big rocks and little trees, where we tie Elmer and Lurch and prepare to make the final descent on foot. What we're looking at is a near-vertical two-hundred-foot rubble of fractured sedimentary boulders, some as big as boxcars and all stained a luminescent lichen green—a formerly proud cliff face reduced by time and gravity to ten thousand angles of repose.

We pick our individual ways slowly down off the talus and onto a grassy bench. Remarkably, the vegetation down here is still verdant, but just a few hundred feet above, out on the tundra, it's all pretty much gone beaver.

Moving parallel to the slope, we walk and walk, and after a while Dennis admits that we may be in for a long search. "I came in a different way before," he explains.

We walk and walk some more, finding only a few scattered elk bones with tiny scraps of crusty red meat still clinging to the folds of their joints, far too fresh to have been lying naked on the ground for several years, and the scenery isn't looking exactly right to Dennis. So we drop down a few hundred yards to the next bench and resume our back-and-forth searching, passing in and out of dark fingers of trees, down and up knolls and lateral gullies, some steep and deep, others broad and shallow.

It's while crossing one of these dry, rocky, snowmelt ditches that I spot a patch of ground maybe four feet across and several inches deep that has been recently excavated, with several big clumps of turf neatly scooped out and flipped down-side up. So fresh is this dig that the vegetation growing on the inverted surfaces of the overturned clumps is still bright and alive, indicating that the greens couldn't have been lying hidden from the sun for more than a very few days. The soil in the dig, however, is dry, suggesting that it has been exposed to sun and air for at least a day.

In keeping with the perplexing nature of all San Juan grizzly spoor, there is no supporting evidence, no tracks or scats. Nor can I guess what the bear had been digging for, though the remains of a ground squirrel tunnel run through the dug area.

"Dennis," I say with feigned quietude, "this may be another grizzly dig. And a real fresh one at that."

"How sure are you?"

Again, it's a good question. It looks just like dozens of Glacier grizzly digs I've recently studied, and I can't imagine what else could have scooped out and turned over such big perfect clods as these.

To document the scene, we photograph each other holding big chunks of the earthy evidence.

When we move on, I find myself stepping more quietly and peering more intently into the shadowy woods ahead, stopping a lot to listen, testing the breeze for any scent of . . . what? As always, even the *suspicion* that a grizzly *could* be lurking nearby snatches me back through ten thousand years of human evolution to a state of pure primitive alertness. This is the most, I realize, that Colorado has ever felt like Montana. My heart is pounding, and not from exertion.

On a knoll several hundred yards north of the dig, a certain fir tree, just one among many, stands out like a billboard, stopping me cold.

Years ago, a Navajo acquaintance and follower of the Native American Church was talking about hunting for sacred peyote cacti in the southwestern deserts. "She hides from you at first," he said. "But if you can find just one of her buttons, and if you sit down right there and eat it, you'll start seeing Peyote everywhere—she'll *reveal* herself to you."

Perhaps those old digs above Cub Lake were my first peyote button for this trip, guiding me on to the fresh dig just back down the way, and now to this . . . a deeply claw-scarred tree, exactly like those Dennis describes having seen around the site of that violent elk kill four years ago.

I whisper Dennis over for a consultation. No, he says, this isn't the place; it wasn't on a timbered knoll like this, but on a gently sloping bench directly above a line of trees. And there were three marked trees, not just the one. What's more, the claw slashes Dennis remembers were higher, "about eye level on me," whereas these come up to only my chest. "But the size and pattern," he says, "look real similar."

I take a small steel tape from my day pack and record the statistics: the three parallel gouges are about three inches long, are spaced nearly two inches apart, are incised a half to three quarters of an inch deep (in pretty hard bark and wood), and have a wide, gaping appearance, as if made by heavy claws, though some enlargement could well have occurred as the injured wood dried and shrank. The scars are, we reckon, about two years old. I haul out the camera and record the evidence, to be analyzed later by those more in the know.

We search for another hour. Dennis wants to drop even farther down into the bowl and make another pass, but I'm thinking about the long climb back to the horses and cleverly weasel out, suggesting that what I'd really like to do is return on another trip when we have more time, hang around camp for a couple of days to acclimate, *then* resume the search. To this plan Dennis readily agrees, and we start the long slow hump back up the boxcar talus to the dozing horses.

While riding back along the rim of the Divide, just as we attain a view of Grizzly Lake—far below, glowing like burnished pewter under the dying sun—Dennis spots a flash of something passing beneath his horse's hooves and calls back for me to check it out. We stop, I dismount, search around for a moment, and pick up an arrowhead black and lustrous as obsidian, which it is. Half an inch wide, a couple long, delicately thin in profile, its cutting edges intricately serrated, its base unnotched. Perfect.

I hand the ancient treasure up to Dennis. This is private land; finders keepers.

As we ride on, we ponder what manner of man might have fashioned and carried the delicate point all the long way up here—hunter? vision seeker?—and how it was lost. It's probably not Folsom, since Folsom artisans rarely used obsidian for small points; it tends to collapse under the rigors of primitive pressure flaking. Nor were their lithic skills so finely developed as this. More likely Ute or Apache. Probably Ute, "only" a few hundred years old.

How, I wonder, did the owner of this tiny ancient weapon perceive his grizzly neighbors?

Back home, I had my Grizzly Lake photos processed and prints made, which I distributed to various experts for their opinions.

In previous conversations with FWS grizzly biologist Tim Thier regarding his role in the 1981 Beck study, I'd asked about the San Juan digs Tim's team had reported as being made by black bears. As he recalled, the suspected black bear dig sites were not in meadows but in high, flat, moist areas dominated by open spruce canopy "and were shallower than what you usually see in grizzly digs." Since returning to Montana, Thier has, on a couple of occasions, seen "similar digs in similar kinds of sites. I believe these [Montana] digs were also made by black bears but can't prove it."

After studying my Grizzly Lake photos, Thier offered some additional thoughts: "Grizzly digs usually contain lots of large clumps of sod, and the San Juan black bear digs we found either had no clumps or only a few small clumps. I agree with your conclusions that because of differences in claw length, it would be very difficult for a black bear to overturn large clumps of sod like a grizzly. I don't know what could make clumps like [those in the Schutz's Hole photos] other than a grizzly bear or a person with a shovel. I honestly don't believe that a black bear could overturn clods of the magnitude you were holding in the photos. The pictures of the older [Cub Lake] digs also look promising, but it's hard to say much more than that, given their age."

There were no "persons with shovels" up there. Nor were either the Cub Lake or Schutz's Hole digs located in moist soil under a conifer canopy, as had been all of Tim's black bear digs; rather, all were in dry, well-drained soil exposed to the sun.

Thier was less encouraging about the claw scars, noting that "the scratch marks on the tree could easily be from a black bear. I've frequently seen where a small or medium-sized black bear captured in a snare will spread its toes and claws and leave large scratch marks on trees."

Doug Peacock, after studying the same photos, said the claw marks "could easily have been made by a grizzly," and that both the fresh and older digs looked to him like the work of grizzlies. Nor did he think the "old" Cub Lake digs were necessarily all that old, noting that in both Yellowstone and Glacier, he'd seen "extensive meadow digs completely revegetated in just one summer."

This confirms what naturalist John Murray observed in Alaska. Over several summers at Denali, Murray noted the conditions of dozens of fresh grizzly digs, returning at intervals to monitor their rates of healing. "With good soil and plenty of moisture like you find in most alpine and subalpine habitats," John told me, "grasses, sedges, and forbs can completely camouflage even an extensive dig in just a few weeks in summer." Like Peacock and Thier, John also believes that both the Schutz's Hole and Cub Lake digs are likely the work of grizzlies.

Meanwhile, former Glacier Park bear manager Neal Wedum reckoned that "the claw marks are certainly a possibility, but not having anything to give the tree some perspective, it's difficult to tell too much. However, the spread in the claws would have to be a substantial black bear or a grizzly. The clumps of earth torn up, to me, are the greatest piece of evidence for living grizzlies in Colorado."

Even the ultracautious Tom Beck reacted positively to the photos of the hot-fresh Schutz's Hole dig, calling it "very suggestive. If I were looking for grizzlies in the San Juans right now, I'd get excited and say, 'Let's go back up there and have another look. One could be there.' But that's as far as you can go with it from a photo; it's not conclusive. Still, if someone shows up with a live grizzly bear from that country someday, it's not going to surprise me in the least."

The only unabashedly doubtful voice was that of Division biologist David Kenvin of Monte Vista, whose specialty is pursuing evidence of phantom species—currently, wolverine and lynx—in the San Juans. Dave hadn't seen my photos, but when I mentioned the Grizzly Lake digs during conversation, he told me of a find he'd made back in 1984: an approximately eight-by-ten-foot bear dig that would seem to nullify the time-honored equation of clods = grizzly.

The Kenvin dig was "in a moist spruce-fir understory at a little over ten thousand feet elevation" on the north-central face of Fox Mountain, just south of U.S. 160 atop Wolf Creek Pass, between Pass and Park Creeks. It was, said Dave, "a place I sure wouldn't expect to see a grizzly bear."

He went on to describe the dig as being "three to four inches deep, in wet ground, with the earth all churned up with some clods as big as eight inches in diameter." It appeared to Kenvin that the bear had been feeding on roots, but the dig was such a mess, he couldn't identify the species of plant being consumed.

Supporting Kenvin's theory that this dig was the work of a black bear were tracks in the fresh-dug dirt that "looked like black bear to me" and measured "no more than five inches across; they were pretty small." Moreover, Dave's high, "moist spruce-fir understory" matches almost verbatim the "high, flat, moist areas dominated by open spruce canopy" that Tim Thier describes as typical of the black bear digs he's seen in the San Juans and in Montana. Both visual evidence and conservative reasoning would seem to validate Kenvin's assessment that the Fox Mountain dig was the work of a black bear, clods and all.

Yet if we were to assume that the rare grizzly traverses Wolf Creek Pass, crossing from the southern to northern San Juans or vice versa— say, north to Snowslide Canyon and back—the travel corridor could easily include the Fox Mountain area. What's more, known Colorado grizzly bears (the subadult Starvation Gulch male, the old Wiseman sow) had footpads measuring only about five inches across.

Even so, I agree with Dave Kenvin that the Fox Mountain dig was probably the work of a black bear. But unlike Dave, I don't believe this negates or even significantly weakens the consensus opinion that the Schutz's Hole dig was the work of a grizzly. The Kenvin dig's "up to eight inches in diameter" clods are barely half the size of those from Schutz's Hole and agree with Tim Thier's observation that black bear digs contain only smaller clods if any at all. But then, *I* found those Tierra Amarilla digs, and so of course I *want* to believe they are evidence of a current grizzly presence; maybe I've inadvertently donned the rose-colored glasses of wishful thinking.

One thing I can say with certainty is that I'll be back. Next summer, Dennis and I will return and scramble again down into spook-haunted Schutz's Hole—looking for blood, hair, and the ground tore up . . . chasing after the tooth-and-claw phantoms of La Tierra Amarilla, perhaps the last best hope.

11

THE GRIZZLY AS PREDATOR

Is the Great Bear a Threat to
Big Game and Hunting?

> *We are kindred all of us, killer and victim,*
> *predator and prey.*
>
> —Edward Abbey

In the early 1990s, the views and actions of the Alaskan hunting industry concerning wolf predation on caribou, moose, and other big game animals became widely known through media exposure of the infamous Alaskan wolf "control" program.

In the end (until the cruelty of the wolf pogrom was revealed to the public by an intrepid photographer and the slaughter halted by public outcry), those with vested interests in Alaska's multimillion-dollar hunting industry chose, in spite of biological evidence to the contrary, to equate fewer wolves with more big game animals. Suppress the wolves, they said, and keep their numbers down, and we'll have more caribou for the human predators who shoot millions into the Alaskan economy annually.

If we were to draw a parallel between the megabuck hunting industries of Alaska and Colorado, and substitute grizzly restoration for wolf preservation, we could predict that a faction of Colorado wildlife managers, hunting outfitters, and hunters would express much the same fears as those being voiced in the Alaskan controversy.

To wit: Wouldn't restoring a predator as voracious as the grizzly have a strongly negative influence on elk populations in the San Juans, thereby reducing opportunities for the human hunters who foot the bill for all wildlife programs in the state? If grizzly restoration is ever to be undertaken in Colorado, this is one of several sociopolitical questions that must be answered.

Certainly, grizzlies kill (or, more often, scavenge) and eat elk every chance they get—and deer and marmots and any other red meat that opportunity offers. That's their function as omnivores. But its love for fresh meat notwithstanding, the grizzly is an inefficient predator whose diet is overwhelmingly vegetarian, with grasses, sedges, forbs, roots, berries, and mast estimated to comprise as much as 90 percent of its annual intake, depending on what's available. With bears, it's not so much preference as opportunity.

Throughout their seven or so waking months each year, grizzlies bulldoze for rodents, fish if they're blessed with spawning streams, and take larger prey as the opportunity presents itself. But unless the habitat has been overgrazed by livestock or in some other way usurped by man, plant foods are *always* there.

So important are greens to grizzlies that if you can predict what plants will be prime where and when in bear country, you've got a good start toward finding your griz. In areas such as Denali, Glacier, and Yellowstone, where they're not persecuted or severely restricted in their movements, in early spring you're likely to spot grizzlies—recently emerged from their winter dens and literally starving—digging for roots and grazing on new sprouts in sunny alpine meadows where the snow has melted early. Any winter-killed animals they happen across at this time are eagerly devoured.

A little later in the season, grizzlies move to shaded slopes and avalanche chutes where the green-up has been delayed by lingering snow. During late summer and fall, berries and mast, including especially squirrel-cached nuts, dominate the grizzly's predenning menu.

Of the minority meat portion of the great bear's diet, it's not fresh-killed game but carrion and moth larvae, grubs, ants, and other insects that make up the bulk. This puts the odds at better than nine to one in favor of finding a grizzly nipping wildflowers, knocking apart a rotten log looking for insects, or gnawing on a winter-killed carcass, rather than ripping the flesh of some large mammal.

Even so, when the resource is rich and the season is right, some grizzlies, having learned the profitability of concerted predation—by watching and imitating their mothers, by observing other hunting bears, or through lucky happenstance—become fearsome and skilled hunters. They stalk, they chase, they ambush, they *plan* their hunts. And most often, their prey are infant ungulates.

Up in Yellowstone, it's established knowledge that the most common strategy employed by grizzlies hunting for elk calves is a slow, methodical search. In one study, searching for hiding calves accounted for 75 percent of the sixty grizzly elk hunts observed. After spotting a lone cow elk, the grizzly approaches, apparently noting some subtle something about her behavior that tells the bear whether or not the cow has a newborn calf hiding nearby. If the signals are right, the bear charges and chases away the cow, then carefully crisscrosses the area where the mother had been, looking high and low, sniffing and listening for evidence of the hidden meal.

In this deadly game of hide-and-seek, if the near-scentless calf has been properly stashed by its mother and is cool enough to remain quiet, it just might escape discovery, death, and digestion. But not always. In the aforementioned Yellowstone study, almost half of all the "slow searches" observed ended with a grizzly dining on fresh wapiti veal.

Of course, Yellowstone is vastly overpopulated with elk, so the bears are doing the ecology (elk included) a favor, although it probably doesn't seem so to the caught calves. And the window of opportunity for catching elk calves is short, about a month in late May and early June, after which healthy calves can generally outrun a bear.

But grizzlies are no mere baby killers.

It was early spring, and Doug Peacock was out doing his thing: watching and studying grizzly bears in the wild. This particular morning, Doug was camped in a backcountry area of the Firehole region of Yellowstone Park. The snow had melted off the open thermal flats but still lay deep back in the woods and along shaded meadow edges. Elk and bison still were gathered in winter herds, and when a grizzly—"a big, black, untagged anonymous bear"—exploded out of the lodgepoles and into a group of wapiti that had wandered near the timber, Doug was there to bear witness.

At first, Doug didn't think much would happen. The elk just loped away, not even seeming all that alarmed, with the grizzly loping along after them. But then the bear picked up on something about one of the cows—old age, disease, something invisible to the human watcher but clearly apparent to the grizzly—and in an instant things got serious. The bear put on a tremendous burst of speed, quickly caught up to the chosen cow, reared up on his hind legs, and slammed both front paws down on her back, collapsing her hips with his weight.

When the cow went down, Doug made a dash back to his pack for his camera. When he returned moments later, the bear was shaking the cow "like a cat with a mouse." When the elk was good and dead, the grizzly eviscerated it with a couple of swipes of claw and dragged the carcass back into the timber to feed . . . shades of "blood, hair, and the ground tore up."

"I'd been tracking this bear every day," Doug told me, "so I knew a bit about him even though I got to see him only twice; he was very secretive. But he was bedding in the same relatively small patch of timber where I was camped, and I was finding his kills everywhere. It looked like he was taking an elk maybe a couple of times a week. He never ate an entire carcass. He'd chew on 'em until he got his fill, then abandon the kill; he didn't always even bother to cover it with debris. But nothing went to waste. As soon as the bear was gone, the coyotes and ravens showed up to finish the job. That griz was feeding a lot of wildlife that spring."

Nor was this a freak occurrence. In the unique, pressure-cooker Yellowstone ecosystem, many have observed what Doug describes as "some pretty weird things regarding grizzly predation on adult elk." Doug cites Number Fifteen.

"He was the bear that went nuts after being trapped and drugged too many times; finally had to be executed after killing a camper at Rainbow Point. But for years, Number Fifteen was a superb big game hunter, taking mature, healthy animals spring through fall, including bull elk. He was the best elk-killing bear I've ever known, especially during the rut. In fact, second to early spring, when the wapiti are still herded up and winter-weak and there's snow still on the ground to slow their escape, the rut is probably the most opportune time for grizzlies to take mature bulls, when the rutting bulls are love-struck and often let their defenses down.

"Certain springs, you see all kinds of elk predation by Yellowstone grizzlies, especially around Gardner and along the Firehole River. I remember one subadult bear who, after running down and killing an elk, would regularly get chased away by a bigger grizzly; he'd have to turn right around and go after another one."

Hearing stories like these, it would be easy to hop to the conclusion that grizzlies are devastating predators—on elk, deer, or whatever else they take a hankering for. But remember, we've been talking about Yellowstone Park, which, by official reckoning, supported some 228 grizzlies and many thousands too many elk as of 1993.

Still, many elk that spend their winters and springs in Yellowstone wander outside the unfenced park and onto surrounding national forest and private lands during the fall hunting seasons, prompting some insecure hunters to argue that every elk killed by grizzlies within the park is one less elk available to them outside the park. Transferring this sort of reasoning to Colorado, some hunters and outfitters worry that if grizzlies were to be restored here, they would make serious inroads into local elk populations.

Would they?

Back in 1972, Glen Cole of the National Park Service's Office of Natural Science Studies published a research paper titled "Grizzly Bear-Elk Relationships in Yellowstone National Park." This paper summarized studies conducted from 1967 through 1971. From the abstract:

Grizzly predation with competitive scavenging was a nonessential but assisting adjunct to other natural processes that regulated the elk population. As an interacting unit, bears of different social rank and an associated scavenger fauna [primarily black bears, coyotes, and eagles] probably helped to dampen elk population fluctuations by culling animals with low energy reserves. The presence of a grizzly population in Yellowstone Park appears essential to have representative natural equilibrium among interacting secondary consumers [i.e., predators and scavengers], to maintain natural relationships between secondary [carnivorous] and primary [herbivorous] consumers, and to retain the scientific values of ecological systems with an intact native biota.

In lay terms, Cole's study suggested that while grizzly predation *alone* isn't essential to maintaining a healthy wapiti herd in the park, the great bear is part of a team of natural forces working to moderate the potentially catastrophic boom-and-crash cycle of herd numbers.

Further, as Doug Peacock observed that snowy morning in the Firehole region of Yellowstone, since a bear or lion or wolf or other predator is going to ferret out the most easily catchable meal—the very young, the old and tired, the sick, lame, lazy, or just plain stupid—the prey population is thus skimmed of its marginalia, ensuring that all available food resources go to those elk best qualified not just to survive but to reproduce and rear healthy offspring.

Biologists see this direct sort of natural selection at work even in bear predation on elk calves, in that the "fittest" cows choose the best hiding places for their young and come to their defense most readily and effectively—usually by trying to distract the predator's attention and decoy him away from the little hider. After this fashion, the young of the cows best adapted for survival have a decided advantage over the young of meeker and less clever mothers.

In summary, Cole felt that Yellowstone grizzlies contribute significantly to ensuring the genetic *quality* of the park herds, even though their hunting leads to a slight reduction in *quantity*.

Two decades later, biologists still hold Cole's conclusions as valid: grizzlies still prey on both calves and mature elk, as opportunities present themselves, but this predation has only an adjunct influence on overall elk mortality and is both natural and positive.

Kerry Gunther is head of Yellowstone Park's Bear Management Office. In the late 1980s, Gunther conducted his own predation study, focusing on the Pelican Valley area. Gunther explained to me that back when park employees used to kill elk to keep their numbers down to around five thousand on the northern range, there were fewer calves to prey on and, therefore, less opportunity for bears to learn how to hunt them successfully. Now, with the northern herd alone numbering in excess of twenty thousand animals, predation (naturally) is up.

Neither Gunther nor any other biologist I've spoken with views such a rise in predation corresponding with an expansion of the prey base as an alarming trend. "The period of opportunity for catching calves is so short," Gunther explains, "that the number of elk lost to predators is insignificant when compared to the number that wander outside the park and get shot by hunters."

(And killed by cars and poachers and winter subdivision dog packs, or starved out by livestock grazing or timbering or real estate development or . . .)

When I asked Gunther about the level of grizzly predation on adult elk in the park today, he explained that carcass surveys suggest *some* bear predation on winter-weakened adult elk during early spring, though no one knows exactly how much. "There's also evidence," he says, "of grizzlies taking a few bulls in the fall, during the rut."

"Predation," Gunther concludes, "is a natural and positive influence on elk and in no way regulates prey populations; the primary regulators are hunting and winter range availability."

Thus all is well and good with predators and prey in Yellowstone Park. In fact, that richly compressed ecosystem could benefit from a lot *more* reduction of elk by predators. But how does that transfer to nonpark elk-grizzly habitat?

Michael Madel is a grizzly biologist for the Montana Department of Fish, Wildlife, and Parks who has the formidable responsibility of managing the bear population and minimizing conflicts between bears and people along much of the length of the Rocky Mountain Front (i.e., the eastern slope of the Northern Continental Divide Ecosystem). His beat includes the Great Bear and Scapegoat Wilderness areas plus a portion of the huge Bob Marshall.

Based on scientific research, Madel is confident that bear predation has little if any influence on local elk numbers across his beat. "We just don't see the type of predatory behavior they regularly observe down in Yellowstone. Beyond the north and west forks of the Sun River, there just aren't all that many elk calving grounds up here that are readily available to grizzlies."

Similarly, elk calving in the San Juans is a shotgun affair, with pregnant cows rarely compressing themselves into rich calf-hunting grounds such as Yellowstone's Pelican Valley. For this reason, rather than being able to concentrate their efforts on specific happy hunting grounds as they can do in Yellowstone, large predators in the San Juans have to cover one hell of a lot of territory between far-flung potential meals, significantly reducing their effectiveness.

When Mike Madel mentioned the Sun River, he was referring to Montana's Sun River Game Preserve, where some three thousand elk spend their springs and summers and human predation is not permitted. Before taking a self-described "cushy indoor job" as the preserve's wildlife laboratory manager, grizzly biologist Keith Aune—the same Aune who inadvertently exposed the likelihood of fraud in the Snowslide Canyon grizzly hair sample—enjoyed a long career studying bears throughout the Northern Continental Divide Ecosystem. (This long, narrow strip of prime wildlife habitat comprises approximately six million acres with Glacier National Park on the north and tracing down the Whitefish and Flathead Ranges as far south as Rogers Pass and Montana Highway 200.) Aune's best estimate is that five hundred to seven hundred grizzlies were living there as of 1993, their densities varying from a low of one per fifty square miles to a high of one per ten square miles.

Interestingly, the distribution of these northern grizzlies appears to be just about the reverse of that of northern elk—with more bears occupying marginal elk habitat and fewer bears in strong elk habitat. Even so, at least on the Sun River Preserve where elk are almost as concentrated as in Yellowstone Park, northern grizzlies do kill northern elk.

"Through radiotelemetry and snow-tracking," Aune told me, "we know that grizzlies up here, like those in Yellowstone and elsewhere, use a variety of tactics, but most especially ambush and stalking. One common ploy is for a bear to use natural cover to stalk close to a group of elk, then run toward them, testing, trying to identify an animal that appears vulnerable."

Aune has also seen strong indications of ambush. He describes finding one place where elk bones and other evidence indicated that the same grizzly had been regularly ambushing calves. Aune described a jungly bottom area where elk feed along a verdant ecotone. This savvy griz, it appeared, would lie there in ambush and jump elk calves that fed past.

"And during the rifle season," Aune added, "bears apparently come down the Sun River looking for wounded and dead animals that have escaped into the preserve from adjoining national forest lands—cleaning up the mistakes made by human hunters."

In the words of Jamie Jonkel, an experienced researcher into the Yellowstone predator-prey relationship, "Hunters shouldn't worry about grizzlies and wolves."

Indeed, perhaps hunters—everywhere—should worry more about the welfare of predators. As indicator species that operate at the pinnacle of the food chain, big predators are the first to fall on hard times when something goes wrong somewhere down the line. In that respect, grizzlies are like the old coal miners' canaries, in that their health in a given area serves as an indicator of the overall health of the ecology.

Down here in the southern Rockies, even the most rosy-eyed, restoration-championing optimists would never hope to see more than a piddling handful of grizzlies extant in the San Juans. Meanwhile, Colorado hosts by far the largest number of wapiti of any state or province in North America: from a low of about 180,000 following the fall hunting seasons to a high of around 220,000 after calf-drop in the spring. Closer to home, just the montane portion of the San Juan ecosystem—in essence, the San Juan and Rio Grande National Forests—is home to a year-round average, near as Division biologists can figure, of some 32,000 wapiti. Plenty of elk meat to satisfy the appetites of all Colorado predators, human and non.

In fact, perhaps too much, with more and more elk winding up mangled and rotting alongside highways every winter, or starved to death on increasingly restricted and overgrazed winter ranges. As the local human population increases, which it has at a horrifying rate since about 1990, and as wildlife habitat shrinks in consequence, local elk are caught in a deadly crossfire. We could, it seems, use a few grizzlies (and wolves) hereabouts to take a little of the pressure off.

I suggest to my fellow hunters that natural predation—whether by grizzlies, black bears, wolves, mountain lions, coyotes, Bigfoot, or scalpel-wielding space aliens—will never cut big game numbers enough to hurt our individual or collective success. Rather, the true enemy of elk and elk hunting is the so-called progress that follows like detritus in the wake of unchecked human reproduction. "Growth for the sake of growth," said Edward Abbey, "is the ideology of the cancer cell." The most obvious symptoms of the growth disease in elk country include excessive logging (and the ecologically disruptive and destructive road-building that facilitates it); untenable, unsound, and unsustainable grazing practices and policies; and the subdividing of large rural properties into ever-smaller residential and commercial lots. *These* are the predators in need of control.

"Progress," said A. B. Guthrie, Jr., "is a word that should imply an improvement in the *quality* of life, but rarely does."

By my lights, saving the last of the San Juan grizzlies, and by so doing, preserving in as near a pristine state as possible the last of their native habitat . . . now that would be progress.

12

"BRAIN-DEAD POLITICAL HACKS" AND OTHER FRIENDS OF WILDLIFE

Black Bear Management in Colorado:
A Grizzly Metaphor?

What goes around comes around.
—Traditional

Well, there's one less bear in the world today.

Round about midnight last night, a man across the creek valley—I'll call him Cal—shot and killed a black bear he feared was trying to break into his house to get at his children, who he says were playing on the living room floor . . . round about midnight on a school night?

In any event, Cal got spooked and popped the bear with a deer rifle. I heard the shots. They woke me from a shallow sleep, and I knew with a preternatural certainty what had happened. So I wasn't at all surprised when warden Cary Carron called this morning to break the news and ask if I wanted to accompany him when he went to investigate the shooting and collect the corpse. At Caroline's request, I declined. Cal is, after all, a neighbor—not a friend, we've never met—but an across-the-valley neighbor nonetheless. Caroline knows me better than I know myself.

It was bound to happen, I guess. We've had at least two bears here in this tacky old vacation-home subdivision off and on all summer. Back in June, a big, black, brown-faced boar walked down the dirt trail that passes for our drive. I was off somewhere looking for bears and so missed it. But Caroline was out front working in her flower beds and got a good close look. About twenty yards before reaching the front door of our humble abode, the bear veered off the drive, ambled past the fire pit and down my archery practice lane, and disappeared into the oak brush and pines.

The same brown-faced black bear had been spotted on another neighbor's deck only a few evenings before, sorting through a garbage can. Standing upright on hind legs, leaning heavily against the sliding glass door, the bear looked, my breathless neighbor reported, "seven feet tall."

The second subdivision regular this summer was the slightly smaller, coal-black boar destined to be snuffed by Cal. Like his brown-faced competitor, he'd been attracted to and was held near the subdivision by the smells of garbage and other tasty, nutritious treats. Every few nights he'd make his rounds, stopping to feast where goodies waited, slipping through unnoticed where nothing edible was left out; it hadn't taken him long to learn where inadvertent handouts were to be had, and where he was wasting his time. Cal's place offered the greatest temptations, what with an open utility trailerful of plastic-bagged garbage, a pygmy goat in the front yard, and more cats scampering about than the Cal clan had even bothered to count.

The only aspect of this sad incident that surprised me was that the bear waited as long as he did to munch the goat. That happened about ten last Saturday night. The Cals were home and witnessed the bear killing the bleating little caprid and toting it off, but they were powerless to stop him; their shouts didn't even provoke the single-minded bruin to glance their way. Right then, Cal called the home of the local game warden (not Cary, who only pinch-hits in this district as necessary) but got no answer; the warden was on leave. He then tried the home of the only other Division official whose name he knew; no answer there either. That really got Cal's goat.

Had Cal known to call central dispatch for Division help, a warden would have come out with a culvert trap on a trailer, baited and caught the bear, and transported it to a far distant place on public land for release. I helped Cary and another warden do exactly that a couple of summers ago. Same scenario: A young male bear was inadvertently baited by the smells of garbage and dog food left out, eventually killing a couple of pet goats penned in a front yard. We trapped and ear-tagged the culprit before releasing him eighty miles away, and he's neither returned nor caused problems elsewhere; a long, bumpy ride in a hot, noisy culvert trap, a shot of tranquilizer, and a plastic tag punched into an ear seem to have provided sufficient aversive conditioning. At least in this case. At least for now. So far as we know.

And just as well for the bear, since, in a recent compromise to mollify predator-phobics who want to see bears and lions destroyed the first time they inconvenience humans (if not before), the Division tightened its long-standing unofficial nuisance bear policy of "three strikes and you're out" to a mandatory two strikes. Henceforth, if a bear is trapped and relocated, then gets into trouble a second time, it will be killed.

But Cal's bear didn't get even a second chance, drawn as he was—you could say helplessly—back to the enticing aromas of that garbage-filled bait trailer. The hungry beast returned the very night following the goat feast and was promptly made into a good bear. The bruin's big muddy paw prints all over the deck and windows, Cary surmised, were more likely indicative of his curiosity about the kittens lounging in windowsills and otherwise swarming around the place than they were evidence of the bear's intent to break in and snatch a schoolchild for a midnight snack.

This time, claiming concern for the safety of his children and having found no relief from the Division, Cal brought out his deer rifle and popped the bear: *Krak!*—(a few seconds pass as I lie in bed and wait)— *Krak!* The doomed intruder staggered as far as the dirt subdivision road, lay down, and expired.

When I saw him this morning, the bear was lying all bloody and swollen in the back of Cary's pickup, his fur wet from the night's rain and shiny and sleek and black as death itself; 250 pounds, we guessed; a robust young adult. Cary remarked that this was the biggest bear he'd seen all summer—goat fattened and ready for the winter den (excavated beneath a nearby vacant cabin) he would never occupy. And a handsome beast he was, notwithstanding the lolling tongue and coagulated blood around his mouth. His front paws measured 5 inches wide by 5$^1/8$ inches from heel to toe tips. The claws were nail-sharp, showed little wear, and extended about an inch beyond the toes.

While Cary and I were talking, Leonard and Dorothy, a retired couple from Arizona and my nearest summer neighbors, pulled in behind us. Having missed the brown-faced bruin that ambled down our drive back in June, Dorothy had longed all summer to see a bear. And she finally had: one night recently a bruin, perhaps the same sleek black fellow, came around at two in the morning and spent forty-five minutes crunching ten pounds of apples left outside. They'd been thrilled to have this hirsute ambassador of wild nature in their yard. Now Dorothy stared at the dead thing in the back of Cary's truck and quietly wept.

After the neighbors drove off, I asked Cary what he planned to do with the bear. "I'll skin him out, I guess, since his pelt is so pretty; we can use the hide for our wildlife education programs in local schools."

Good. Maybe if kids can be taught how to live with wildlife, they can educate their parents.

I do wonder why people who obviously fear wild nature—biophobics —choose to live at its door. Time and again, romantic fools move to the country "to be close to nature," then soil their Skivvies and cry for help the first time they encounter any wildlife larger than a squirrel.

Cal told warden Carron he shot the bear because he feared for his children. And he probably did. Still, if you're that concerned about bears, why keep bear baits in your yard all summer, even after you know a bear is about and your neighbors have tried to warn you?

Why, indeed? Taking Cal's side for a moment, let's surmise: There is no curbside garbage collection out here in this mountainous rural subdivision (a private entrepreneur tried to make a go of it once, but failed owing to muddy and snow-packed roads and too many customers neglecting to pay their bills). If you want to buy special containers and haul your garbage down to the blacktop county road, a private service will pick it up, but the cost and hassle put most people off, myself included.

Meanwhile, the city of Durango nails county residents with stiff fines for depositing their trash in city Dumpsters (there for tourists only, it seems). The distant county dump station charges outrageous prices because the county claims it can't afford to subsidize this absolutely necessary public service (even, ironically, as it annually squanders some $12,000 on Animal Damage Control to quiet a handful of bleating sheep ranchers). So you don't want to be running out to the dump every few days with just a couple of bags of garbage. Consequently, many rural residents, like Cal, stash their trash in utility trailers and visit the dump as infrequently as possible.

Furthermore, Cal *had* tried to contact the wildlife authorities, to no avail, though he could have tried a little harder. *After* shooting the bear, he finally hit on phoning the county sheriff's dispatcher, who went down the list until she found a warden, good old Cary, who would answer a Sunday midnight phone call at home.

It's a messy situation, with plenty of fault to go around. Only the bears, in my eyes, are blameless.

Given this sorry state of black bear affairs, what kind of welcome can we expect for grizzlies here in the San Juans?

In November of 1992, eleven months before the Cal incident, the citizens of Colorado voted overwhelmingly—70 percent to 30, with high voter participation—to adopt a state ballot initiative, dubbed Amendment 10, ending spring black bear hunting and banning the morally repugnant practices of using trailing hounds and bait piles to "hunt" the bruins. The anatomy of this pivotal event in Colorado bear management is worth dissecting here for what it reveals of the personalities, philosophies, and political tactics of some of the same factions that will be major players in any grizzly bear restoration debates in Colorado.

The best summary of the feelings and events that led to Amendment 10 is found in a brochure prepared and distributed by CUB, the acronym for the ad hoc citizens' group Coloradans United for Bears. On the cover of the CUB brochure is a photo of an infant black bear. Above the photo appear the words, in bold capital letters, "KILL THE MOTHER AND THE CUBS DIE TOO." Below the photo is the plea, "HELP STOP THE SPRING BEAR HUNT." The pitch reads:

HISTORY: In November 1991, the Colorado Wildlife Commission (CWC) voted to lengthen the spring black bear hunting season by two weeks, to May 31, and to extend the length of time in which hounds and bait can be used to kill bears. This decision ignored the Division of Wildlife's recommendation to end the spring bear hunting season; in fact, Division staff declared the spring hunt "indefensible." The CWC also ignored the public's overwhelming opposition to the spring bear season and bait and hound usage for bear hunting. Comments to the Division ran 16 to 1 in opposition to spring hunting and 122 to 1 in opposition to baits and hounds.

In the last three years, the Division has commissioned two public attitude surveys with highly reputable independent polling companies. In the 1989 survey, 90% of the public expressed opposition to spring bear hunting, while 75% expressed opposition to the use of bait and hounds. In the 1991 survey, a strong majority again disapproved of spring hunting and, as in the previous poll, 75% opposed hound or bait hunting of bears. . . .

HOUNDS: Hunting bears with hounds violates the ethical hunter's fair-chase standards. Hunters use packs of hounds (often fitted with special radio-tracking telemetry collars) to chase and drive an exhausted bear up a tree, and then shoot the bear out of the tree at point blank range. . . .

BAIT: Like hound hunting, bear baiting is unethical and unfair. Weeks before the hunting season starts, baiters dump rotting meat and sweet-smelling foods into bait buckets. The bears smell the food and begin daily feedings at the bait station. Then, hunting season begins and the hunter shoots the unwitting bear over the bait from point blank range. The Intermountain Region Regional Forester of the U.S. Forest Service stated as recently as November 1990 that "the use of salt as an attractant to draw elk and other game animals is illegal for ethical reasons. The Forest Service believes these same standards should apply to all game species, including black bear." Besides being unsporting, baiting also habituates bears to human food sources. Baited bears not shot by hunters will raid garbage cans or turn into general human nuisances.

Amendment 10, as it appeared on the ballot, read:

An amendment to the Colorado Revised Statutes to prohibit the taking of black bears by the use of bait or dogs at any time, and to prohibit the taking of black bears by any means between March 1 and September 1 of any calendar year, and subjecting violators to misdemeanor penalties and a loss of hunting privileges. (Legislative Council, 1992)

The "hunters' rights" lobby—fueled in largest part by industry contributions and given voice by hook-and-bullet magazines, the National Rifle Association, the hunting industry's political action group Wildlife Legislative Fund of America, and kindred organizations—responded predictably. Employing a paranoid mentality that equates to "Let them have our assault rifles today, and they'll be back after our BB guns tomorrow!"

the hunting lobby charged that Amendment 10 was the work of a tiny coterie of animal rights fanatics and represented but the first skirmish of a war to end all hunting in Colorado—and after Colorado, of course, the world.

The anti-10 forces were of course right about radical antihunting groups attempting to use the Amendment 10 victory to further their avowed goal of ending all hunting; but, as has always been the case, the hunters vastly overestimated the strength of their enemies. Wayne Pacelle, national director of the Washington, D.C., lobby group Fund for Animals, wasted no time in petitioning the Colorado Wildlife Commission to ban bowhunting for bears, claiming that archery equipment is ineffective and thus cruel. Patently and verifiably untrue. In reality, bowhunting is a popular target for antihunters simply because bowhunters are relatively few in number—a weak and disorganized lobby—and thus viewed as easy prey.

To its credit, the CWC sent Pacelle packing with a flat refusal even to consider his proposal. As *Rocky Mountain News* writer Ed Dentry observed in an article titled "Anti-hunting Group Snubbed in Colorado":

> Clearly the . . . animal rights organization misinterpreted the implications of Amendment 10. . . . Fund members will wince to know their blunder puts them in company with many Colorado hunters. . . . The anti-hunting group, which sent money to instate backers of Amendment 10, assumed it could use the amendment's passage as Step 1 in its stated goal of whittling away at all hunting. It expected those who pushed the amendment to support them in Step 2—doing away with bowhunting for bears.
>
> Many hunters assumed the same. They were wrong. Backers of Amendment 10 have insisted all along the measure was not part of an anti-hunting drive. In recent weeks—and again Thursday—they said they resented the fund's Step 2 invasion into Colorado hunting issues. They have refused to join the Fund in its attack on bowhunting.

If only both sides could rise above their differences and come to see and deal with the truth: antihunters are not the greatest enemy to hunting, just as hunting is not the greatest enemy of "animal rights." Rather, it is human overpopulation and the transmogrification of wildlife habitat into "resources" and "real estate" that are the great destroyers of the natural nobility of wildlife and the forces that will eventually put an end to democratic hunting and "the American way of life" in general.

When I interviewed Colorado bear biologist Tom Beck in early November of 1993—a year to the day after the passage of Amendment 10—we discussed that historic ballot initiative at length, chewing over both its roots and its implications for the future of wildlife management in Colorado and elsewhere. Following is a distillation of Beck's views on Colorado black bear management, politics, and many pertinent peripherals, with no static interference from me. Beck's caveat: these are personal sentiments and have not been reviewed or endorsed by the Colorado Division of Wildlife (and most certainly not by the Colorado Wildlife Commission). In his own words, here's his piece:

I don't believe anyone who's informed on the issues favors wildlife management by general ballot. It should be a scientific and social process, not political and populist. But then, we biologists are in part to blame for letting things get so bad that Amendment 10 became necessary—because wildlife management in America has *always* been more political than scientific, and we have never sufficiently protested that state of affairs.

I'm a member of the International Association for Bear Research, a group of bear biologists involved in research and management. A decade ago, in the early 1980s, I moved to get the group to come out with formal positions on the crucial issues, but my proposal was greeted with little interest. Most members ran from it, using excuses like, "We can't tell my agency what to do. It's too political! It's too controversial! This will make our lives a lot more miserable, and we won't do it." That was the response from the people who, more than any others, hold the fate of the world's bears in their hands. And if *we* won't take the role of advocates for the bears, who will? Even concerning an issue as egregious as the sale of bear body parts, biologists refuse to take a solid position.

My point is that society has changed in the past fifty years, but wildlife management has not. Certainly, we're more technologically advanced today, but philosophically we're half a century behind the times. We should be the leaders in modernizing wildlife management, but we're not. At a recent public meeting in Michigan, when one of my colleagues, for whom I otherwise have great respect, was asked—by a ten-year-old child—"How can baiting bears be fair?" he fell back on the standard agency answer: "As long as the overall *population* of bears isn't being hurt, how hunters go about killing individual animals isn't our concern as biologists."

That's not only an obvious dodge, it's absurd. In effect, it's saying we *don't care* how an individual animal dies.

But society cares. To me, this disparity of compassion is the number-one credibility problem of wildlife management agencies today in the eyes of the nonhunting public. I'm not speaking of antihunters, that minority who are philosophically opposed to killing animals under any circumstances, but of the 75 percent of the American public who have no problem with hunting per se, but who do want it carried out in a more biologically sound manner. This nonhunting majority very much cares about the individual animal, and hunters and professional wildlife managers had better start showing that we care too. How individual animals die *is* important.

Coming full circle, maybe if we Colorado wildlife professionals had been able to find the guts early on to state some obvious truths and hard opinions on black bear management, the necessary changes would have come about from within the Division, rather than being forced down our throats by an exasperated public. I don't believe the Division did a very good job of educating either the public or our own people about the real issues, the real problems.

Bear management in Colorado began in the 1930s, when the state legislature first designated black bears as game animals and gave them the protection of a temporary moratorium on hunting, followed by a regulated annual season. But the cop-outs began almost immediately: In response to protests from ranchers, who'd always been allowed to kill predators at will, it was decided that stockmen could continue to kill bears that "pose a threat" to livestock. The only requirement was that all such kills be reported to the Division. Many ranchers loved the killing part but didn't care much for the reporting; compliance wasn't good then, and it still isn't today. Livestock people don't want to report the killing of protected predators, bears and lions, because they fear we'll send somebody out to check up on them, to verify that stock in fact is being lost to bears.

Colorado had very conservative black bear hunting seasons through the mid-1950s, generally limited to the month of September. Then, when archery deer and elk hunters were given their own season, that pushed bear hunting out of September; we didn't want the two overlapping. After that, through the '60s and early '70s, we went through a number of different bear season structures, experimenting with spring, summer, and fall hunts, often running all three.

Then, during the mid-1970s, we started seeing a tremendous increase in bear-human conflicts. This caused a clamor among bear hunters and others for a more liberal spring hunting season with a liberal variety of methods—including especially the use of baits and hounds.

Naturally, hunting outfitters loved this idea, since catering to spring bear hunters provides a lucrative source of income during a season when guides and outfitters traditionally are out of work. The livestock industry can be relied on to lobby in favor of liberal hunting seasons on predators. So all of this was stacked against the bears, with no one to speak *for* them, and with the whole shooting match based on the assumption that sport hunting helps to reduce bear-human conflicts, even though a substantial body of research from several states showed that sport hunting very definitely *is not* an effective antidote to the problem of nuisance bears.

Another significant event of the middle and late '70s was a dramatic increase in the amount of attention paid by the hook-and-bullet magazines to shooting bears over baits; the outdoor media, in effect, helped create the current craze for bait hunting. Consequently, by the 1980s, killing bears in the spring over baits was enjoying an unparalleled boom in every state and Canadian province where it was legal.

It was at this point, in Maine and elsewhere, that bear-advocate groups first formed to speak out against the spring hunt. In effect, Maine fought the same battle Colorado was destined to fight, with the same outcome, but a dozen years earlier. And were we professional bear managers paying attention? We were not; we learned nothing from that history.

So by the 1980s a tremendous push in favor of maintaining a liberal spring bear season had evolved in Colorado. Everyone liked it—the livestock industry you bet, hunters, outfitters, even many within the Division, laboring under the false impression that by keeping down the overall bear population we were helping to lessen human-bear conflicts.

Meanwhile, I'd begun my Colorado black bear study in 1977. We went into the field in 1978 and started trapping bears the following year. As an adjunct to my field studies, I lobbied the Division to start collecting better data on the annual bear kill: numbers, sexes, ages, locations, dates, methods of take. Beginning in 1979, the Division instituted a mandatory bear check. For the first three years of this program, I personally summarized the data and compiled reports. And in the doing, I identified some trends that really worried me.

Basically, in a lot of Colorado's more popular bear-hunting areas, the number of bears being killed was beginning to show a decline, suggesting an overall reduced population. But at the same time, the percentage of female bears killed increased dramatically. This indicated that we had overshot our male bears, which are more vulnerable to baits, and were starting to cut into the female population. Simultaneously, the size of the bears being killed, both male and female, was getting smaller and smaller. It was as if we'd killed off all of our larger, older bears. What I was seeing suggested strongly that we were overhunting some parts of the state.

Our first attempt to halt this trend was to shorten the season. We started by eliminating the summer hunt, then we shortened the spring hunt. But surprisingly, this didn't significantly impact the total kill; the greatest hunter success was still occurring during the last two weeks of the season, no matter whether that last two weeks fell in May or June. However, by shortening the spring season we did see a big change in the sex of the bears being killed: the earlier the season closed, the higher the percentage of males compared to females. Males leave the den earlier than females, and May 15 seems to be the turning point: before that we killed mostly males, after that the number of females, some of them nursing cubs, increased dramatically.

Predictably, the more we shortened the seasons to try and correct these problems, the greater the opposition we met from all those groups who wanted to maintain a liberal bear season for their own ends. By about 1982, the Colorado Wildlife Commission had grown weary of listening to these arguments, and instructed the Division to come up with a detailed analysis of bear hunting in Colorado that recommended "significant changes." As is typical for a bureaucracy, the Division did nothing. That really infuriated some Commission members, who retaliated by appointing a citizens' task force—comprising hunters, nonhunters, stockmen, outfitters, and other groups—to study black bear hunting in Colorado. This *could* have been a good idea.

But it quickly became apparent that the task force leader was not going to let the group address the critical issues of hunting *methods, ethics, and orphaning of cubs,* but insisted on keeping the focus narrowed to the single problem of overhunting. Consequently, what the task force came up with was a limited license system for spring bear hunting, in which the number of tags issued for each hunting area was dependent on the perceived health of the bear population in that area, with all licenses being given out by a lottery drawing. Otherwise, the spring hunt, baiting, and hounds all survived intact.

Nor did this change impact the fall bear season, which remained unlimited. But because baiting and hounds are not allowed in the fall, that portion of the season structure has always been peripheral, accounting for only 15 to 25 percent of the annual kill. But at least the limited spring license system worked to stop the overhunting problem, and we stuck with it through the mid-1980s, leaving the issues of methods and morals to flounder on the sidelines and planting the seeds of public discontent that would eventually mature into Amendment 10.

I was always concerned that baiting disturbed the natural feeding patterns of bears and added significantly to the number of "garbage bears." And I believe that the tremendous number of bear-human conflicts we had in May and June during the first spring that bear hunting was not allowed following [passage of] Amendment 10 arose from the sudden end of baiting. In years past, there were always four to six thousand barrels of bait scattered around the state waiting for hungry bears the moment they came out of den. Bears that didn't get killed became conditioned to that rich source of postden nutrition and learned to go straight to the nearest pile of meat scraps or pastries. Then suddenly, no more baits, which prompted bears to look elsewhere for garbage. I believe that in a few years, when our current bait-trained bear generation is gone, we should see a significant reduction in garbage bear problems.

The theory, widely held by the public and some within the Division as well, that killing no bears this spring was the reason for the sudden increase in problems is based on ignorance. People who believe that haven't looked at the numbers. Colorado has about twelve thousand bears. Killing 350 to 400 in spring has a negligible impact on the total bear population and thus on bear-human conflicts. It doesn't matter if you have a hundred bears on a mountain or 97; if the right conditions are there—something to attract the animals, particularly if exacerbated by a dry spring and summer like we had this year—you're going to have problems.

But getting back to the issues that precipitated Amendment 10: the spring hunt, in a lot of people's minds, was a motherhood issue—"kill the mother, and the cubs die too," as CUB proclaimed. But because of the tremendous opposition to further limiting the spring season, nobody in a position of responsibility would act: the Division refused to address the problem; the citizens' task force on bear hunting declined to address it; even professional bear biologists and managers wouldn't touch it. So it sat there and simmered, year after year through the late 1980s.

And this in spite of the fact that as early as 1984, a poll of our field people—biologists and district wildlife managers—had revealed a strong belief that we needed to stop the spring bear hunt, at least in the southwest region of the state. Our reasoning wasn't that we were short on bears, but that a spring hunt with bait and hounds is very hard to morally justify. The survey results and a proposal to stop the spring hunt were submitted to the Division's top administration—and overruled.

The administration's rationalization for keeping the spring hunt was that "well, we're only killing twelve to fifteen nursing females per year, with an average of two cubs each; statistically, half those cubs would die even if the mother lived, so the spring hunt accounts for the deaths of only twelve to fifteen cubs per year, which is not a significant impact on the population."

Trouble was, this line of thought ignored the issue, which was the *morality* of hunting bears during a period when young are totally dependent on their mothers. As our critics pointed out, we didn't allow this sort of abuse of any species but mountain lions and bears, the state's two largest predators. Coyotes, of course, a third stock-killing predator, receive no protection at all and can be killed year-round, using any method.

So, more and more in the late '80s, the Division was being asked: "Why do we hunt bears in the spring? How can you justify the unsporting practices of baiting and dogs?" We had no good answers, and the criticism intensified. Over the years, a handful of the most dedicated of our critics—all of them at this point, I should mention, were Colorado residents and some of them hunters; no outside agitators or organized antihunting groups were involved—educated themselves in bear biology and, through the school of hard knocks, became adept at addressing the politics of wildlife management in Colorado.

For a long time, these people tried to effect changes from within the system. They even tried good old-fashioned political compromise, suggesting repeatedly that if the Division would back off on maintaining the spring hunt, they would back off on the issues of hounds and bait. But the organized hunting groups and outfitters weren't willing to compromise, clinging to a paranoid domino theory mentality that says if you give the opposition an inch, you're going to lose the whole race.

The Division's last chance to straighten things out on its own came in 1989, when the hunting-season structure was set for the next three years. At that time things were relatively quiet; the critics of the spring bear hunt had backed off, giving us the room to make the right moves on our own without losing face. But the administrators chose to continue the spring bear hunt, squandering their last opportunity to make necessary changes in a nonvolatile arena.

Finally, 1991 rolled around, and it was time to set another three-year management plan. Again, the Division's field staff, speaking through their regional biologists, recommended that we needed to get away from spring bear hunting, primarily on the grounds that it was morally and ethically insupportable. The director took that recommendation to the Commission, which didn't like it and requested that it be revised before the next meeting. At that next meeting, the director returned with his biologists, who again insisted that the spring hunt be terminated. *Finally,* we had made the right decision, the right recommendation, and had mustered the guts to stand behind it.

This put the director in a bind, with the Commission pushing him one way and his promise to his biologists that he wouldn't arbitrarily overrule us pushing the other. To his credit, the director stuck by us as we met repeatedly with the Commission, trying to get them to understand the correctness of our position.

Meanwhile, the Commissioners were hearing the hunters' rights advocates screaming that all management decisions should be based on biology alone. But we've never done that; wildlife management decisions are *never* made based on biology alone. I'm not sure why representatives from the various hunters' groups could never come to recognize the importance of how hunters are perceived by the nonhunting public.

So by 1991, on the one side we had those aligned against the spring hunt fighting it as an ethics issue, and the other side fighting it as a hunters' rights issue; lots of polemics but very little communication taking place. The Commission pretty much sided with the hunters, which left the Division stuck in the middle: our critics protested that we hadn't campaigned long or hard enough to end the spring hunt, which was true, while hunters charged that we'd abandoned the group whose license fees pay our salaries; hunters seemed to feel that we should go along with anything they wanted.

By this time, the debate had caught the attention of a number of major environmental publications, bringing the big national-level animal welfare and hunters' rights groups into the fray. I believe the big animal rights groups saw the issue as an easy win, a potential feather in their caps, and a good issue for fund-raising—because from 1979, when it all really started, to 1991, when it became an issue of national magnitude, they hadn't been involved. And they were right: the hunters' lame arguments and moral dodges and avoidance of the real issues were destined to give the critics a freebie; the spring bear hunt advocates essentially handed it to them on a silver platter, put parsley all around, and said "Happy Thanksgiving!"

So that was the situation in 1991, when the CWC voted to continue the spring hunt. In what I guess they saw as a major effort to compromise, though, they instituted a program they hoped would wean hunters away from the spring hunt: the first year, limited spring bear licenses would be cut by half, from two thousand to one, with the other thousand issued for a new September hunt and no open fall bear season; the second year, we'd issue only six hundred spring licenses and up the September hunt to fourteen hundred; with the third year set for a ten/ninety split.

This scheme was designed to give the *appearance* that we were phasing out the spring bear hunt. But it didn't fool many of the critics, who said, "Wait a minute. What about year four? There's no guarantee that three years from now we won't be right back to the same old debate. We don't want to wait three more years to have this settled; we've been fighting it for ten years already." Similarly, the bear hunters recognized that, "yeah, we're going to get pounded for three years, but then we'll come back prepared to fight hard for a more liberal spring season."

Thus the Commission never clearly stated their intent relative to the spring bear hunt in the long-term; they left *everybody* hanging, feeling shortchanged. Not only that, but they *lengthened* the spring season by two weeks. During the previous three years, the spring hunt had opened April 1 and closed May 15, and now the CWC extended the closing date to May 31. This move basically reiterated that the cub issue was unimportant, that total bear population was the only concern. It was demoralizing to the Division staff who had worked so long to develop a reasonable position and, in essence, dared the critics of the spring hunt to throw their best punch.

But the straw that broke the camel's back fell when the Commission chairman got up and gave a very emotionally charged speech in support of what I view as the radical right wing of the hunting-rights movement, wherein he charged, in harsh words and tones, that the spring hunt critics' clamor to save helpless bear cubs was just a smoke screen for a hidden antihunting agenda, then challenged them to a head-on battle. All of this is preserved on tape. That November '91 Wildlife Commission meeting was absolutely horrid; there was even evidence that violence might erupt, and people were searched for weapons before being allowed to enter the meeting chamber.

The upshot was that a leading critic of the spring hunt, a Boulder-area man named Michael Smith—who was not an antihunter but who nonetheless had taken the brunt of the Commission's insults—responded to the effect that "for ten years now, I've been trying to get the Division and the Commission to see that the spring hunt is bad—bad for the bears, bad for the Division, and most of all bad for hunting. It's clear now that you're *never* going to listen, so I'll take the question to the citizens of Colorado with a ballot initiative. Further, I'll recruit whomever I can get to help me win."

That meant the antihunting group Fund for Animals with its large, highly motivated membership and fat purse. Additionally, Smith withdrew his previous offer to let baiting and hounds continue in exchange for ending the spring hunt and vowed to go for the whole loaf. Thus, through its stubbornness, the CWC *invited* the national antihunting movement to join the fight.

Ironically, on two occasions before November 1992, the Division had commissioned professional polling services to measure the public's opinions on all of these issues, and on both occasions, the results accurately predicted the outcome of the ballot vote, with an overwhelming majority of the public opposed to all three issues: spring bear hunting, baiting, and hounds.

After the resounding triumph of Amendment 10, we commissioned yet another survey, dubbed the Amendment 10 Post-Election Voter Analysis, intended to discover *why* people voted the way they did. And this one should be an eye-opener for state wildlife agencies and hunters' rights groups everywhere. The primary concerns of those who voted in favor of Amendment 10 were perpetuation of the bear resource and *ethical hunter conduct*. Meanwhile, the primary issue in the minds of those who voted against the amendment was hunter rights, with hunter conduct and perpetuation of the bear resource way down the line. Another big concern among anti-10 voters was that the ballot initiative was the wrong way to answer wildlife management questions. Interestingly, the pro-10 voters felt the same way.

From both camps, then, the vote was a condemnation of the way the Commission and the Division had handled the bear-hunting issue. Public officials and agencies can get away with an awful lot, but if you really get out of step with the public pulse, and then get *arrogant* about it as well, populism is going to rise up and swat you back into place. Everyone on both sides seems to be aware of the inherent dangers of writing wildlife legislation with a ballot initiative, yet when things get bad enough, when the representative system breaks down, populism is likely to step in and squash the misguided oligarchy.

I don't share the fears of the hunters' rights groups that Amendment 10 will prove to be the precursor of a whole barrage of wildlife ballot initiatives aimed at destroying hunting. History has shown that *nobody* likes this form of legislation, and before a core group of people will go to the monumental effort and expense of collecting enough signatures to put an issue on the ballot, they must be absolutely convinced that the powers that be are horribly wrong and absolutely unreformable. Consequently, we're not going to see this happen for every little wildlife management issue that comes along.

Looking at it statistically, the number of resident hunters in Colorado is 15 percent; the number of bona fide antihunters is around 10 percent; that leaves 75 percent as nonhunters, and this majority will control every election. *That's* the group the agencies and the hunters need to listen to. And one way of doing that is to pay attention to what the antihunters are saying. I'm not suggesting that we roll over to every demand of the antihunters, but only that we should listen carefully to their charges as a way of identifying valid issues that could someday be embraced by the nonhunting majority.

I discern two different groups of antis. The first is philosophically and immutably opposed to any form of hunting. The second, and I believe far larger, group is not anti*hunting* but only anti*hunter,* their feelings based on the observed behaviors of hunters, individually and collectively. That's the group we need to listen to.

As hunters, we're a minority and always will be, and it will only be through the grace of the nonhunting majority that we're allowed to continue to pursue this ancient and essentially honorable activity. We'll never survive by continuing to rely on straw-man arguments and brute force to get our way, right or wrong. We're just too small a minority, too weak, and too often wrong. Our only hope for survival is to develop a group image and a group *reality* of even-mindedness, responsibility, and ethical behavior. Then, when we're *unfairly* challenged by antihunters, we'll have the weight of both biological science and ethics on our side, we'll be able to win the nonhunting majority over to our side, and we will persevere.

It's not the antihunters, but a few selfish and unethical *hunters* and the groups that support them who will someday kill all hunting if things don't change. Consequently, as an ethical hunter who wants to keep hunting and not be ashamed of it, I'm compelled to speak out against what I know is wrong. And for that, I've been branded a traitor by some. So be it.

In addition to the "Amendment 10 Post-Election Voter Analysis" mentioned by Beck, the Division, much to its credit, commissioned a second study in an effort to make the most of this valuable if painful learning experience. This report, titled "The Colorado Black Bear Hunting Controversy: A Case Study of Human Dimensions in Contemporary Wildlife Management" (prepared by the Department of Natural Resources, Cornell University, in consultation with the Colorado Division of Wildlife), was published in the spring of 1994 and confirms Beck's recollections of and opinions on the black bear controversy right down the line. Not surprisingly, the Cornell report comes down hard on the CWC for ignoring the dominant public sentiment as well as the recommendations of the Division's biologists, field personnel, and (belatedly) director to end spring bear hunting. From the abstract:

Perhaps states need to assess wildlife decision-making systems where an agency mandated to represent all citizens' interests in wildlife is overseen by a commission that by design disproportionately represents specific interests.

Farther on, in its "Conclusions and Implications," the report hits again on the problem of a politically appointed wildlife commission holding veto power over the Division:

We conclude that the Commission saw its role [in the black bear hunting controversy] as primarily representing traditional hunting and agricultural stakes; whereas CDOW staff attempted to incorporate broader interests among Coloradans, as reflected in survey results, with those of the traditional groups. This difference in the Commission's and the staff's use of human dimensions data may reflect an inconsistency between CDOW's mandate to manage wildlife for *all* of the people of Colorado and the appointment criteria (and therefore expectations) for the Commission. Inherent in the process of selecting commissioners is a representational bias favoring farmers, ranchers, and hunters. These are the only stake-holders specified in the selection criteria and are ensured to be represented in wildlife management decisions. Such representation is not assured for other minority interests.

In other, less tactful words, selection of Colorado's wildlife commissioners needs to be removed from the Good Old Boy arena of political appointment; I have been told by knowledgeable sources that "you needn't apply for a Commission seat unless you know the governor personally or represent a significant lobby; appointment is a political plum."

One bold attempt to reform the CWC has already been made and quashed since the passage of Amendment 10, by Sinapu, a Boulder-based group devoted to restoring wolves to Colorado wildlands. As outlined in its newsletter "Colorado Wolf Tracks," Sinapu's Commission reform proposal would

provide for new selection criteria for wildlife commissioners, so that
never again would half the Commission represent an industry (ranching) that employs less than one percent of the population. Two of the
commissioners would be biologists, and two would be elected. The
remaining four would represent, respectively, agriculture, hunting/
fishing, tourism, and biodiversity interests.

This modest, commonsense proposal was embraced by State Representative Dorothy Rupert of Boulder, who introduced a modified version
as part of a wildlife protection bill. The Rupert/Sinapu proposal was cut
down in its infancy, of course, in part at least because of rural political
prejudices against its origins in Boulder, the "New Age Capital of the
Rocky Mountain West." But perhaps now, in light of the Cornell study,
something *will* be done to remove political cronyism and agricultural
dominance from wildlife management in Colorado. As the Cornell study
summarized the problem, "The process of selecting wildlife commissioners must involve the public more comprehensively."

A more colorful view of the radically unbalanced CWC as it existed
at the time of Amendment 10 was expressed by *Denver Post* writer Bob
Ewegen. In his September 21, 1992, column, under the headline "A
Brain-Dead Political Hack Belches the Stupidest Statement of 1992,"
Ewegen wrote:

> Forthwith we doth give the Stupidest Statement of 1992 Award to
> state wildlife commissioner Eldon Cooper, for vilifying as atheists
> those citizens trying to protect lactating bears and their cubs with
> Amendment 10 on the Nov. 6 ballot. *"If you believe in the Bible, you
> must vote against this amendment,"* Cooper roared stupidly to the press
> on Sept. 17.

Eldon Cooper, of course, is the selfsame "brain-dead" Commission
chairman who railed so churlishly against Michael Smith and others at
the November 1991 public meeting and thereby directly prompted
Amendment 10. The good news: in 1994, Cooper finally retired from
the CWC.

Clearly, if the grizzly bear is ever to stand a chance of survival in
Colorado—and even with all grizzly considerations completely aside—
the Colorado Wildlife Commission must be reformed. Or, perhaps bet-

ter—given that the CWC is an expensive, cumbersome, and sometimes arrogant appendage that often works at odds with the Division, at such times giving the Division no recourse for relief other than to petition the very governor who appoints said commissioners—Colorado wildlife and Colorado citizens both might be better off if the Colorado Wildlife Commission were permanently retired; it does nothing the Division couldn't do faster, cheaper, and more democratically on its own.

Tom Beck is a bit more optimistic, forecasting the evolution of "a smarter and better balanced Wildlife Commission in the future." I hope he's right; that would be the easiest fix. For the time being, however, the slow healing process continues, laboring under the same old clunky system (minus, gladly, the biggest clunk of all).

Meanwhile, to avoid being caught ever again in a position of having inadequate data on Colorado black bears (including regional populations, sex and age ratios, longevity, mortality, vulnerability to hunting, reproduction rates, denning, habitat use, migration patterns, and other pertinent management considerations), the Division is currently embarked on a major field study, with Tom Beck at the helm.

Concerning people-bear conflicts—that prime motivator of many of the policies that culminated in Amendment 10—the Division is finally coming to recognize, it seems, that focusing all of its energies on handling "problem" bears—trapping and relocating, killing when all else fails—is fruitless so long as humans continue to create situations that invite bear problems.

"The future and hope of nuisance-bear management," Tom Beck is convinced, "lies in educating the public. We've got to create peer pressure among rural subdivision residents to keep things cleaned up. We've got to get the cooperation of county commissioners, so that when they approve new housing developments in prime bear habitat, there are covenants requiring bear-proof garbage containers and responsible behavior by residents. And these covenants must be rigidly enforced. The root of the problem is that we're leaving food out to attract bears."

I reflect on my own little mountainside subdivision, on my neighbor Cal and that goat-eating black bear that died for our collective sins. "It won't be easy," I tell Tom.

"No," he agrees, "it won't be easy. We're like an aircraft carrier trying to make a U-turn at full speed—it'll take a while. But then, the Berlin Wall eventually *did* come down."

• • •

Lessons we can hope have been learned: if the San Juan Grizzly Project, or anyone else, should ever decide to launch a serious campaign for grizzly restoration in Colorado (though no such move is currently afoot) they would do well to begin by studying the events and attitudes that precipitated Amendment 10 and use this knowledge as a road map to facilitate public and agency discussions. Thus, perhaps, they could minimize the risk of provoking a nasty Amendment 10–style showdown with opponents . . . who, in this case, would be the hard-liners of the Colorado ranching community and their powerful economic, political, and philosophical allies.

Similarly, if and when grizzly reintroduction becomes an "issue," the Colorado Division of Wildlife should do as it did with the controversy over spring black bear hunting and take the public pulse—but only, as Tom Beck has suggested, *after* the public has been fully apprised of the pertinent facts and issues on both sides of the question.

If this unbiased opinion poll shows that the people of Colorado support grizzly reintroduction, then the Division, in cooperation with the U.S. Fish and Wildlife and Forest Services, should conduct a thorough and aboveboard environmental assessment—therein inviting yet more public input—and present its recommendations to the Colorado Wildlife Commission.

And if those recommendations favor an attempted grizzly restoration, on any level, the CWC should use the lessons it *should* have learned from the Amendment 10 debacle and take the advice of the Division, listen to the will of the people, and steel itself against what is sure to be a roar of opposition from a well-organized, vocal minority.

On the other hand, if public and agency support for grizzly restoration are lacking, the great bears' champions should gracefully acknowledge defeat.

But before either eventuality can triumph, the presence of a remnant grizzly population in Colorado must be proved beyond any reasonable doubt and officially and publically acknowledged. And that remnant *must* be protected, swiftly and completely.

13

TASTING THE SOIL

The San Juan Grizzly Project Revisited

> *We need to get on the ground and taste the soil if we are to tell the story right.*
>
> —Jim Tolisano and Jim Sharman

In early August of 1993, just before embarking on my marathon Snowslide Canyon wild-grizzly chase, I went backpacking with the San Juan Grizzly Project. More than a year had passed since my initial outing with this group, and I wanted to see how the field program was evolving.

I arrived at the trailhead early and stepped into the fragrant forest, where waist-high ferns sparkled with dew. Within earshot of the road, I found a moss-covered blowdown for a backrest and took a seat on the damp ground. Thus comfortably situated, I quickly found myself mesmerized by dewdrops clinging precariously to the leaves of wild strawberries (not unlike the last few Colorado grizzlies clinging to their San Juan redoubts), running out of space, running out of time, running out of luck. Inevitably, one by one, the liquid gems slipped from their delicate perches and fell to earth, where they were immediately absorbed and as gone as if they had never been.

After a while I heard two vehicles rattling and growling up the Forest Service road. I walked over to investigate. An old beater pickup and a compact with the stereo blaring had just parked and were dislodging eager young bodies, only two of which I recognized.

I'd met Round River instructor Kevin Holladay once before, briefly. Though I hardly knew the man at all, I knew his credentials and was impressed: master's degree in interpretive ecology plus extensive field experience at Denali and Katmai National Parks in Alaska and Glacier in

Montana. Kevin was in his mid-thirties, of medium height, enviably mesomorphic, scruffy of beard, soft-spoken, serious, professional, pleasant . . . a fit successor to Jim Tolisano, who'd moved up to overseeing ecological research for all Round River field projects.

We shook hands, then Kevin provided a quick introduction to his students (whom Round River addresses as "research assistants"). Now in its third summer, the San Juan Grizzly Project had settled into a pattern of one twelve-week session overlapped by two four-week sessions. Thus research assistants—most of them college students here for the education, credits, field experience, and adventure—can come and hike and camp and search for ursine ghosts and dirty their hands in the local ecology for either a month or the full high-country summer. This group was the last for the '93 season, and the five included four in the second of their four weeks, plus one long-haul veteran.

In a whirlwind of handshaking, I learned that Rebecca and Amy were both from the Northeast and new to the Rocky Mountains. Tall, friendly C.J. from Salt Lake City introduced himself as Dennis Sizemore's stepson. Tom had recently received a degree in geology from Fort Lewis College in Durango. Kevin's fifth charge, Paul, would join us a day or two hence, hiking in with co-instructor Matt Black of Montana. Paul's grandfather had died, and he'd taken leave from his twelve weeks here to fly back to Rhode Island for the funeral.

Kevin and I consulted a topo map, and I pointed out the area I wanted to explore. It was essentially the same montane environment as the trailhead—a fecund riparian and spruce-fir understory jungle at the ankles of a spur range off the Continental Divide; a hike of a handful of easy miles. Hiking out from base camp, I hoped to find a way to the top, then explore along the narrow subalpine ridge line. It was up there, somewhere, that Rick Bass, back in 1990, had picked up that big old scat containing laboratory-confirmed grizzly hairs. I wanted to look the place over for myself, and bears or no bears, the views promised prolonged visual ecstasy. On the map, a big avalanche chute looked as if it might offer access up through an otherwise solid wall of cliffs guarding the crest; we'd camp near its base, right at ten grand.

This would be an embarrassingly easy hike compared to what Kevin's crew had been doing all summer. Even so, the area had not previously been searched for grizzly spoor, although grizzly scat and hair had been found in the vicinity. The Division had once considered it possible grizzly habitat and set a baited camera in the area. Because it was a trailless old-growth forest untouched by livestock, it provided a secluded magnet for shy wildlife and thus was one of the few places so close to a road to which an anthrophobic grizzly might risk venturing.

After about a mile, where the path fords Lower Creek, we jumped off-trail and bushwhacked up-creek, through an alder thicket where the sandy stream banks were pocked with the cloven prints of elk and deer and one clear front track of a small black bear. The latter was no great surprise; this was prime bear habitat, with giant cow parsnips, cress, sweet cicely, vetch, meadow rue, and many another edible growing in mad profusion, plus an obvious abundance of deer fawns and elk calves for the finding in spring.

Within minutes of leaving the trail, I found myself wishing for a machete. During a couple of hours of slow going, we skirted around or legged over scores of blowdown trees, weaving first nearer, then farther from the creek in search of the least problematic route. Every now and then, Kevin would hang out a strip of red engineer's tape, which Matt and Paul knew to follow and collect.

Bear sign was abundant: rotten logs ripped open, big rocks turned over, wide swaths of vegetation flattened where a bruin had charged through, and scats aplenty. The students bagged three samples even before we found a little bench near the creek we decided to call camp.

Such as it was—nary a lump-free place anywhere large enough to accommodate a tent, a conifer canopy so thick it blocked the sun almost entirely, flies swarming. Even so, it was more open and level than any-place else we'd seen, the creek was low-banked and free of the alder tangles that lined most of its course, providing easy access to the clear cool snowmelt in which swam a few small and very nervous trout, and the avalanche chute, so said my map, was within easy striking range.

It was late afternoon by the time we got the tents pitched and the evening's firewood gathered. Too late in the day to launch an exploration, so Kevin put the students to reading one of the weighty ecosophic texts they all lugged in their packs. I wasn't tired and had nothing to read and the flies were on you the moment you quit moving, so I opted for a quick hike to check out the vicinity.

Only a few minutes out of camp, while working up a gentle slope toward a cliff wall (typical for south San Juan mountain flanks), I spot-ted, a quarter mile ahead, the dark oval of a large alcove at the head of a box canyon. Always a sucker for caves, I altered course toward it, moving slowly and quietly through chest-high understory, paralleling along above a gully maybe fifty feet across and nearly as deep.

I hadn't gone far on this new course when some large animal jumped up just ahead and streaked across close in front of me, right to left, disappearing into the sheltering forest. The streaker was big but low, shaggy, and blond: a bear.

In the instant of adrenalized recognition, perhaps because of subconscious wishful thinking, my mind flashed "grizzly." But even as the possibility occurred, it melted away. This was a smallish bear even for a black, 150 pounds tops, and blondish blacks are common in the south San Juans. But then, I argued with myself, it could have been a subadult of *either* species. As certain as I was that it had been a black bear, the possibility that it *could* have been a young grizzly, no matter how remote, changed everything; suddenly, standing there alone and unarmed, I was no longer necessarily the biggest dog on the block.

For a long time I stood quietly: watching, listening, waiting for I didn't know what. Only after several minutes had passed without hearing or seeing anything more of the bear did I inch forward in hopes of picking up its trail and finding a print. Having no such luck, I backtracked and found where the animal had been shaded up beneath a spruce in the bottom of the wash. The nest was essentially identical to an elk daybed.

In the course of a long looping return hike to camp, I found more bear and elk sign, the latter everywhere. Hoof-plowed elk byways slashed through the understory this way and that, joining and diffusing and crossing in patterns that appeared helter-skelter but surely were not. Elk droppings—the formless piles that evidence grazing on soft, moist summer vegetation, looking like small cow pies but smelling a whole lot better—were ubiquitous, as were elk beds.

But I met no more bears, just one muley doe that bounded away and the normal quota of cranky gray jays. The noisy arrival of our human parade, no doubt, had driven the spooky wapiti entirely out of the tight little valley. And had any shy grizzlies been lurking about, we'd have chased them away too—an unpleasant but unavoidable side effect of large-group travel.

At dusk, my fellow campers prepared and ate a hearty hot communal feast whose finale was an instant creek-water cheesecake—while I munched a cold pittance of trail mix, dried fruit, and home-jerked elk flesh. Afterward, as the crew lazed around a modest campfire, Kevin reviewed their summer for me.

The first trip had been a nine-day, early June hump into the high country. Their intent had been to search the upper edges of the avalanche chutes that vertically striate this precipitous little mountain range, looking for bear sign in general and den sites in particular. But (I could have told them) early June proved at least a month too early to be that high after a heavy-snow winter, and they found the chutes all still clogged.

So back down they went, and out onto the aspen benches just below snow line. There, said Kevin, they found "some really good bear habitat but no bears and very little bear sign. Even down in the subalpine, I guess, we were still a little too early."

For their second effort, the searchers crossed the San Juans to the vicinity of Platoro, where they climbed under their packs and headed into some of the most remote canyons to be found east of the Divide. A couple of these, said Kevin, were "classic bear habit" but, perplexingly, held little sign.

A third outing took the Project back into the subalpine forests on the San Juan side of the Divide. "In one drainage up there," Kevin recalled, "we found thirteen bear scats, while the next drainage over held none. Hard to figure."

Now, following what had developed into a leap-frog summer, the expedition jumped back to the Rio Grande side and reentered one of the canyons they'd explored a few weeks earlier. "It looked so promising," Kevin explained. "We figured we must have been in there too early the first time, and wanted to see what it looked like in midsummer." Another disappointment.

But there were exciting moments as well.

"The simultaneous high and low point of the season for me," Kevin said, "was the morning we had a bear almost walk into our camp. We'd just finished the morning's lessons and were sitting around looking at maps and discussing our search strategy for the day. All of a sudden, one of the students, Will, said, 'Oh, my gosh . . . it's a bear!' He pointed, and there, maybe fifty yards away at the far edge of the little meadow we were camped beside, was a medium-sized bear, maybe two hundred pounds.

"The thing that excited Matt and me wasn't its size, but its light-brown coloration; we'd both seen a lot of grizzlies exactly that color. It also appeared to have small, rounded ears like a grizzly. But that was it; I looked and looked—the bear was moving gradually closer, ignoring us, and we could see pretty good detail—but I couldn't make it have a dished face or long front claws or a shoulder hump.

"So there we were, all of us staring holes through this poor bear, trying to wish it into being a grizzly. I worried that so much mental energy focused on it would scare it off. But instead, it sat down and started scratching its neck; classic displacement behavior—'I'll just pretend I'm not the least concerned that you guys are all staring at me.'

"But before long, the bear stood and loped off down the creek, disappearing into the alders. The sighting probably hadn't lasted more than a couple of minutes, but it was enough to get everybody real excited. When we were sure it was safe, we went over and searched for tracks. We finally found some fresh prints in the creek sand, and they were clearly black bear.

"For me, the experience was sobering. I've seen lots of grizzlies in Alaska and Montana, and Matt has seen lots in Glacier—and here was a bear that resembled a small grizzly but wasn't. If experienced field biologists can make that mistake, even for an instant, how many lay people who report grizzly sightings are likely wrong?

"Another time—I wasn't in on this one—Dennis Sizemore and several others got a close glimpse of a bear that Dennis said looked a lot like a grizzly. Again, its hair was the right color, but they couldn't determine whether or not it had a dished face or shoulder hump, so Dennis wrote it off as another black bear.

"My only other sighting this summer was when we saw a large, dark-colored bear from quite a ways off. No way to tell what species it was.

"Perhaps the most encouraging discovery of the summer was when Dan McNulty and John Wickersham found some huge bear scats up in a side drainage of Snowslide Canyon in the Weminuche Wilderness. Lots of water and food there, good cover, all tucked into a small pocket away from any trails. Dan and John are strong hikers and experienced woodsmen, so we sent them out on their own to reconnoiter the Weminuche. They bushwhacked into places where very few people ever go, but those big scats are the only potential grizzly evidence they found."

Yes, I thought, and they aren't worth the crap they're made of until such time as Round River can raise the big sackful of bucks necessary for mitochondria/DNA analysis.

I was glad it didn't rain that night. My ultralight packing experiment (no real food, no real tent) was pretty much a flop already, and rain would have ensured a disaster. Morning eventually came, revealing another heavy dewfall. The clouds had returned, though not nearly so magically as the day before. Rain appeared likely.

Since we expected a long hard day of hiking and climbing, Kevin agreed to forego the morning lessons. We rushed through breakfast (for them, oatmeal, toast, and jam; for me, a fistful of trail mix, dried apricots, and a swig of Tang), filtered some creek water into our canteens, stuffed a few essentials into our day packs, and struck out to conquer the top of the world. Rebecca, not feeling quite up to snuff, elected to stay in camp and read and nap.

Off we went—Kevin, Amy, C.J., Tom, and me. We retraced my path of the evening before, at their request, so that I could reconstruct the bear sighting for them and we could explore the big cave. The cave proved to be shallow and void of any sign of life save for rat scats and a few deer tracks in the dusty floor. From there, we paralleled along just below the cliffs, looking for a way up—which, it turned out, the big avalanche chute did not offer; it, too, was stoppered at the top by impassable cliffs.

On we hiked, picking up a weighty wealth of bear scats as we went, most of which went into dynamo Tom's pack. On one little bench just below a major game trail, in the midday shade of an old-growth spruce, we found a well-used bear bed, double-wide, with a big pile of big-bear scats at one end, a little pile of little-bear scats at the other. Into the bag with the lot.

Eventually, we came to a deep sidehill drainage that held some promise in that we couldn't see any cliffs above us. Trouble was, we couldn't see its top. Only one way to find out, so up we went, huffing along the cluttered bottom of the drainage until it narrowed and petered out, then switchbacking up a final stretch so steep that we found ourselves clawing hand over foot, with abundant deadfall to negotiate for added amusement.

But all things pass, and eventually we topped out on a narrow side ridge angling up toward the ultimate crest and agreed to break for lunch before making the final push. The view from the far side of this anony-

mous spine was long and green and wild, offering the greatest expanse of
nothing-but-trees I'd yet seen in the lower reaches of the south San
Juans. Plenty of room for bears to roam undisturbed and undetected. Or
so it appeared from above.

Onward.

For a while our little ridge remained wide enough to trail along
confidently. But soon we encountered the first of what became a chain of
big conglomerate hoodoos. Skirting around these natural roadblocks via
the treacherous scree slopes at their flanks was just dicey enough to be
interesting.

Circumnavigations one and two went well enough, but while scrambling around the third hoodoo, I heard a strange little sound behind me.
I turned to see Amy frozen midslope, hands and boots clutching desper-
ately to the scree, letting slip a little whimper with every hyperventilated
breath. She was, both mentally and physically, petrified.

And then it started raining.

I called for the others, and we encircled Amy protectively, offering
what clumsy reassurance and encouragement we could. The slope Amy
was stuck on, I pointed out, while steep and high—we were well above
eleven grand—was not so very dangerous; a fall would mean a rough
tumble of a few dozen yards, at which point trees would intervene.
Maybe a few bruises, but no worse. Probably. It was not, in my view, a
life-threatening situation.

But my view didn't count. Amy lived at sea level and was new to real
mountains and had no previous experience with scree skating; she'd gone
to her limit and beyond without a word of complaint, and even the
whimpers were involuntary. No one found fault, nor was there any fault
to find; this was no Iron Person contest. Still, our climb was stifled, our
quest unfulfilled.

Gentleman C.J. took Amy's hand and led her off the scree and down
into the trees, and the crisis was over. Not yet soaking wet, I donned my
rain poncho, while the others produced—umbrellas! Lavender, blue, and
yellow, these grizzly hunters beneath their parasols looked more like a
bunch of Morton salt girls. It was to laugh. At least at first. But after
we'd hiked long enough that I'd become sweat-soaked beneath my clingy
nylon tarp, I began to wonder.

"We discovered this by accident early in the summer," Kevin explained. "You can buy these things for three bucks at Kmart; they weigh

nothing and fold down small enough to fit easily into a day pack. I'll never hike without an umbrella again."

Nor will I, I suppose, though I'll try to find one less bright and gay.

Kevin glanced at his watch and suggested that a good way to rescue the remainder of the day would be to conduct a few "plot surveys." The three research assistants seconded that motion, walked off a ways with purpose, dumped their packs, set aside their umbrellas, extracted steel tapes and notebooks and pencils and charts and magnifying glasses, and went to work. Conveniently, the thundershower had passed.

I took a seat and asked Kevin to explain what was up.

"Circular plot sampling," he said, "is an important part of an extensive biotic inventory we're conducting to assemble a useful body of on-the-ground information about the San Juans. Bruce Baizel has been talking with Rick Metzger, the Rio Grande Forest biologist, who says that by the end of next summer Round River will have a more detailed insight into the ecology of the San Juans than the Forest Service, which has pretty much restricted its efforts to timber surveys.

"We choose plots more or less at random, selecting spots that are representative of a larger area—including scree slopes, alpine tundra, subalpine, and montane forest types. When we come to a likely spot—like right here—we stop, then take fifty paces in any random direction, and that becomes the center point for a circular plot tape-measured at thirty-six feet in diameter. We divide that pie into four equal slices, and four research assistants—three today—conduct the survey, using a standardized biotic inventory form.

"The inventory starts with a general site description that includes altitude, aspect, and slope. We then assign a biotic community type according to the guidelines in David Brown's *Biotic Communities of the Southwest*—subalpine grasslands, montane coniferous meadow, and so on, as determined by altitude and dominant plant types. Next we measure the quantities of dead and down wood and count the standing trees, cataloging them by species and height and recording their diameters at dbh [data base height, about four feet up the trunk] and the percentage of overstory, or canopy, they provide.

"Next we look at the density of ground cover and inventory the plant types in that cover. We measure the depth and composition of the soil litter, including the percentage of rock. We have a list of plants that are important foods for bears, and we carefully identify and count all of those we can find. We also search for insects and other invertebrates, ground squirrel tunnels, and such, assessing the potential grizzly prey base. In fact, we record all wildlife spoor for all identifiable species, such as deer and elk tracks, beds, and droppings.

"And, of course, we look for bear sign: beds, scats, hairs, tracks, and digs. Finally, we rate the overall quality of the area as grizzly habitat. This rating is simultaneously quantitative, qualitative, and subjective; all things considered, does the area appear to be poor, good, or excellent habitat?

"In addition to the plot samples, on a larger, forest-wide scale, we use a 'disturbance index' to measure such negative influences as soil erosion along ATV trails, litter, grazing impacts, mining and logging disturbances, and so on.

"And that's the quick-and-dirty of it."

Hardly quick, what with three people having been working in that one little circle for half an hour and still at it. But dirty, yes; down on hands and knees, probing, sniffing, even tasting the soil. I was impressed.

I asked Kevin how many such plots they'd cataloged over the summer.

"We're not done yet, but let's see—three months, with at least twenty days a month spent in the field. That's sixty days at six plots a day. Conservatively, by summer's end we'll have sampled three hundred plots."

"And then?"

"We plan to convert the raw data into biotic maps using a standardized computer program. That done, we'll make the information available to the Forest Service and other management agencies, updating it every summer. It could prove useful not just in determining the quality of various parts of the San Juans as grizzly habitat but in a broad variety of other applications as well. Our goal out here, in addition to finding proof of living grizzlies, is to help forest planners and wildlife managers make wise decisions based on reliable, up-to-date biological information."

Such a deal for the agencies—Round River doing their work for them, for free—*if* said agencies will only condescend to accept such "nonprofessional and possibly biased" data. Could be; Rio Grande National Forest planners, I hear, have been meeting and talking with Round River of late, and forest chief Jim Webb seems open to change. We'll see.

"Bottom line," Kevin concluded, "is that we're concerned with a lot more out here than just grizzlies. We use the bear as our flagship species because the grizzly is a universal metaphor for wildness. We could just as easily use the wolverine or the lynx or even some endangered invertebrate, but the grizzly gets people's attention like nothing else, gets everyone excited.

"The ultimate question we're raising is: How wild do we want the San Juans to be? Whether the grizzly is here or not, the information we're collecting is invaluable as a tool to help protect the San Juans; it stands alone as a measure of the current wildness of the ecosystem and reveals its potential for the future."

When the students finished and walked away from their plot, you couldn't tell they'd ever been there—low-impact, high-yield field biology. After we hiked back down into the alder biome along the creek and the students located another sample plot, I asked Kevin, "Just how wild *are* the San Juans? Do you think these mountains can continue to conceal and nurture a minimal viable population of grizzlies?"

"We've spent a lot of time this summer in high lush canyons and up on the alpine tundra in places without trails," Kevin began, "hiking for as long as nine days at a stretch without seeing other people and few if any signs of human activity. Judging from those experiences, together with my academic background in biology and my experience in grizzly country, there's no question in my mind that there's plenty of room up here for a few grizzlies to live and roam without getting into trouble or even being seen. We only need to give them a little respect, a little slack, a little elbow room."

This reminded me of something Doug Peacock wrote in *Grizzly Years:* "I wonder why the park and forest services have not figured out that if you leave every other backcountry drainage without trails, you create entire regions to which animals like grizzlies can escape during the peak months of human travel."

Here in the south San Juans, that would not be *physically* hard to arrange; in fact, one of the features that makes the southern mountains so much wilder than the Weminuche is that there *are* entire drainages void of trails. But hardly every other drainage, and it could be a political nightmare trying to get rid of even a few existing trails. Once people, especially horse and ATV people, become accustomed to using trails, they'll fight like devils to keep them open.

"Concerning habitat quality," Kevin continued, "the San Juans are as rich as anyplace in North America."

But what, I asked, about the arguments that (a) the San Juans are too small to accommodate a reintroduced "viable population" of grizzlies, and (b) there are too few native grizzlies left to be genetically viable without augmentation?

"I think we can look to Europe for a hopeful paradigm. I'm encouraged that in Romania, in the Abruzzo Mountains of Italy, and in other heavily populated areas, there are small isolated populations of brown bears that have learned to live among people and livestock and almost never get into trouble. Even more importantly, the people in these places, most of whom take their livings from the land, have learned to live with the bears; mutual acceptance born of necessity. It's generally believed that any surviving San Juan grizzlies have evolved to be extraordinarily shy and primarily nocturnal—exactly like the European brown bears. Nor, apparently, have these little island populations suffered any negative effects from inbreeding.

"All of this bears directly on the San Juans and is encouraging. So yes, I think there's plenty of room here for a small population of grizzlies. Flying over the San Juans, especially the south San Juans, or looking at a map, this ecosystem appears pretty small. But after hiking and climbing through these mountains all summer, they seem huge, remote, and wild. It's like Jim Tolisano says: in order to really know a place, you've got to get down on the ground and taste it."

After a couple more days of poking around with Kevin and his crew—during which we never did find a way up through the cliffs and Matt and Paul finally arrived—I said my so longs and hiked out alone.

All the good work the San Juan Grizzly Project has done notwithstanding, I've accrued some nagging worries during the three years and more I've watched its progress.

I worry, for instance, about the instructor turnover. Although Jim Tolisano remains one of the driving wheels of Round River, he is no longer involved day-to-day with the Grizzly Project. And since my brief outing with them last summer, Kevin Holladay and Matt Black have both moved on to other endeavors.

Moreover, with simultaneous projects in Colorado, Arizona (wolves),

Honduras (jaguars), and British Columbia (old-growth forests), plus a start-up planned soon for the La Sal Mountains of Utah (cougars)—with all these far-flung overlapping efforts, I worry that Round River's energies may be spread too thin.

Then there's the ongoing chore of recruiting enough students to keep the research ship afloat and pay the bills. Round River's field programs, of necessity, are not free; they're not even cheap. Will the students keep coming?

Moreover, after three years working in the San Juans, the Grizzly Project is still considered by both the Division and the feds as mildly suspect, a status no private-sector advocacy group is ever likely to rise above. And this notwithstanding that the Project has performed professionally and honorably throughout.

Of less importance, perhaps, but still worrisome to me are the limitations of the group approach to ghost chasing. Jim Tolisano's tactic of having search groups of two or three fan out daily from a mobile base camp seems tenable but isn't workable for every group, for every student. Even getting to useful high-country base camps is limited by the abilities of the group's least-capable member.

Finally—this is my most profound concern—potential conclusive evidence of a living grizzly presence in the San Juans (mostly in the formless form of scat samples) is literally growing mold waiting to be processed. DNA analysis has thus far proven too rich for Round River's limited budget—something like $20,000 just to establish a database and get the ball rolling. Meanwhile, hair samples have become essentially useless since the feds have refused to accept them as conclusive proof, in effect impaling Round River on the horns of a dilemma, with the necessity for DNA analysis on the one side, its financial inaccessibility on the other.

With these concerns and more weighing on my mind, I phoned Round River projects coordinator Bruce Baizel, warned him I was going to play devil's batboy, then read him my worry list. He listened quietly, then responded right down the line.

"Granted," said Bruce, "keeping top-notch instructors is an ongoing challenge, but it's not unique to Round River. The combination we look for is appropriate education and field experience, self-motivation, leadership and people skills, plus an ability to work within a fairly relaxed organizational structure. We also need people with the physical stamina and outdoor skills to spend an entire summer camping and backpacking in the mountains, no matter the weather.

"That's a demanding and specialized wish list, and there aren't all that many folks around who fill the bill. Last winter, we had to fire two instructors from our Arizona program. That was bitter medicine but a valuable learning experience as well. One of the upshots was that we asked the affected students to put together a job description detailing what qualities *they* want in an instructor, and we now factor those things in as well. There is, fortunately, a small pool of excellent people out there, and it's our challenge and responsibility to find them.

"As for retention—we're dealing with young, highly qualified people, some of whom are working toward established career goals. Not many people can make a career of working at nonprofit-level wages, although we try to be competitive. It's become clear that to be successful as a Round River instructor, you have to *want* to be doing this kind of work. It can't be just another job, or you won't last. The other side of this issue is that we have to work to find ways to avoid the burnout that so often dogs the field research professions. We think we can develop a rotation and mix of work that will prevent this.

"With all that said, I believe we've got a couple of excellent field leaders for the '94 San Juan season. John Wickersham has finished his Ph.D. course work and is writing his dissertation, which explores the way people in the West react to grizzlies. In the summer of '93, John volunteered to go on an extensive bushwhack with intern Dan McNulty; as our point team, they went places larger groups and less physically capable individuals could never go, scouring some of the most remote pockets of the Weminuche, slipping in and out without causing any noticeable disturbance to the environment. John is one of the stronger woodsmen we've had.

"Our second Grizzly Project instructor this summer is Dwight Barry. Dwight is working on his master's in conservation biology at Yale but is a Colorado native; his wife, in fact, is from Durango. Dwight's strong biological background is the perfect complement to John's varied skills.

"Concerning student recruitment, last summer we had four students in the first four-week program, one for the whole summer, and four in the second program, for a total of forty-four student weeks. This year, we have four twelve-week students, one for the first month-long program, and five for the second, for a total of seventy-two student weeks. That's approaching our maximums. Former students have provided our best advertising, and if the trend continues, by the summer of 1995 the San Juan Grizzly Project will have a student waiting list.

"Regarding the danger of spreading ourselves too thin—so long as we can continue to recruit first-rate instructors for all of our projects, there's no strain. Our goal all along has been to maintain field projects in a variety of locations where we see pressing ecological concerns not being addressed by the responsible agencies. Each project takes on its own personality, and I view that diversity as a strength, not a weakness.

"As to group size, discounting occasional visitors like yourself, we've never gone out with more than eight, instructors included. Granted, even a group that size, as you experienced last summer, can sometimes be clumsy and limiting. It is, however, a good size for combing a large area fast, and it facilitates broad-scale biotic plot sampling. Meanwhile, we'll continue sending teams of two or three of our most capable people into the more remote and difficult places. And to minimize disruption of potential grizzly enclaves, John and Dwight plan to concentrate this summer on refining and employing techniques of low-impact, low-visibility camping; we want our camps to be paradigms for what grizzly-country camps should be.

"Concerning the future direction of the Grizzly Project—the questions of 'Are there grizzlies in the San Juans, and if so, how many?' are symbolic of the bigger question of *how we relate to the land.* As the Project has evolved, we've changed our perceptions somewhat regarding all of these concerns. In hindsight, looking back to 1991 when we first launched the search, we may not have been ready to deal with rapid success. We hadn't yet thought through the next steps to be taken after finding proof of grizzlies in the San Juans. Nor were the agencies prepared to deal with a grizzly suddenly dropped in their laps.

"Now, after three years of being continually reminded that yes, there *are* a few native grizzlies left in the San Juans, the agencies are finally starting to come around. The Forest Service, in particular, seems interested in what we have to say, and even the Division is talking seriously about grizzlies, if only internally. These things would never have happened without the San Juan Grizzly Project. Only the U.S. Fish and

Wildlife Service remains reluctant to talk about Colorado grizzlies, notwithstanding the token mentions of the San Juans in their Grizzly Bear Recovery Plan.

"And too, we've come to realize that the agencies are going to be the significant players in grizzly management, here as elsewhere. What we're working toward now is to have specific, workable recommendations for grizzly and habitat management ready to submit simultaneously with proof of the bears' existence.

"Concerning proof, as you suggest, Round River has been pushed into a corner in that the only evidence the agencies will accept—other than a bulletproof photograph of a grizzly or a grizzly track in an identifiable locale in the San Juans, neither of which we're liable to be lucky enough to come by—is DNA. Modern mitochondria analysis can nail down not just species but regional subspecies and perhaps even local family groups, surmounting the suspicions of fraud that dog hair samples. But DNA analysis, so far, has proven financially beyond our grasp, leading to a backlog of potentially conclusive evidence. We plan to make the resolution of that problem a priority in the coming months; if we can't raise the money or work something out with the DNA lab in Salt Lake City, we may approach the feds to explore the possibility of them doing the DNA work. We don't know if they will, and right now we don't even know if they can, but we intend to ask.

"Those are our primary goals for the immediate future: moving forward with processing existing evidence, and adjusting our field methodologies to minimize intrusions and maximize the usefulness of our data."

In all of this, I wish the San Juan Grizzly Project all the luck in the world. They're going to need it.

14

GHOST GRIZZLIES

Is There Is, or Is There Ain't?

> *What is it that slides invisibly among my*
> *thoughts? . . . Always at the corner of my eye,*
> *just beyond the focus of my vision, something*
> *moves, disappearing when I turn toward it.*
> —Edward Abbey

Here is the story as it was told to me.

On a morning in late June 1993, Arthur Trujillo of Denver was backpacking in the south San Juans. It was his second day out, and he was just approaching the alpine tundra. Hiking alone, off-trail, in a place so high and rugged is not an activity likely to appeal to many. But Arthur Trujillo was not new to the area; he is a vigorous off-trail hiker who explores the south San Juans every summer armed with a camera, then returns with a rifle each fall to hunt elk.

The Trujillo roots, in fact, go deep into local history, with Arthur's forebears among the beneficiaries of the original Tierra Amarilla land grant of 1832, though they were never able to settle there owing to the fierce resistance of local Indians. Arthur tells of one relative who, in the 1880s, went exploring alone into the T.A., returning home a few days later considerably the worse for wear. Indians—Southern Utes or Jicarilla Apaches—had ventilated the unfortunate Trujillo with arrows, woven his hands and jacket sleeves into his horse's tail, and sent the horse trotting homeward. Trujillo Meadows, Trujillo Reservoir, and a Forest Service campground on Los Pinos River above Cumbres Pass all are named for this old-line Hispanic family.

But on this June morning in 1993, there was no threat of Indian hostilities. In fact, danger of any kind was the last thing on Arthur Trujillo's mind as he hiked over undulating, hill-and-gully tundra beneath an overcast sky. Then the bear appeared, shuffling up a gully directly toward him: a big, light-brown bruin with dark legs, rump, and head, and grizzled guard hairs across a muscular back. Trujillo describes the beast as being the second-largest bear he's ever seen, and slightly bigger than the biggest (640-pound) grizzly of three at the Denver Zoo —a lot of bear.

At first, the beast seemed unaware of the man. Then, at a distance Arthur says he later paced off as a knee-knocking twelve yards, the animal either saw or scented him, stopped suddenly, stared, then started "bouncing up and down on its front legs and huffing. I could see its muscles rippling with every move." Only later would Trujillo reflect that he "might have been only a heartbeat away from becoming bear shit."

But the hiker stood his ground, and after a while, the bear simply turned and walked away. Trujillo dove into his pack for his 35mm camera and attached a big 500mm reflector lens. Lacking a tripod to steady a tube that long, he dropped down and rested the cannonlike lens on one knee. Rather than trying to pan the moving bear, the experienced amateur photographer picked a spot ahead of the animal and focused and metered on a patch of dwarf willows there. When the bear entered the frame, at a distance Arthur estimates at about 150 yards, he fired the shutter. The animal topped a rise and was gone before the photographer could set up for another shot.

The result was a well-composed, properly exposed and focused image of a distant bear that not only looks very much like a grizzly but closely resembles the Wiseman sow: dark brown legs and face, light brown body with silvery guard hairs, stocky build, a distinct hump of shoulder, and a clearly dished facial profile.

Only the one ear that shows in the photo looks possibly wrong. It's long and pointed, rather than short and rounded like typical grizzly ears. In fact, the ear is too long and pointed for *any* species of bear, more canine than ursine. Close inspection of a transparency made from the photo and projected on a screen reveals that a small dark rock lying on the ground behind the bear—the area is clearly littered with them— lines up just so to create the optical illusion of a long, pointed ear. The true ear profile appears to be short and rounded.

But, of course and as usual, none of these physical features—color, build, hump, facial profile—nor even all taken together, is conclusive.

Color is a notoriously unreliable ursine species identifier, with both black and grizzly bears ranging from black to blond. Similarly, a black bear will often appear to have a shoulder hump when its head is held low, as when feeding. The Trujillo bear's head, however, is held in a neutral walking position and a distinct hump is still present, with the shoulders noticeably higher than the hips.

According to Colorado bear biologist Tom Beck, not even the length, curvature, and coloration of a bear's front claws are always definitive when viewed from a distance. As Beck pointed out while we were examining bear remains at the Denver Museum of Natural History recently, some grizzlies have claws as dark and short—the latter character due largely to digging wear—as some exceptionally long- and light-clawed black bears. Furthermore, a given bear's claws can appear alternately light or dark under differing conditions of illumination. The claws on the Trujillo bear are obscured by angle and vegetation.

While Tom Beck's impeccably cautious approach to species identification is scientifically laudable, not all bear experts agree that such "pedantic specificity" is necessary. They argue that a combination of physical features, the grizzly *gestalt,* if you will—including build, color, hump, dished face, and long front claws—can generally be trusted to identify a bear as black or grizzly. And even Tom Beck won't say the Trujillo bear is definitely *not* a grizzly, but only that "there's absolutely no way I could make a convincing argument either way."

Concerning the similarity of the Trujillo bear's coloration to that of the Wiseman grizzly, Beck explains that the south San Juans are home to some very large black bears, with varying shades of brown being the dominant color. Further, "a lot of our brown-colored black bears have dark legs in summer because of differential molting and hair bleaching," frequently fading during the course of the summer to full blond. This phenomenon, says Beck, can produce a multicolored black bear with dark legs and head and a light, even blond back—mimicking typical grizzly markings. Furthermore, this grizzly-chameleon cycle peaks in late June, precisely when the Trujillo photo was taken.

"The minute I saw that picture," Beck told me, "I predicted it had been taken the last week of June."

Doug Peacock feels it could go either way, admitting that he's been "totally fooled a few times when looking at bears from a distance," but adds that in his opinion, "the likelihood is far greater that it's a grizzly than not." Likewise, I'm told by an informed source in Denver that "most agency biologists who view the photo feel it's a grizzly."

Whatever the species of the big bear, this was the fourth possible grizzly sighting Arthur Trujillo has reported from the same general area of the south San Juans in recent years, albeit the first time he was able to get a photo. Observations one and two came in fall 1990 and spring 1991, and in both cases, says Trujillo, were big bears that looked to him like grizzlies.

But more exciting, says Arthur, was his third sighting, which occurred in October 1991—exactly one year later and in the same general area of the Schutz sighting, and not all that far, says Arthur, from where his June 1993 photo was taken. Trujillo says he was out elk hunting that autumn day and had climbed long and high. As he approached the rim of a cliff, hoping for a panoramic peek down into the Tierra Amarilla, he heard a considerable commotion below. He crept up and peered over the ledge and saw, some twenty yards below him, "a *much* larger bear than any others I've ever seen, in the wild or in a zoo."

In his field notes, Arthur recorded that this behemoth brown-colored bear had a large shoulder hump, was silver-tipped across its back, and appeared quite agitated. He suspects the bruin sensed his presence but couldn't pinpoint him and was taking his angst out on the local scenery: body-slamming and clawing trees, pawing the ground, and "snorting and farting" loudly. Big piles of fresh bear scat lay here and there, suggesting—whatever the bear's species—that Trujillo had probably stumbled upon the immediate area of the bruin's winter den just prior to bedtime.

Trujillo reported this third sighting to the Colorado Division of Wildlife, as he had the first two, and was dismayed that "nobody was interested enough to go back up there with me." Trouble was, it was elk hunting season and a frantically busy time of year for Division personnel.

Division officials say they've never doubted that Trujillo was seeing some big bears he thinks are grizzlies. But then, there could hardly be as many grizzlies in the San Juans as people report seeing every year; everyone these days, it seems, is on the lookout for forest ghosts. Moreover, it struck the Division as a little odd that one man made three sightings within the space of a single year—fall of 1990 through fall of 1991, and a fourth less than two years later—while no one else has reported seeing a grizzly in that area in recent years.

But then, most folks who hike or ride horseback through that rugged terrain stay on or near established trails and tend to travel in chatty pairs or noisy groups. Contrarily, Arthur Trujillo generally hunts and hikes alone, moves quietly, and travels extensively off-trail. Further, whether or not there have been other grizzly sighting reports in the same area depends on your interpretation of "area"; both the Schutz sighting and the Wiseman grizzly fight took place only a handful of miles from where Trujillo says he took his photo.

In any event, Trujillo's picture got the Division's rapt attention. When Arthur returned to the San Juans in October of 1993 for elk season, Pagosa district wildlife manager Glen Eyre and Division spokesman Todd Malmsbury from Denver met him with three horses, hoping he could lead them to "the place." Of necessity, the trio headed for the area of the sighting by a different route than Arthur had taken on his leisurely and circuitous backpacking trip back in June. Consequently, says Trujillo, nothing looked familiar.

In the end, the three men rode for several hours without finding a vista that matched the sparse alpine scenery in the photo, though by the time they called off the search both Trujillo and Eyre felt they were "getting close."

It was a great disappointment, and a little perplexing. Even so, Trujillo's inability to home directly to the photo site didn't entirely destroy warden Eyre's faith that the shot had in fact been taken in the south San Juans.

Nor mine. The picture looks like hundreds of places in the San Juans, while bearing no resemblance whatsoever to anything I've seen in Yellowstone, Glacier, Canada, or Alaska—none of which places Trujillo says he's ever visited. Moreover, Glen and I both know from personal experience how difficult it can be to navigate back to a specific off-trail spot, especially when you weren't paying any attention to how you got there the first time.

Even so . . .

Meanwhile, in Denver, after inspecting the five-by-seven-inch color print Trujillo provided to the Division, chief big game biologist Rick Kahn asked Arthur to send the negative so a computer-enhanced enlargement could be made and studied. Trujillo says he put the small negative in an envelope along with a letter, a map, and a drawing of the bear's tracks, and mailed it first-class across town to Division headquarters. When the envelope arrived at Kahn's office, one corner was ripped open and the negative was missing.

"It looks like it happened in the postal machinery," Kahn told me. "The postmark is partially on the envelope and partially on the papers inside. Come look at it for yourself if you want."

I didn't want; stuff happens, especially at the post office, and I suspect no foul play though others may choose to. Instead, I arranged for a springtime flyover of the area. In an hour or so of air time, bear picture and topographical maps in hand, I hoped to locate the scene of the Trujillo photo and get a panoramic overview of the many places I've visited on horseback and afoot in recent summers.

But first:

In February 1994 I met Tom Beck at the Denver Museum of Natural History to examine the Wiseman bear's remains and reconfirm Tom's original proclamation, made shortly after the old lady was killed in 1979, that the enlarged size and darkened pigmentation of her teats provided immutable physical proof that she had suckled cubs at some time during her life. Even though other wildlife biologists who've examined the hide have confirmed Beck's opinion, Tom had since studied more than a hundred additional female bears and wanted another look.

The reproductive history of the Wiseman sow is, of course, critical to forecasting the continued existence of grizzlies in Colorado; if she was barren, she might well have been the last San Juan grizzly. For that reason, Denver Museum curator of mammals Dr. Cheri Jones, Montrose area wildlife manager Mike Mclain, and I watched as Beck inspected the hide and found . . . nipples almost as large as pencil erasers and black as you like.

"You can quote me," proclaimed the most conservative wildlife biologist I know, "that this bear *definitely* nursed young at some time during her life."

But how long ago? That is, how old might the cubs be today if any survive?

Estimates of the Wiseman grizzly's age vary widely. According to a dental-cementum-annuli count (a procedure analogous to tallying the growth rings of trees), she was "at least sixteen" when she died. Other estimates run as high as twenty-four. As we examined the hide and skeleton of this most recent "last" Colorado grizzly, I asked Tom for his all-things-considered opinion.

"Old," he said. "I don't give much credence to the dental-cementum estimate of sixteen, even as a minimum. It's not all that reliable an aging technique for ursids to begin with, and the ability to accurately age a bear by its teeth decreases dramatically with age. It's my gut feeling, considering her overall physical condition, that the Wiseman grizzly was probably in her mid-twenties when she died."

I am no wildlife pathologist, but it's hard to look at all the dental problems—severe wear and cavernous abscesses—the healed-over battle scars on jaw and shoulder, and the gruesome arthritic gnarling of virtually every joint in her skeleton, and still accept that the Wiseman grizzly was only sixteen, barely middle-aged. Clearly, this bear was, as Tom Beck so succinctly puts it, "old."

That established, if we were to assume that the Wiseman sow gave birth early in life and only once, her cubs would by now be almost a decade beyond the mid-twenties life expectancy for wild grizzlies. (There are exceptions: The U.S. Fish and Wildlife Service's griz guru, Dr. Christopher Servheen, told me of one northern Rockies sow that was thirty-five and still kicking when she went into den in the fall of 1994, though she's an anomaly.)

But what if the Wiseman sow gave birth late in life—say the early or mid-1970s? In that case, her cubs could still be around. And who's to say that she had only one litter during all those years? Further, even if all her original offspring are dead, the Wiseman grizzly's grandcubs would still be in their prime today. In fact, they could well be the selfsame bears Arthur Trujillo, Dennis Schutz, and others have reported seeing in recent years.

That "others" includes Rick Lapin, who operates the upper Banded Peak Ranch, just above Dennis Schutz's digs, on the Tierra Amarilla. Says Lapin: "I truly believe there are a few grizzlies left up here. I *think* I ran into a sow and two cubs back in the early fall of 1987. It was one of those 'you see, you run' deals. A cousin and I were working over in one of the high back valleys, opening up an old logging road that hadn't been used in twenty years or so, when I heard what sounded like a couple of sheep bleating. I wandered across the creek and up the hill toward a big berry patch to check it out.

"The bleating continued, and the next thing I knew a little bear cub, just a baby, came streaking out of the brush, skidded to a stop not far from me, stood up on his hind legs, looked at me, and went *ba-a-a-a.* When he spun around and ran back into the brush, I realized that he'd been calling for his momma and I'd better get the hell out of there.

"About then, my cousin Charley came up behind me and asked what was going on. As I was telling him about the cub, I saw a huge, chocolate brown bear's head—the ears on it were a good eight or ten inches apart, a *big* head—rise from about twenty yards away and start swaying back and forth, trying to get our scent. I said to Charley, 'She's over there,' and started backing up. Charlie says, 'Where? Where? Oh my God!' and we both ran back across the river.

"We returned the next day and looked the place over, and I found the sow's tracks where she'd been standing down in a gully and had reared up so that I could see her head. I went down and stood exactly where she'd been and couldn't see over the tops of the bushes. That meant that when she reared up, in order for me to see her entire head from where I was standing, she must have stood over eight feet tall. One clear hind track measured about nine inches from the rear of the heel pad to the front of the toes, with claw marks way out front of the toes; a big bear. I've always felt certain those bears were grizzlies.

"Another time—this was quite a few years ago—my mother-in-law was fishing up near the top of the ranch, not far from where Ed Wiseman met his bear. She'd caught some trout and left them lying in the snow while she continued fishing on downstream. When she returned later, the fish were gone and there were tracks in the snow and in the wet sand, the latter still filling with water. They looked to her like grizzly tracks, with claw marks way out front of the pads. Our ranch superintendent, Johnny Miller, was with her, and he felt certain it was a grizzly. Johnny's been here for sixty years, and he knows his bears.

"I hope we're right. The grizzly is welcome here."

MAY 11, 1994: SOUTH SAN JUANS, COLORADO

Ace mountain pilot Mike Schlarb and I meet early for a stick-to-your-arteries breakfast at Oscar's Cafe, one of the last old-style diners left in recently Californicated Durango. Oscar's is the kind of place where lazy blue smoke from hand-rolled cigarettes spices the atmosphere, '50s nostalgia seeps from an invisible jukebox ("For yourrrr pre-shus lu-u-uv"), and the clientele dine in T-shirts bearing such universal proletariat sentiments as "Work sucks—I'm going to the lake!"

After breakfast, we drive out to the Val-Air glider park in the Animas Valley just north of town, preflight, gas up, and take off from a grass runway. (In an airplane, of course.)

Half an hour later, Mike sits the single-engine tail-dragger down at the Pagosa Springs airstrip, where we take on ballast in the form of Glen Eyre and Dennis Schutz. A few minutes more and we're skimming along low above the glittering, snow-bound Continental Divide. As always, no matter the perspective, I am awestruck by the raw beauty of these rocky old massifs.

After a few minutes, Glen directs Mike to bank right and follow a little hiccup of mountains jutting out from the Divide like the spur on a wild turkey's leg. In moments we're over the area where Arthur Trujillo says he took the photo that has recently caused so much excitement and confusion in Denver. But there's still a lot of snow, and try as we may, circling time and again, we can't see anything that looks just right.

"It may be down there," I shout to Glen above the roar of the engine as Mike climbs sharply to vault us over the saw-toothed rim of the spur range and down into the valley of the Navajo River, "but we're not going to see it today." We all agree that if the place is ever to be verified, it will probably have to be done on horseback or afoot. Unfortunately, Arthur Trujillo has moved to Idaho and won't be around to help. Until the place can be found, the Trujillo photo is doomed to remain stuck in a purgatory of official doubt.

We droned on up the narrowing valley, following the white thread of the Navajo into a V-necked canyon a thousand feet deep. Even though Mike has been climbing at a steady rate of five hundred feet per minute, we're about to run out of sky in front of us, with crumbling gray conglomerate cliffs looming *above* us—to port, starboard, and dead ahead. I'm thinking we *might* make it when Mike mumbles "Nope" and dips the left wing to crank us around down-canyon.

Now Mike pulls up and grinds into a patient spiraling climb, going for altitude enough to lift us safely above the stone teeth all around. (There are old pilots, and bold pilots, but not many old bold pilots.)

Mike's prudent caution in this butt-puckering kind of flying is more than commendable, it is critical.

"Feels strange to see this place from the air again," says Glen from the cramped backseat.

I'll bet it does. Down below the cliffside ledge, directly beneath us now, near where Ed Wiseman fought his griz, Glen points out a narrow shelf where he spent a frigid February night a few years ago after the helicopter in which he was riding during a bighorn sheep count "popped a fuel line" and crashed. I jockeyed choppers for five years in the Marines, and peering down there now I can't imagine how Glen's pilot managed to put his wounded bird down safely. Glen, like a lot of experienced Division people, rarely volunteers to ride in helicopters these days.

I identify the Wiseman site, then ask Mike to bank right and head for "Grizzly Lake." As we approach, I look but fail to see. I know it's down there, somewhere, but it escapes me until Dennis points it out, still hiding under a melt-wrinkled blanket of snow with only the distinctive little clump of spruce around which I watched that horny September bull chase his reluctant date whiskering up from the plain of white to reveal the lake's sleeping presence.

On the flight back down the Navajo, we dally briefly above "Willow Creek," circling a couple of times, enjoying a raven's-eye view of the place where Dennis saw his big-bear family three and a half years ago. No bruins down there at the moment, nor any tracks in the immediate area.

But there *are* bears out and about. In several of the many avalanche chutes we've overflown this morning—including one in the general area where the Trujillo photo was supposedly taken, one near Willow Creek, and one in the Navajo canyon almost directly across from the Wiseman site—big, roundish, obviously ursine tracks emerge from the trees just below timberline, then beeline or switchback down-chute to where the snow is gone and fresh green stuff beckons. All of these probable den-emergence sites are located at close to twelve thousand feet—as high as trees occur—no matter the aspect.

Common biological belief holds that only grizzlies den that high. But in Tom Beck's west-central Colorado study, he found that approximately 3 percent (males and females averaged) of a study population of 120 black bears denned at 11,220 feet or above, the record being 11,310 feet. "They'd have denned even higher," says Beck, "except in that part of the state you run out of mountain about then."

But even if black bears do den higher in the southern Rockies than they're known to farther north, it's tempting to think that a few of the den sites we've seen this morning may have sheltered grizzlies through the recent winter; some of those tracks down there are outlandishly big.

Our pleasant morning's work done, having established nothing except that a lot of big bears hereabouts den as high as possible in the timber near avalanche chutes, and with my bladder distended and aching from too much Oscar's coffee, I suggest to Mike that he put the pedal to the metal and make all good haste back to Pagosa and homeostasis.

As the south San Juans fall behind us, I reflect with great anticipation that as soon as what's left of the most recent annual reenactment of the Ice Age melts away—late June, probably—I'll be back down there, tired and happy again, hunting for the elusive site of the enigmatic Trujillo photo, then returning with Dennis to Grizzly Lake to resume last summer's search for those hirsute ghosts that continue to slide invisibly among my thoughts, just beyond the focus of my vision.

A while back I got a call from Glen Eyre, who asked if I'd heard "the big news."

I admitted I had not.

"Well," said the good warden, his voice fairly brimming with uncharacteristic excitement, "there's been a confirmed grizzly sighting, and only six miles south of Pagosa Springs!"

"No kidding!" said I, shocked and delighted. "A *confirmed* sighting! And only *six miles* from Pagosa!" I tried to visualize the place.

"Yeah," said Glen, something different in his voice now . . . "at the Rocky Mountain Wildlife Park."

Ho, ho. I'd been had. The grizzly to which my comedic friend was referring does in fact exist, incarcerated in an outdoor cell at a small private indigenous wildlife zoo located—I should have seen it coming— six miles south of Pagosa Springs.

I took no umbrage at Glen's little prank, chuckling right along with him. I knew he hadn't meant to imply that he thought believing in the continued existence of a few last Colorado grizzlies was a joke. To the contrary, like the majority of informed locals I've spoken with, Glen is a cautious believer; he was merely passing along a joke circulating among doubtful Pagosa-area residents, many of whom—ranchers and hunting outfitters and such—had lived, worked, and played in the San Juans for a lifetime and seen neither hide nor hair of any grizzly bear. Except, of course, at the local zoo. In spite of its sometimes self-serving motivation, I respect such pragmatic skepticism as a necessary balance in the "Is there is or is there ain't" San Juan grizzly controversy. To a disinterested observer, this polemic is a little like perusing an autumn haystack from across the pasture and pronouncing conclusively whether or not it contains a few hidden needles.

As things now stand, if you're inclined to believe a few grizzlies still haunt hidden refugiums deep and high in the sprawling San Juans, there's plenty of convincing evidence to support you, with more coming in every summer. But evidence is not proof, and should you choose to believe that the Wiseman grizzly was the dead last of its breed in Colorado, the end of a multimillennial occupation, you can rightly claim that no evidence exists that's so sound as to prove you absolutely wrong.

In rebuttal, believers maintain that the existence of a remnant Colorado grizzly population *has* been proved beyond a reasonable doubt, enumerating the hair samples retrieved by the San Juan Grizzly Project and identified by an independent laboratory as grizzly; the several finds of huge, grizzlylike tracks; the highly credible Schutz sighting; the Trujillo photo; and other intriguing, albeit inconclusive evidence, including the hot-fresh, big-clod dig Dennis Schutz and I found near Grizzly Lake in September 1993.

Thus, say champions of Colorado grizzlies and grizzly-quality wilderness, pointing to the Endangered Species Act, the time has come for the responsible management agencies—the U.S. Fish and Wildlife Service, the Colorado Division of Wildlife, and the U.S. Forest Service—to quit hiding behind a morally suspect curtain of "no conclusive proof," admit the obvious, and take action *now* to protect the last few southwestern grizzlies and their besieged enclaves.

Meanwhile, doubters both within and without the agencies counter that it would be a waste of precious resources of manpower and money to take any protective steps before proving conclusively that we have some grizzlies left to protect.

The irony, of course, is that no agency is officially looking for that proof, nor even aiding in any significant way those who are.

Is there is, or is there ain't?

You choose.

15

"ONLY A MOUNTAIN NOW"

Grizzly Recovery in Colorado: A Forum

*Love of the land is the basis for the unending
struggle of those who really care, against those
who see only material rewards.*
—Sigurd Olson

In January of 1994, the U.S. Fish and Wildlife Service released its long-awaited "Grizzly Bear Recovery Plan," prepared at great expense of time and money (four years and millions), by the FWS's Grizzly Bear Recovery coordinator, Dr. Christopher Servheen of the Interagency Grizzly Bear Committee. The 181-page Plan is intended to "delineate reasonable actions that are believed to be required to recover and/or protect the species."

The Plan opens by quoting Aldo Leopold's poignant essay "Escudilla," which eulogizes the killing by a government trapper of a latter-day Arizona grizzly dubbed Old Bigfoot, the sole ursine inhabitant of an isolated mountain called Escudilla:

> The government trapper who took the grizzly knew he had made Escudilla safe for cows. He did not know he had toppled the spire off an edifice a-building since the morning stars sang together. . . .
>
> Escudilla still hangs on the horizon, but when you see it you no longer think of bear. It's only a mountain now.

Alas, the Grizzly Bear Recovery Plan was not written by Leopold and almost immediately the Wilderness Society, Sierra Club, the National Audubon Society, and the Greater Yellowstone Coalition petitioned Interior Secretary Bruce Babbitt to withdraw it, calling the Plan "a road map to extinction." Their primary criticisms are that the Plan would allow the delisting of isolated grizzly populations as "recovered" in spite of insufficient numbers to ensure long-term stability, that it fails to establish standards to protect essential grizzly habitat from new logging roads and other proven threats, and that, in general, the Plan relies on "bad science."

Before the arrival of spring, a second coalition, this one including seventeen environmental groups, announced plans to sue the FWS "because its Grizzly Bear Recovery Plan will fail." By fall 1994, the number of plaintiffs had grown to twenty.

But at least one wildlife advocacy group so far has declined to join the anti-Plan stampede. Hank Fischer, Montana spokesman for Defenders of Wildlife, discounts the "road map to extinction" claims, saying that the real threat to the survival of grizzlies in the lower forty-eight isn't the lack of a "perfect" recovery plan, but continued delays in putting *some* plan into action. In other words, counsels Fischer, quit studying, quit bickering over details, and *start recovering*.

On page 15, in the "Needs for Recovery" section, the Plan states that it addresses

> seven areas in the conterminous 48 States where grizzly bears are known or thought to have been present in 1975 [when they were listed as "threatened" pursuant to the Endangered Species Act of 1973]. These seven grizzly bear ecosystems either presently have or recently had the potential to provide adequate space and habitat to maintain the grizzly bear as a viable and self-sustaining species.

Colorado's San Juans rate seventh on that list of seven "grizzly bear ecosystems." A passage on page 16 justifies that low priority by noting:

> There is no firm evidence suggesting the recent presence of grizzlies in the San Juans. The lack of information in the San Juans is due in large part to limited reconnaissance and research efforts. Decisions concerning the status of the San Juans as an evaluation area are pending.

Then, on page 121, under the dazzling heading "Evaluation of the Potential for Grizzly Bear Recovery in the San Juan Mountains and

Other Possible Recovery Areas Throughout the Historical Range of the Grizzly Bear," the Plan states that a "subgoal" is to

> evaluate the feasibility of grizzly bear recovery in the San Juan Mountains of Colorado and other potential recovery areas throughout the historic range of the grizzly bear. This analysis should focus on habitat values, size of the areas, human use and activities in general, relation to other areas where grizzly bears exist, and historical information. This analysis is expected to take 5 years, at which time a report should be presented to the IGBC [Interagency Grizzly Bear Committee].

Finally, Appendix G, "Summary of Public Comments," notes that among the five thousand or so comments received and supposedly cranked into the drafting of the final Plan, a whopping 449 said, in effect, that "the plan should include the San Juans Wilderness [*sic*] of Colorado as a grizzly bear recovery zone, and/or the plan should include the specific details necessary to begin the evaluation of the San Juans for grizzly bear recovery."

Meanwhile, only three comments were "opposed to the recovery of grizzly bears in the San Juan Mountains of Colorado, and/or opposed to the evaluation of the San Juan Mountains as a grizzly bear recovery zone." That's a public preference ratio of 150-to-one in favor of grizzly restoration in the San Juans.

The Grizzly Bear Recovery Plan leaves me with several questions, which I passed along to Chris Servheen in a lengthy letter. To wit:

- What, exactly, does the designation of the San Juans as a "grizzly bear ecosystem" imply?
- Does the FWS in fact intend to conduct a recovery suitability evaluation for the San Juans, as stated in the Plan, and if so, who will conduct it, who will pay for it, when will it begin, and what will it entail?
- What is Servheen's position on grizzly restoration in the San Juans, "including why you would or would not favor a restoration attempt, and what conditions would have to exist before restoration would be undertaken."

- Does Servheen personally believe there might be any surviving grizzlies in the San Juans, and why or why not?
- If it were proven that native grizzlies do in fact exist in the San Juans, would this mandate a federal study, would Endangered Species Act protections—such as a proscription against black bear hunting and removal of livestock from core grizzly areas—automatically be put into place, and would it immediately change the way the San Juans are managed by the Forest Service?
- Short of a full-blown recovery attempt, what is the advisability of a "limited, experimental augmentation of, say, one male and two females every few years—phasing the bears back in slowly, as it becomes evident they can adapt here?"

Dr. Servheen's response included the following comments:

"The San Juans is an area where we would like to undertake a five-year habitat evaluation similar to those we did in the Bitterroots and North Cascades. We have not undertaken such an evaluation because we have no funding for it. It would be done, pending funding, by a cooperative effort with the USFS, Colorado Dept. of Wildlife, and the Fish and Wildlife Service. It would be funded by federal recovery and Forest Service funding. It would entail habitat mapping, bear food quantification, mapping, and evaluation of the type and extent of human uses and their impact on grizzly bears, and an assessment of the space available to maintain a grizzly bear population.

"I have never said I am not in favor of restoring grizzly bears to the San Juans. . . .

"My opinion on surviving grizzly bears in the San Juans is irrelevant. I have not seen any conclusive evidence of grizzly bears since 1979. Any 'proof' of a grizzly bear would have to be just that. . . . No 'federal search' would be 'mandated' should such proof arise. . . . A single bear is not a grizzly population, nor is there evidence that the area could support a population pending the habitat evaluation. . . .

"There are limited numbers of bears available to augment existing populations as we are doing in the Cabinet Mountains, or to introduce new populations into suitable areas as we are planning to do in the Bitterroot ecosystem. Any available bears will go to the areas with the highest potential for development of a population. There is no such thing as a free lunch. Efforts in one area do impact efforts in another."

• • •

Beyond the shortage of funds mentioned by Servheen, there are social, political, legal, and biological concerns that must be addressed prior to any restoration effort. By way of exposing some of these concerns to open discussion, I've asked a few key people for their thoughts on grizzly restoration in Colorado. It is, I believe, a representative forum, including the opinions of extractive forest users (hunters, trappers, outfitters), landowners, grizzly advocates, plus representatives of the Colorado Division of Wildlife and the U.S. Forest Service. Chris Servheen has already stated the positions of the U.S. Fish and Wildlife Service and the Interagency Grizzly Bear Committee.

Cary Carron: Wildlife Manager, San Juan District, Colorado Division of Wildlife

I don't hold out much hope for the grizzly in the San Juans. Even if there are a few left, there probably aren't enough to find each other for mating, which means that when the current generation dies out, the distinct native species will be gone from Colorado forever. Still, it would be nice to think there are a few left; grizzlies add something to wilderness.

Concerning reintroduction, I don't believe there's enough habitat to support a full-blown "viable population" of grizzlies in the San Juans. It would, therefore, probably be a death sentence for transplanted bears. Better to put the time and money toward keeping established grizzly populations in Montana, Yellowstone, and elsewhere healthy. *Limited* reintroduction, on the other hand, could be an interesting experiment. Radio-collar the new bears and conduct a well-designed follow-up study. That would be a fascinating experiment.

But grizzly reintroduction on any level is unlikely to happen here unless and until the traditional agricultural influence in the Colorado legislature can be won over.

Glen Eyre: Wildlife Manager, South San Juan District, Colorado Division of Wildlife

I think it's possible that a few grizzlies remain in the San Juans. Because it's tough to tell the difference between some grizzlies and some black bears just by looking at them, and because they inhabit remote areas, a few grizzlies could exist without ever having problems with man or even being seen.

If proof of the grizzly's existence were produced, I'd like to see the habitat managed to keep them around for as long as possible. That would include the elimination of livestock grazing in the immediate area so that the potential for conflict would be reduced. We'd also need to conduct an intensive educational program for forest users, designed to minimize potential people-bear conflicts.

If there are a few bears remaining, it would be nice if they could continue to exist without the introduction of new grizzlies. The native San Juan grizzly gene pool would be unique, and I'd hate to see the natives crossed with outside bears.

Before any reintroduction of grizzlies could take place, we would need to determine if there is enough habitat for them to coexist in reasonable harmony with man. Also, the people of Colorado and, more importantly, locals, would have to want such a reintroduction. At this time, that level of support is not evident. And, too, there's the questions of where we'd find bears to introduce here; we don't want other people's problem animals.

I'd sure like to know if they're still out there. But even if I never know for sure, the thought that a few grizzlies might still inhabit the San Juans adds something to my experiences in the woods. I'll always be looking for them.

Rick Kahn: Chief Big Game Biologist, Colorado Division of Wildlife

I believe there may be a few grizzlies left down in the south San Juans. One thing I've learned in my years as a game warden and wildlife biologist is that any time you go looking for a small population of animals, particularly when they're shy creatures like bears, they're damned hard to find. Talk to the guys who've worked with grizzlies in the Selkirks, for instance—they had solid evidence, they *knew* they had grizzlies there, yet they couldn't find a one.

We know the 1979 grizzly had given birth and nursed. We don't know how often or how recently before her death, but she definitely had been a reproducing female and she lived a good long life. It's certainly not presumptuous to assume that at least a couple of her offspring are still out there.

Even so, by the early 1950s the Colorado grizzly had probably already passed the point of maintaining itself as a viable population. And there's nothing we can do about that now, short of introducing more bears. And even then, the southwestern grizzly as a distinct race would still disappear. In that sense, I agree with Tom Beck's feeling that even if we should determine conclusively that a few San Juan grizzlies are left, there's nothing we can do for them but to follow the situation more closely and try to slow their inevitable slide into extinction. Reintroduction is a workable possibility, but they wouldn't be native Colorado bears, only hybrids. And only then if the new bears can find and will breed with the natives.

The bottom line is that if we were to decide we want grizzlies in the San Juans again, a decision I personally would endorse, instead of wasting money on another search to prove we still have a few natives left, we should just go for it—spend the money on reintroduction. It can be made to work, but *only* if the people of Colorado want it to. It's really irrelevant if the Division wants to. The public should make the decision.

The Division's problem is that we have just one little pot of money, funded through our Nongame Wildlife Program, dedicated to recovering all the state's endangered species. How should it be spent—on the controversial restoration of a single high-profile species like the grizzly? Or on several less-glamorous but endangered native species: river otters, sandhill cranes, and on down the line? What's best for the people and the wildlife of Colorado?

Ernest Wilkinson: San Juan Mountain Man

I can't see closing entire areas to human use in favor of preserving or restoring the grizzly in the San Juans. We're getting along just fine without the grizzly. Maybe there is a grizzly left up there. He's not going to come down to where there's a lot of civilization; he's going to stay in remote areas. The main thing [grizzly advocates and the agencies] have to do is to educate the public, so that if a hunter sees a bear, instead of shooting it thinking it's a black bear, he'll take time to try to identify it, and not shoot if it looks like it could be a grizzly. Put some of this [research] money into educating the public, so that if there is a grizzly left, people can identify it and not shoot it. They can do all the research they want, but if a hunter shoots the last grizzly, it hasn't done any good.

Ed Wiseman: Hunting Outfitter and San Juan
Grizzly Mauling Survivor

I don't think grizzly restoration should even be attempted here. If you take the geographic requirements of a grizzly bear and superimpose them on Colorado's wilderness areas, you'll see that there are practically no areas that will fulfill the bear's needs and allow him to exist without confrontation with man. Colorado is too settled.

Because of the grizzly's natural inclination to prey on livestock and to be king of the woods—which he rightly deserves—any grizzly without sufficient wilderness to roam in is eventually going to come into hostile contact with people, be designated a "problem," and be destroyed. I don't think that's fair to the bear; he's been put into a situation where he can't behave naturally.

For that reason, I don't endorse grizzly reintroduction here—not because of any danger the bears would present; I think we could learn to live with that part of it, and a lot of us would even welcome it. But you've got to look at the population as a whole. Consider a person who gains his livelihood from the forest by grazing sheep or cattle, and a bear comes in and starts tearing up his way of making a living. That bear's going to be in trouble, law or no law. A grizzly bear can't help but be a grizzly bear. And people are going to be people. And when the bear's rights and human rights come into conflict, the bear will always lose, legally or illegally.

Rick Lapin: Banded Peak Ranch, Colorado

We truly believe we still have a few grizzlies up here, and that's good news to us. They don't bother us, and we try not to bother them. I'd like to see every native species living here today that was here before the ranch existed. It's our goal to maintain an ecosystem here on the ranch that can support all native species, including grizzlies.

We don't hunt bears, and we don't run livestock except for a few horses, so we have no objection if the Division of Wildlife or whoever feels that it's necessary to stop bear hunting and sheep grazing in critical grizzly habitat. Even grizzly reintroduction probably wouldn't bother us. To have a balanced ecosystem, you have to make concessions for your neighbors, even when they're grizzlies. And likewise, these grizzlies up here have always made concessions for us; they're very shy.

We'd even welcome gray wolves back . . . though some people around here definitely don't feel that way.

Dr. Tony Povilitis: Wildlife Biologist, Life Net

In the contiguous states, the grizzly is now essentially confined to the northern Rockies, a tiny fraction of its former geographic range. It can't assume its ecological role or realize its evolutionary potential in the American West under these circumstances. There are only a few places outside of that limited northern area where it can be restored (or for that matter where the full complement of native species and ecosystems can be restored). One of these areas is the San Juans.

If the grizzly is to reestablish itself in the San Juans (or be successfully reintroduced), it will need a sizable habitat core area and a relatively secure buffer around it. The core area (in this case, the main stem of the San Juans) would be cooperatively managed as a primary wildlands zone, which would in effect ensure that the San Juans are "forever wild."

We run into a special problem in the San Juans, since there is no "fire-free [no hunting] zone." This makes it extremely difficult to secure a grizzly population, much less restore one. The key for the San Juans would necessarily be to keep human-caused mortality down to essentially zero. This means no accidental shooting by hunters, outfitters, sheepherders, and other armed persons, and no poaching (the primary cause of grizzly bear mortality in national forests elsewhere).

I know how reluctant some people would be to shift their work or recreation in deference to wildlife. This is because we have tended to place wildlife last in almost all circumstances when it comes to any apparent conflict. But I think times are changing as people realize how quickly we are losing wildlife and nature and how few options remain for restoring them.

For example, I think most people would support seasonally restricted access to the south San Juans in order to save surviving Colorado grizzlies *if* they better understood the dilemma and were assured of alternative places for their activities. Strong leadership and commitment on the part of all interested citizens and groups (and especially the Forest Service) would be needed to work out the necessary agreements.

In the long run, for the grizzly to live in the San Juans, the overall region will have to be relatively wild. This becomes problematic given the rapid influx of newcomers into the area and current accelerating land subdivision. A more complete answer is required—one that could make the San Juans one of the twenty-first century's premier regions of the world.

Tom Beck: Bear Biologist, Colorado Division of Wildlife

The thoughts I offer here are my own ideas, based on my professional experiences. They do not represent the position of the Colorado Division of Wildlife, though I do not believe they are in opposition to current official policy.

Like a lot of people, I believe we may still have a few grizzlies here in the San Juans, and I like that idea a lot. But I'm not sure we're going to do those bears any bloody good by exposing them. Because as soon as we do . . . well, humans want to overmanage every blasted thing, and the vested interests aligned against the grizzly are as strong today as they've ever been.

The heart of the problem is that right now we don't have enough people, on either side, capable of sitting down and talking reasonably about grizzly management in Colorado. If we come out and say we've got half a dozen grizzlies here, there's one extreme that will clamor to shut down all human activity in the south San Juans to protect those few bears. And an opposite extreme will tell you right to your face that "by God if we can find those bears, we're going to shoot the SOBs and be done with it"—the old shoot, shovel, and shut up philosophy. And, too, there are the ski area developers and the loggers and the outfitters and the off-road vehicle groups—all those multiple use positions joined together against the grizzly and grizzly quality wilderness.

Most people are probably somewhere in the middle. But the polarized elements, the "wise use" crowd on the one hand, and the radical animal rights groups on the other, are going to dominate any debate on grizzly management in Colorado. And I'm not sure that will do the bear, or the San Juans, one bit of good. We can look to Yellowstone for an example.

Have you seen any significant improvement in how the national forests have been managed around the perimeter of Yellowstone and Glacier National Parks across the last twenty years or so, since the advent of the Endangered Species Act? The only change I've seen is an *increase* in oil and gas exploration and mining, continued heavy logging and heavy grazing, and more roads. And how is that good for grizzly bears? I'm not sure the Endangered Species Act has enough clout to force any agency in any direction it doesn't want to go.

Of course, we *know* a lot more about grizzlies and their habitat needs than we did before. But too often, studying a problem year after year is merely an excuse to delay having to make the tough decisions. Grizzly management in the northern Rockies has evolved into a self-serving bureaucracy, an intellectual sellout—they're literally studying the problem to death. We don't need that here in the San Juans.

Back in 1980, I believed that if I could demonstrate that grizzlies still lived in Colorado, the agencies would respond with appropriate policy. That's why I wanted so badly to catch a grizzly. I wanted to see the Forest Service and the Colorado Division of Wildlife pushed up against the wall. I wanted to see them have to make the right decisions. But I'm convinced now that they'd have figured a way out of it, and they'll figure a way out of it today or tomorrow. The easy way out for the Division is just to say, "OK, all San Juan grizzly bears are protected." With that, we've done our part as the state regulatory agency, and responsibility shifts to the federal government to mandate that nobody can do anything that's "proven" to be detrimental to the bear. And what does that mean?

I'm not an optimist concerning the long-term future of grizzly bears in Colorado. There are a lot of people in this state, with more arriving every day. And as a society, we tend to be pretty selfish; we want to be able to do anything, everything, anywhere, everywhere. For grizzlies to survive here, we're going to have to learn to share and to give some things up.

Consequently, if I were going to try and restore grizzlies to the San Juans, I'd begin by assessing the social climate. Anything less would be grossly irresponsible. I'm not the king of Colorado, and I have no business making decisions that ultimately may affect the whole state. But even before that, we need to make a *serious* effort to go out and explain to the public the costs, the consequences, the gains, the losses—educate people as thoroughly as we can, using the best information available. Only then can we accurately and fairly gauge the social acceptability of grizzly restoration in Colorado. I'd have to see that happen, see those results, before I'd make another move.

Unless I got a *very* strong direction from the public, I would not propose grizzly reintroduction because all we'd accomplish is to kill bears and alienate people. There are a lot of self-servers out there trying to use a few controversial species, like the grizzly, to bring down the entire Endangered Species program. The agencies have already made some mistakes in trying to comply with the act—we've sometimes gone a little overboard—and the enemies of the ESA are making the most of those foibles, focusing on them to portray the act in the worst possible light.

A law is no better than the agency that has to enforce it. Regarding the Fish and Wildlife Service's handling of the ESA—I'm not terribly impressed. I say that based on their track record across the country on many species. And what have they really done for the grizzly bear? Have they stood firmly against the development interests? Have they significantly increased the number of grizzlies in the lower forty-eight? Have they guaranteed a more secure future for grizzlies in the northern Rockies? I don't see it, and consequently I'm not real keen to see the FWS come down here and spend a lot of money and go swarming all over the wilderness conducting another study that I don't think is going to do a whole lot of good for the bears. If we're going to restore grizzlies here, we should do it ourselves.

The Division should start by initiating massive rounds of public meetings as well as using the media to get the word out, especially television, because that's where the biggest audiences are. We should arrange to have responsible people from both sides of the grizzly debate explain the pros and cons of restoration.

This would be an expensive and time-consuming effort. I envision it as an *honest* Environmental Impact process, very different from the norm, where you have alternatives A through G, with all of them stacked in favor of a preordained choice, which is the way the Environmental Impact Statement process has developed in all agencies. Of course, we'd provide options: no grizzlies; a small population augmented as necessary to maintain what's determined to be the optimum number for the available habitat; a self-sustaining population, and so on. But they'd be *honest* choices with no built-in bias in favor of or against any specific outcome. Then—with the education completed and the alternatives presented— put it to a vote; what do the people of Colorado want?

That's what I think *should be* done, but there's little or no chance of the Division ever sponsoring such a program. The Colorado Wildlife Commission has stated a clear and stringent antigrizzly position, and I don't see them welcoming an effort by the Division to find out if the public agrees or not. I may be wrong here—the board of commissioners who passed that antigrizzly, antiwolf resolution several years ago has retired, and the present board may be more open-minded. Who knows? But without the Commission's endorsement, the Division is never going to sponsor either a public education and polling process or even another grizzly search. Much less reintroduction.

The whole restoration scenario—the big questions to be asked and answered, the potential risks and losses—can be walked through as an intellectual exercise right here and now.

If we have, say, five grizzly bears left, the first question should be: Is that a sufficient population to assure that we'll still have grizzlies here fifty years from now? I think most people would agree that we've got to have more, which means we'll have to bring them in from somewhere else.

Which leads to the question of where these supplemental bears are going to come from. We have to know before the fact—taking into consideration the percentage of imported bears that will be killed one way and another—how many grizzlies will it take to reach our restoration goals, and where do we get them?

For argument's sake, let's say the supply problem is overcome, and we arrange to bring in some Yellowstone grizzlies to augment our five Colorado natives. At this point, we can make some biological predictions about what's going to happen next. And the most significant of those predictions is that most of the adults will try to go home. And that raises the possibility, the *likelihood,* of human-bear conflicts. Those animals are going to be stressed from having been trapped, extensively handled, and released in strange country. They're going to try to get back home—with an awful lot of people in the way.

Some people have suggested that bringing in subadults who haven't yet established a territory of their own would largely overcome this problem. And I'll grant that the subadult female is the easiest bear to relocate; she has a tendency to stay put where released if the habitat is sufficient to meet her needs. And the San Juans are superb bear habitat. But the subadult male has as strong an instinctive drive to roam as the female does to settle down. Any reintroduction would have to include both males and females, so we're still looking at wandering grizzlies coming into conflict with humans. And those conflicts are going to push the agencies up against the wall and cause significant problems for the whole restoration program.

There are also legal ramifications. If we know in advance that some imported grizzlies aren't going to stay put, and if we know they're stressed and unpredictable, is it prudent to bring them in? There are some serious biological problems to be overcome, but the highest hurdles are social and political: Do the people of rural southern Colorado and northern New Mexico and the Southern Ute and Jicarilla Apache tribes —the groups that will be potentially directly affected by reintroduction—want grizzlies here badly enough to be willing to make the necessary changes necessary to coexist with the bears? And are they willing to make those changes *fast?* If not, all we'd accomplish with reintroduction is dooming many of the new bears to swift, violent deaths.

An analogy is what has happened in recent years with cougars wandering into Front Range suburbs near Boulder. What we hear at the Division is "Help! Get this thing out of here, quick! It's on my porch!" Most people just aren't very tolerant of big predators. They admire lions and bears in the abstract, but not when one is standing in their front yard.

As much as I'd love to have a viable grizzly population in the San Juans, maybe we'd be better off forgetting about restoration and all its potential problems in favor of doing everything we can—right now, no further delays—to make sure that any native grizzlies we have left will be able to live out their full natural lives. We have to ask: Where is our money and energy best spent? We could, if we really wanted to, enact those protections without even proving the existence of a single grizzly in the San Juans.

But even such a moderate approach as preservation can and will run into resistance. As I said before, as soon as you find legal proof of grizzlies, you're dealing with the U.S. Fish and Wildlife Service; there's no way at that point to keep them out. And because the bears are living on federal land much or all of the time, the Forest Service is going to have to consult with the FWS on every single move it makes, every single activity that might affect the bear. Thus the FWS will wind up being very much the lead agency concerning the grizzly's future in Colorado.

On the question of handling bears: If I were asked to do another grizzly study that required the use of leg snares—which tend to cause injuries to bears that fight them—or radio collars, and if I wasn't convinced that the study was absolutely necessary for the benefit of the bears, I'd refuse. It's a trade-off. A strong part of me says, "Don't catch and tag any Colorado grizzlies." Another part says that if we really want to do something for the bears, we're going to have to know more than just that they exist. Let's say we catch three bears. If we had information about how and where they live, what could we do to make things better for them? If I could not clearly see that the knowledge gained by collaring those three bears would help them, I'd say forget it. Knowledge for its own sake in this case—considering rarity, mystique, and the awe I have for grizzlies—isn't justified.

Bottom line: If we should choose to let any remaining Colorado grizzlies live out their lives without attempting restoration, I would not trap, handle, tag, or collar a one. But should we decide in favor reintroduction, then yes, I would, because we need to know something about where and how they live.

Doug Peacock: Wilderness Philosopher
and Grizzly Advocate

It's important to understand that we're dealing with a different kind of bear here. The San Juan grizzly is an incredible survival story; it has been programmed to avoid humans at all costs, at any expense. At the same time, because there have been so few of them for so long, and because they've been so relentlessly persecuted, I believe these last few Colorado grizzlies have become incredibly social, to the point that I doubt that they ever completely cut ties with their mothers. If I'm correct about this, it destroys the argument that they can be written off because there are so few grizzlies left in the San Juans, scattered over such a wide area that they couldn't find one another to breed. Can you imagine being the last of a species—how lonely that would be? I believe every grizzly in the San Juans knows where to find the others at any given time.

Concerning augmenting those last few bears with new grizzlies—I'm not sure. I know what reintroduction means in the abstract, but in real terms, you're talking about uprooting and relocating individual young bears that have mothers and wild homes of their own. A far happier ending to the Colorado grizzly saga would be to discover a tiny remnant breeding population of native bears that somehow have defied all biological abstractions concerning viable populations, interbreeding, and so on. Wildlife managers talk about "genetic drift," but what does it really mean? Even the experts know very little.

We don't know, for instance, what constitutes a "viable gene pool" for grizzlies. How genetically lost *are* these last few Colorado bears? Since older females seem to be the key, the essentials among bear societies, we may be talking about just four or so generations. Maybe it takes thousands of years for genetic stability to disappear in isolation. We can't pronounce these bears genetically doomed until we learn exactly what population numbers over how long a time dictate irrevocable genetic damage.

The fact that these grizzlies seem to be reproducing doesn't make any more sense to me than it does to the scientists. But somehow, it seems to be happening, and we need to keep it going. Consequently, I don't think I'd want to propose any level of augmentation for a while. I'd rather just pull out all the stops to protect the bears we still have left, then watch and see.

I haven't yet seen a San Juan grizzly with my own eyes, but I believe they're out there. The question is: Are we sure we want to prove it? There's a deep ambivalence in my heart, more than in my mind, concerning the best course of action. Whatever attributes have allowed these grizzlies to survive against all odds for so many bear generations is something that's utterly heroic and should be honored and rewarded. I treasure those abstract attributes. By proving the presence of bears in the San Juans, we could be undermining those very qualities. So if I really thought you could protect a remnant population of grizzlies by ignoring them, that's what I'd do. But I don't believe that. If we ignore them, they will definitely die out. I believe we have to act, and act fast.

Consequently, we need to start right now formulating a battle plan to protect not just the individuals that are left, five bears or whatever the number may be, but also to safeguard their instincts and learned behaviors, their unique tricks of survival. If we prove the bears are there, then step back and leave it to the feds to move in with all of their apparatus and bureaucracy—and even given the best of intentions on their part—it will be too clumsy and heavy-handed. We're talking about a very delicate and sensitive ursine population that has been naturally selected over the past century and more to avoid people, poisons, baits, and traps.

Ideally, I would like to see the fact of their existence established simultaneously with the announcement of a workable plan to save both the bears and their unique survival qualities. I don't want a collar on every one of these animals; that will destroy them. On the other hand, we can't afford to lose a single individual, so we need to know what's going on with them. My hope is that modern DNA technology will give us that necessary knowledge without seriously disturbing the bears' daily activities; we can just follow them around from a polite distance and pick up some of their scats and analyze them. Among other things, individual animals can be identified by their DNA fingerprints; their seasonal ranges, social interaction, and diet can be plotted—a lot of knowledge can be gained without resorting to radio collars and handling.

But before that, before anything, we need to get all the fools with guns out of the grizzly's core habitat. Get rid of black bear hunting and discourage elk and deer hunting in those areas—we're talking about just a tiny piece of the south San Juans up along the Continental Divide.

This needn't all be done by regulation. Certainly, we can't afford to have continued bear hunting in grizzly habitat; even experts can't always tell the difference between a black and a grizzly out to the limits of rifle range, which is several hundred yards. But most of the rest of it can be accomplished simply by making wilderness access a little tougher, closing a few access roads, prohibiting ATVs on Forest Service trails, discontinuing maintenance on a certain few trails in the south San Juans, and so on. We don't need to mandate any closed areas; no "shut outs"; just make it a little harder to get into critical grizzly habitat and encourage people to go elsewhere to hunt and hike and ride their horses.

Of course, we have to consider the possibility of crazies going after the bears, and we'll have to deal firmly with that. Realistically, intentional poaching in the San Juans probably isn't a very big problem, but it's nonetheless a possibility that must be planned for . . . one man with a rifle or one poisoned bait could wipe out the bulk of the remaining population—say, Dennis Schutz's sow and three cubs—in minutes.

And domestic sheep should be removed from core grizzly habitat in the south San Juans immediately. The incompatibility of grizzlies and sheep, and grizzlies and sheep ranchers, is proven. There's something about the nature of sheep that lures big predators to commit slaughter—their endless whining and bleating and run of excreta. I'm serious: recent studies have shown that there's something universal about the sonic quality of what's being called the "primordial whine" of sheep and other prey species that invites rampant killing by predators. Sheep and sheep ranchers are the premier whiners of the universe. We simply can't have sheep and grizzlies in the same place.

In the past, ranchers and federal trappers have simply barged in, killed the grizzlies, and assumed control of any public land they want, which is almost all of it. But this time, it's the ranchers who will have to go. There are plenty of vacant grazing allotments throughout the San Juans they can be moved onto. It's not like they'd have to quit business, though they'll carry on like it's the end of the world. With a few noble exceptions, wool growers have no generosity, no imagination, and never willingly compromise. There is absolutely no room for argument here: in order to save the last of the San Juan grizzlies, the sheep have to go.

We're talking about such a small area that's so high, we don't really need *any* commercial activity up there. The economic value of grazing and outfitted hunting in the high south San Juans is negligible in the big picture and insignificant even in regional economics. We can't continue bowing and catering to every extractive forest enterprise that comes along. That's what spelled the end of the grizzly and wolf in the Southwest in the first place. Cattle took up most of the more easily accessible grazing land, which pushed sheep into every little corner of wilderness. The loss of one cow or sheep was viewed as economic disaster, so ranchers blew away every predator that moved.

This same "us against them" paranoia continues today, and it's no longer acceptable. I'll fight that self-serving mind-set, that local whining about "economic necessity," with all my power. Most of the time, when these people talk about wanting to ensure the economic welfare of their children and their children's children, it's just a smoke screen for personal greed and spiritual impoverishment.

So we put the necessary protections into force immediately, and we use minimally intrusive measures to track the bears and learn how many there are and what their seasonal territories are and where they den, we draw a genetic map of these bears; with DNA analysis, it's even possible to learn where San Juan grizzlies came from originally—where are their closest living relatives today? Ideally—and this is what the FWS and other responsible agencies should be working toward—we could someday establish linkage zones to reunite the various tiny island populations of related grizzlies, or wolves, lynx, wolverines, jaguars, so that they could naturally augment one another.

Only after we've taken the San Juan survivors out of immediate harm's way and learned all we can about them without invading their privacy and disrupting their daily lives, only then should we look at the possibility and advisability of attempting to find some way of supplementing that population without destroying its unique survival adaptations.

Where would the new bears come from? I don't think we have an excess of wild grizzlies anywhere, and I don't believe it's ethical to take a wild bear from one place and dump it somewhere else. Even subadult wild grizzlies have already spent two and a half years learning the intricacies of their environment and the nuances of the social system among local bears, and I don't believe it's moral to take them out of that familiar setting and drop them into a whole new world.

Perhaps the best source, and one rarely discussed, is zoos. Grizzly cubs are always available from excess zoo populations. Conditioning and releasing captive-born bears into the wild may offer a more humane and workable way of going about restoration than trapping and moving wild bears.

But no matter where the bears come from, we'll need to establish a halfway house for them. I have a couple of local ranches in mind that would be perfect. I can't tell you exactly how this should be done, but I do know we have enough biological knowledge to figure it out. It's been done with wolves, and we can do it with bears. I'm not worried about that aspect of reintroduction. For one thing, grizzlies seem to have an instinctive knowledge of which natural foods are best, and in what types of terrain they occur and when.

But all of this should come way down the line, if at all. Protections for the remaining native San Juan grizzlies should be implemented with

all possible speed. Restoration should be considered carefully and implemented one slow step at a time. Even then, there would be some attrition
among the new bears. But attrition is the norm for all grizzly populations everywhere, even in zoos. We just have to do everything slowly and
carefully in order to keep losses to an absolute minimum.

The idea that any grizzly that wanders down from the mountains and
into an inhabited area will get into trouble and wind up dead has been
proven wrong time and again. It's entirely possible for grizzlies to use
human-inhabited fringe areas of their habitat and not even let people
know they're there. This has been happening in the North Fork Valley of
Montana, just outside Glacier National Park, forever. Up there, grizzlies
are everywhere. And so are cows and cabins and people and their gardens,
and there's almost never any problems. You see fresh cow pies with huge
grizzly and wolf prints in them, and yet there's no livestock predation.
Most people never even see the bears. These are modern grizzlies; they
have learned how to survive around humans. Which is more than can be
said for most humans.

Most people know nothing about bears, and that's why they're terri-
fied of them. Rather than taking the time and effort to learn how to live
with bears, our culture has always preferred just to blow them away. The
problem is not the grizzly; it's human ignorance, intolerance, and lack of
imagination.

Without a doubt, the greatest political enemies of the grizzly are
rural locals who view the bear as a threat to their traditional way of life,
to working and playing in the national forest. Certainly, we need to
listen to these people with respect and then answer them in kind. If
they're willing to be reasonable, to learn, and to compromise, so should
we. But you can't reason with an unreasonable person, especially when
that person is ignorant and proud of it. If they want to play that old
bully game, we'll have to be ready to fight back; the stakes are too high
to do otherwise. A relative handful of locals whining about "traditional
uses" simply cannot be allowed to continue to dominate at the expense of
western wildlands and wildlife and the best interests of the majority of
Coloradans and Americans.

I'm sorry, but sheep ranching and logging are no more "traditions"
than asphalt pavement. White culture, especially in the West, is the new
kid on the block. We've lived in North America just a heartbeat of time;

we haven't been here long enough to consider *anything* we do as traditional, especially not when you're talking about the good of the land.

It's like the northwestern loggers who are resisting being retrained for new careers on the grounds that logging is a family or local tradition. Well, they can change jobs now, or they can wait until they've cut what little is left of the old-growth timber there, *then* change jobs. It's inevitable; their "traditional" way of life has logged itself out of viability in less than a handful of generations.

Before whites came into the San Juans, there were Navajos and Utes and Apaches, and before them the Anasazi and way back were Folsom hunters and gatherers. All of these people considered the San Juans to be "theirs," and all of those "traditional" ways of life are gone today.

In the long run, the only tradition worth honoring is one of sustainability. Anything less is just get-it-fast-as-you-can, to-hell-with-posterity, slash-and-burn greed. There has to be a sense of reciprocity between people and the land that supports us. And we've never had that with grazing and logging and mining, and certainly not with recreational off-road-vehicle use. These are not traditions worthy of continued survival. The South San Juan Wilderness is not some giant free supermarket; it is a living, suffering organism.

These local "traditions" have brought Colorado's wilderness to the point that today it is widely and rightfully considered the least wild in any Rocky Mountain state. But the San Juans could easily be returned to a true wild state. In fact, the San Juans hold the potential to become a paradigm for all wilderness areas in the lower forty-eight.

Contrary to what the feds would have us believe, we don't need a lot of money to save the grizzly and grizzly wilderness in Colorado, and we certainly don't need the Interagency Grizzly Bear Committee. The IGBC talks about not having enough money to restore bears in the northern Rockies as well as help Colorado's grizzlies. But a big part of the reason for that is that the IGBC is not cost-effective.

All organizations, movements, committees, and causes are born to serve a purpose and die. The IGBC has evolved into an albatross. Go to their meetings and count the lobbyists for antiwilderness, antigrizzly interests hanging about, especially the aides to those Wyoming, Montana, and Idaho congressmen best known for sucking up to rich ranching interests. It's gotten to be the most political, antiproductive, antilife forum imaginable. I believe the time has come to disband the IGBC. At the least, we don't need them in Colorado. They're not worth what we pay them. The grizzly doesn't need them. We can do it better and cheaper without them. In the field, all the feds know is collaring bears, writing reports, and wasting time and money. We don't need or want that with these last few Colorado grizzlies.

How do we do it on our own? We forge an alliance with the Forest Service and the Colorado Division of Wildlife and—if they're willing to *participate* without having to run the whole show—the Fish and Wildlife Service, to protect the remaining bears. We fight to slow and stop habitat loss, and eventually we think about linkage zones; we think about wilderness *expansion,* not shrinkage.

Collectively, all we're currently doing is fighting a war of attrition. In Yellowstone, for instance, the agencies have done a pretty good job of cutting grizzly mortality, resulting in an elevated reproduction rate. But even if we have more grizzly cubs in Yellowstone this year than we've had in the past twenty, it doesn't mean dogshit, because the habitat there, and consequently the carrying capacity of the ecosystem, is shrinking radically every year; not enough has been done to protect the *habitat.*

Local forest managers should take the lead in preserving the remaining grizzlies and grizzly wilderness. The Rio Grande and San Juan National Forests should design a management plan that includes both forests, the private land within and surrounding those forests, and migratory wildlife corridors linking it all together. The bedrock problem is the poverty of our minds. The poverty of our minds makes us desperate and greedy.

The qualities that make us human are generosity, reverence, awe, and humility. *These* are the things worth saving—not the so-called traditional lifestyles that brought wild nature to its knees in the first place and are keeping it there today.

Jim Webb: Supervisor, San Juan and Rio Grande National Forests

Since participating in a grizzly bear workshop at Yellowstone Park in 1993, I've given a lot of thought to the grizzly's place here in the San Juans. If knowledgeable people are saying that perhaps we have a few bears left here, I'm willing to go along with them. I'm even comfortable going ahead and taking some protective actions based on that "perhaps." We're going through forest plan revisions for the Rio Grande right now; our draft will be out in October [1994]. And we're gearing up to do the same for the San Juan side.

I think the first thing we need to do, across both forests, is to start requiring forest users to take reasonable actions to avoid habituating *any* bears, blacks or grizzlies, to human food. I think we should institute the same backcountry bear precautions here as are currently in effect in the Yellowstone ecosystem and elsewhere: bear-proof panniers, hanging food and garbage out of reach of bears, and so on. These things are minor inconveniences to forest users, and I think we might as well get on with it; I'm ready. Probably the most effective way of going about this would be to require a permit to enter potential grizzly areas.

As for allowing trails to deteriorate in areas where grizzlies may be present—by and large, those areas are so remote that the trails into them don't carry a lot of traffic, and most aren't that great anyway. And even without Forest Service maintenance, trail users, especially riders, will clear fallen logs and cut detours around slides and whatever else is necessary to keep the way open; all experienced horse people carry saws or axes with them. In the end, I don't think letting trails deteriorate will prove to be an effective inhibitor to their use.

Concerning sheep—any remaining grizzlies have managed to survive in the proximity of sheep. Still, I understand the potential for disastrous conflict. Certainly, we have a lot of vacant grazing allotments throughout both forests. And the sheep industry is in such a struggle for survival right now, that given monetary incentives, most sheepmen, and cattlemen too if that's deemed necessary, should be willing to swap their south San Juan grazing permits for allotments outside grizzly habitat. And others, for a little compensation, may just say, "To heck with it, this business is no longer worth it," and simply give up their allotments. I would have no problem with either of those alternatives: transferring allotments or buying back grazing permits. To some extent, this is happening already, with some sheepmen relinquishing their permits voluntarily and getting out of the business, and others letting their allotments go ungrazed because it's no longer profitable.

Of course, there will be one or two ranchers who are sentimentally attached to a particular allotment, and they're going to say, "No, by God, I don't want to give it up!" But even here, my sense is that if we sit

down with them and explain the situation and offer some kind of compensation, they'll be willing to cooperate.

Certainly, we shouldn't be allowing any ADC [Animal Damage Con-
trol] activity in potential grizzly areas. If problems develop between
cattle or sheep and bears, we should just reimburse the ranchers for their
losses, as the Division of Wildlife already does, and have them move their
animals out of harm's way. We shouldn't be killing bears, for any reason,
in areas where grizzlies may be present.

Just as important, I think, is to limit bear hunting in potential
grizzly habitat. Just announce, "Hey, no more bear hunting in these
certain areas until we find out what's going on." That shouldn't infringe
on all that many people's "rights" or be much of an inconvenience to
anyone. Between the Forest Service, the Division of Wildlife, and the
U.S. Fish and Wildlife Service, we certainly ought to have the guts and
gumption to say, "Hey, this is important, and this is the way it's going
to be, at least for a while."

One thing I learned from my experiences in Yellowstone is that it
can be damned difficult to tell whether you're looking at a grizzly or a
black bear, especially from any distance. If there are, say, five or even ten
grizzlies left in the south San Juans, not a single one is disposable; there's
absolutely *no* room for people with guns to make mistakes. I'll go along
with whatever the wildlife management agencies suggest is necessary to
protect any surviving native grizzlies in the San Juans.

And once we get the survivors protected, studies should be conducted. If those studies suggest that we need to introduce more grizzlies
—enough to keep the native gene pool from crashing—I have no problem there. Perhaps the first step should be for the Division to conduct an
unbiased public opinion poll to determine the level of support for grizzly
reintroduction.

When I look at the "Grizzly Recovery Plan" recently published by
the Interagency Grizzly Bear Committee, I worry about their proposed
five-year study plan for the San Juans and professed lack of money to
conduct it. Rather than waiting for the IGBC, I'd like to see all the
concerned agencies, plus private groups such as the San Juan Grizzly
Project, get together and pool our resources and build a plan to conduct
the necessary vegetative and habit analyses, and to do some intelligent
fieldwork to confirm or deny the presence of grizzlies in the San Juans
once and for all.

I'm open to all of this and more. The one thing I'm *not* open to is closing off areas of national forest to any human access.

We're in the process right now of doing what's called an integrated resource inventory, which is a fairly intensive mapping of all four million acres of the San Juan and Rio Grande national forests. Consequently, my question to a number of people in other agencies has been: "When we get into suspected grizzly habitats, what kinds of things should we be looking for?" Maybe there are certain plants whose abundance we should pay special attention to, and so on. We're going to be out there covering the acres anyhow, so we might as well go in armed with the best possible knowledge relative to grizzly concerns and come out with the best possible information, which we can then share with other interested parties. Why should we cover the ground today, only to have another agency go back over the same ground tomorrow? We can handle the vegetative analysis—*if* the wildlife agencies will just tell us what information they're interested in. I've made that offer several times already, and I plan to keep making it. But so far, I haven't seen a lot of interest.

I'm concerned that if we don't get the Division of Wildlife, or somebody, to start coordinating grizzly bear issues in the San Juans soon, it could turn into a great big mess with all the different agencies and private groups charging around in the woods trying to help the bear, tripping over one another, and in the long run being more of a detriment than a help. I don't care who takes the reins, federal or state wildlife people, but *somebody* needs to do it, and soon.

Under the Endangered Species Act, our joint responsibility—the Forest Service, the Fish and Wildlife Service, and the Division of Wildlife—is to protect the grizzly. But trying to get anybody to acknowledge that it's time to get together and act on that responsibility has been difficult so far. Working together and taking action *now* is our only morally sound option, and a hell of a lot better than continuing to deny the possibility of grizzlies in Colorado, then down the road a few years from now wishing we hadn't.

The Forest Service is ready to cooperate fully. If somebody would call a meeting to get the process rolling, we'd be there and we'd participate with gusto. The Forest Service is not dragging its feet. For me personally, it's exciting to think there may be grizzly bears in the San Juans. It adds a whole new dimension to being in the woods.

Bruce Baizel and Dennis Sizemore:
Round River Conservation Studies

Doug Peacock has thought long and hard about the many questions surrounding the San Juan grizzly, and we're comfortable with the tone and substance of his opinions. We would, however, like to add a few specifics.

Based on our fieldwork, together with hair samples, tracks, digs, photographs, and sightings made by individuals not associated with us, we believe it's highly likely there are grizzlies in the San Juans. We note that the accumulated evidence is nearly as strong as, if not stronger than, the evidence for grizzlies in the North Cascades, where "proof" is no longer an issue. Further, it's our observation that demands for further "proof" come primarily from those who would rather not see grizzlies here. We believe that the evidence available so far is sufficient to answer this question positively, whether from an ethical, a land-management, or a legal standpoint. The real issue is what responses are appropriate.

We've identified five categories of response that we feel should be undertaken immediately and simultaneously:

1. A review by the Forest Service, to be completed within six months, of all human activity on the national forest lands in question. Where current human activity poses even a moderate level of risk of mortality to grizzlies, it should be deferred pending development of interim management measures. Such a deferment may require cooperative efforts by other state and federal agencies.

2. Development and initiation of a public education program regarding grizzly bears and appropriate human activity in grizzly country. This program should be presented, at a minimum, to hunters, outfitters, other forest users, schools, local residents, and local outdoor-related business owners.

3. Completion of an assessment of currently suitable grizzly habitat, beginning with the south San Juans, focusing on the quality and extent of that habitat, as well as identification of causes of degradation of suitable grizzly habitat.

4. Establishment of a task force charged with speaking for the grizzly in all issues actually or potentially affecting the bears in the

San Juans. Membership in this task force should be based on two criteria: residence in the greater San Juan area and a commitment to ensuring the continued presence of a healthy grizzly population in the San Juans. The task force should probably be no larger than five people, with no more than two of the five being employed by agencies.

This group should have no legal decision-making authority. Rather, its authority would be moral and ethical. It could call upon agency staff, scientists, forest users, and elected representatives for advice, as needed. Its job would be to consider issues related to grizzlies in the San Juans and to make recommendations concerning what would be best for the bear in various instances. It would be up to agencies, local residents, and members of local organizations to put these recommendations into practice.

5. Establishment of a monitoring committee charged with ensuring that, to the greatest extent possible without disruption of the grizzly's current living patterns, threats of mortality are reduced as much as possible. This committee should probably include both agency and citizen members, and might consider such issues as antipoaching efforts, prevention of human-bear conflicts, and continued observation of grizzly activity at a discreet distance.

Finally, at this time, we believe it's premature to talk about grizzly reintroduction in Colorado.

I had hoped to conclude this forum on grizzly recovery in Colorado with an authoritative voice from the Southern Ute Indian tribe. But that voice has not been forthcoming, so I must venture the part myself.

In virtually all primitive human societies, wild animals, especially those more powerful than humans, command respect, admiration, even ritual worship. The modern worldview is different, usually favoring extermination of any creature that threatens our safety, income, or even convenience.

The Southern Ute tribe today is caught between these two divergent worldviews. As a people, they still consider bears of any species sufficiently holy not to allow their killing on reservation lands; yet many modern Utes are ranchers, and ranchers, as a group, fear and hate all large predators.

The traditional Ute perception of the grizzly bear epitomizes the "natural man" worldview. An ancient Ute creation myth holds that when the Great Spirit wished to create humans, he coupled with a female grizzly. The daughter of this powerful union was destined to become the mother of the Ute people. This "Bear Mother" theme, with regional and cultural variations, is perhaps the world's oldest and most widespread creation myth, cherished by native cultures worldwide. Consequently, the Utes have always respected and revered bears as relatives and elders. The most obvious manifestation of this respect is acted out in the oldest of Ute religious rites, the annual spring Bear Dance.

According to legend, one spring night long ago, a dreaming Ute man entered the den of a sleeping grizzly. Seeing that the bear had long overslept and fearing it would soon starve to death, the man awakened the great bear. The grizzly was most grateful and by way of thanks led the man to a secret place in the woods where local bears were performing a sacred dance in celebration of their annual rebirth. The bears invited the man to join their dance, teaching him the music and steps. When he awakened, the man told his people of his dream, proclaiming that henceforth the Utes should perform the Bear Dance each spring to celebrate— and perhaps to help ensure—the end of winter.

Meanwhile, contemporary Utes on all four Colorado reservations, for better and worse, have for the most part jumped into the mainstream of twentieth-century capitalism. The Southern Utes augment their ranching-based economy with income from natural gas royalties, a horse racing track, a gambling casino, and other lucrative business ventures. They are adding land to their 411,000-acre reservation as fast as they can buy up adjoining parcels, and have lobbied long and hard (and expensively) for the Animas-La Plata Project, the last of the great federal pork-barrel water projects and the last gasp of the Bureau of Reclamation. Animas-La Plata would pump water (using coal-generated electricity) from the Animas River up and over a large hill into a reservoir, from which the Utes could draw water both to sell to thirsty desert states such as California and Arizona and for slurry mining their rich coal deposits.

Consequently, contemporary Utes are caught in a societal purgatory, still clinging to such traditional values as their proscription against killing bears and their observance of the Bear Dance, even as a dominant contemporary "white" capitalistic outlook is manifest in the way they conduct daily business.

How do the Utes feel about the possibility of having their Bear Mother back among them? As Colorado bear biologist Tom Beck has noted, the Utes' opinion must be considered in any restoration scheme, because there is nothing to stop grizzlies planted in the south San Juans from roaming onto adjacent Ute lands. Either way, for or against, the Indians stand to lose: sheep and cattle, perhaps (albeit a minor risk of a minor loss), if they welcome the grizzly's return; traditional values and cultural pride if they don't.

Perhaps that is why they declined to comment.

16

"KNEE-DEEP IN ITS ABSENCE"

A Modest Proposal

> *The thought of what was here once and is gone*
> *forever will not leave me as long as I live. It is as*
> *though I walk knee-deep in its absence.*
>
> —Wendell Berry

In early July 1994, I drove to northern Montana to accept retired Glacier National Park bear manager Neal Wedum's offer to show me some grizzlies, which he did.

Late the first afternoon of our three-day backpack trip, the dark grizzly appeared in my binoculars: a summer-fat beast loafing across an acre of granite down in the mile-square subalpine bowl called Bear Valley. For the next half hour, Neal and I spied as the grizzly explored a quiltwork of wood and meadow, digging for roots, upending rocks, and knocking apart rotten logs in a slaphappy search for sustenance. The animal was a deep glossy brown, almost black, with rippling muscles and a casual demeanor. But what I remember most vividly about the dark grizzly is the low sun sparking in tiny eyes, hard and impenetrable as obsidian. Here walked the perfection of freedom, the flesh-and-fur incarnation of the wildness where, as Thoreau reminds us, the preservation of the world resides. Suddenly the dark grizzly quit its bemused perambulations, jerked its muzzle skyward, sniffed the air, and bolted away over a low rise. Gone. No people down there; Neal guessed the big bear had gotten a whiff of an even bigger bear, a beast we never saw.

We found the ruddy grizzly the second afternoon. For half an hour we watched as this huge auburn bruin nosed around, browsed, and dug. At one point, amid a particularly prolific patch of glacier lilies, the ruddy bear settled back onto its ample haunches and used both "hands" to roll back a huge wad of turf. Through my spotting scope I could see the ivory claws clearly, thick and long as a big man's fingers; with them, he lifted the prize to his parchment-colored muzzle and nibbled, looking for all the world like a hairy fat man eating corn on the cob. Neal and I both were saddened when this exceptionally entertaining bear eventually wandered out of sight.

Later that same evening Neal spotted the blond grizzly. She was huge and lovely, at least four hundred pounds, with hair the color of ripened wheat. Even knowing this blond bombshell could have ripped my lungs out with one flashing swipe of scimitar claws, I felt a compelling affection for her and a foolish desire to get closer. Fortunately, before I could act on this potentially fatal attraction, she withdrew into the evening shadows, fading into the realm of fond memory like a dying love.

I have never felt anything quite like that in Colorado.

AUGUST 6, 1994: "GRIZZLY LAKE,"
TIERRA AMARILLA, COLORADO

Yesterday, Banded Peak Ranch foreman Dennis Schutz and I hiked the long, lung-burning path up through Heavenly Valley, over "the Devil's trail," out onto the tundra by Cub Lake, and past the old grizzly digs we'd stumbled onto there a year ago, over the Continental Divide, and down to Grizzly Lake.

Today, we plan to scale a different shoulder of the Divide and drop down into Schutz's Hole, a place remarkably reminiscent of Bear Valley in Glacier. It was there we found the fresh bear digs and claw-marked tree last fall, and it was there that Dennis once happened upon the bloody-fresh remains of an adult elk killed in a violent struggle with some unknown large predator.

Last night, toasting our return with George Dickel and Grizzly Lake water, I managed to get myself just a couple of toasts shy of toasted. I rise at daylight, hangover notwithstanding, drag on damp, cold-stiffened clothes, and stagger off toward the Schutz's Hole overlook, figuring to spy from there with binoculars and scope until Dennis gets his morning horse chores done and joins me.

But it has been nearly a year since my one and only previous visit to the overlook, and I am not precisely sure of the way there. "Head north and stay high," advised Dennis last night, so off and up I go. And up. In little more than half a mile, my pocket altimeter says I've gained four hundred feet. Winded, my head pounding, I stop just below the rocky crest of a little knoll to catch my breath and clear my throat. This mild commotion prompts a loud crashing of limbs from just over the rim as some large animal explodes into flight. Probably an elk; I counted over a hundred of the big deer grazing on the open slope across from camp last evening. To confirm that guess, I bound up to the rim and peer over, hoping for a glimpse of the fleeing creature, but arrive a moment too late and see only trees and an open grassy lane winding off between a pair of low, wooded ridges: an immaculate natural stage devoid of its players.

Figuring the grassy lane to be as good a path forward as any, I follow along its curving course, which I find littered with three, four, five fresh bear scats. In passing, I poke at the poops with a stick; one and all, the grassy loaves exude the sweet aroma of damp alfalfa.

A little farther on, around a slow left bend, I find two more scats. Like the others, these are large but not huge, old enough to have blackened but still fresh enough to remain uncrusted and moist. It strikes me as more than a little odd to find such an abundance of bear droppings in one small area up here on top of the world, where Dennis says he has never seen a black bear and finds little to no bear sign. And now, just beyond the last of the dung heaps, I spot an even less likely sight: an extensive area of what could be fresh bear digs. Feeling a bit foolish, I look around uneasily as I retrieve a canister of pepper spray (a Glacier souvenir) from my pack and attach it to my belt before moving ahead to inspect the scene.

These clods, unlike those down in Schutz's Hole last September, have not been flipped upside down (as if the digger were after roots), but sit upright beside the holes from which they were torn. Nor is any dig-talus visible. In one place, more than a dozen big sod chunks form a drunken plow line. Most peculiar.

Just beyond, where the narrow lane opens into a broad subalpine meadow, the grass is dotted white with an exuberance of alpine bistort. And from the midst of these flowers sparkles a cluster of prismatic dewdrops perched atop a clump of animal hair. I walk over and pick up the quarter-sized wad of damp, flattened fur and hold it up to the morning sun: blond to orangish in color, silky-fine and wavy. From the nucleus of underfur project a score or more guard hairs, each several inches long, mostly blond-orange but a few entirely clear. Ho boy.

I stash the hair in a plastic bag, stuff the bag in a shirt pocket, and race back down to camp, where I catch Dennis just preparing to leave. I blurt out my story, show the hair, and we're out of there, huffing double-time back up to what I've optimistically dubbed Grizzly Knoll.

While I'm taking photos and bagging scat samples for the long-hoped-for, potentially conclusive mitochondria-DNA testing that I'm beginning to doubt will ever come about, Dennis explores the knoll. After a while he returns and asks what bear "nests" looks like. I say they resemble elk and deer beds, usually located at the base of a shade tree with a breeze and a view and most often with a litter of bear scats nearby.

"Follow me," says my friend, not offering where or why.

Dennis leads us back along the grassy lane to where I had first topped out this morning and scared off that unseen large animal. There, beneath a low bushy spruce, he points to a slight depression in the earth, just in front of which lie three big fresh bear scats.

By George! I recall the beautiful blond Glacier grizzly and wonder about the size, and especially the species, of this Colorado blond I apparently almost met face to face.

We continue our inspection of the knoll, and in an area of little more than an acre between the nest and digs tally sixteen scats. Dennis says he has ridden or walked close past this knoll dozens of times but has never paid it a moment's heed. Only by lucky accident did I literally stumble onto this fecund little refugium.

From Grizzly Knoll, we wander on toward the Schutz's Hole overlook, searching carefully for more bear spoor as we walk. Around midmorning, we are crossing open tundra close below a granite cliff when I spot what looks at first glance like a mound of horse droppings. I ask Dennis if he has ever ridden through this area.

"No," he says, returning to where I'm kneeling beside the big, straw-colored, desiccated pile. "But that's not horse anyhow; that's bear."

"Naw," says I. "Too big."

With a spall of rock, I invert the massive dung. Sure enough, the underside is black, tubular, and segmented, in obvious opposition to the biscuitlike leavings of horses. Viewed from this angle, it is clearly an ursine product, the biggest I've ever seen. Anywhere. I break off one

section of the monster flop, measure it at 2⅛ inches in diameter, and bag
it separately from the comparatively modest-sized samples collected on
Grizzly Knoll. Prime meat for DNA testing.

At home a couple of days later, I phoned Rick Kahn at Division headquarters in Denver. As it happened, Tom Beck was there with him.
When I asked, they agreed to submit my bear hair sample—channeled
through Judy Sheppard, who heads the Division's Nongame Wildlife
Program—to the Wyoming wildlife forensics lab for species analysis.

"We've got a brand-new draft contingency plan for dealing with
grizzly reports," Tom told me, "and this will be our first opportunity to
use it."

I've known for some time that a state grizzly contingency plan was in
the works, and even in draft form it is potentially the best news I've
heard yet from the Division regarding the Colorado grizzly controversy.
If nothing else, it reflects a shift away from the agency's staunch, long-
held "no grizzlies left" public stance and reflects a willingness to weigh
evidence, possibly even to take action.

The conception of the Division's grizzly plan came about in early
1994, when Judy Sheppard asked Tom Beck to draft a letter outlining
his recommendations for dealing with what Beck terms "the continuing
furor over the presence/absence of grizzly bears in Colorado." Among
other things, Beck suggested the plan should provide "a definitive, published set of criteria for assessing the validity of a sighting of a grizzly
bear or sign." All sightings would be graded by the Division official
taking the report, with those scored "probable" or "definite" being forwarded to an interdisciplinary "grizzly bear committee" for evaluation
and a final grading.

Said committee, according to Tom, "should be composed of biologists with field experience in the study of bears from CDOW, USFS, and
USFWS; non-agency biologists with bear experience; bear hunters/outfit-
ters; and laymen from private advocacy groups" such as the Colorado
Grizzly Project. Thus the Colorado Grizzly Bear Committee envisioned
by Beck would comprise at least half a dozen members, probably more.

It is significant that Beck clearly intended far greater responsibilities
for his proposed grizzly committee than merely grading evidence. In
addition to passing judgment on the validity of the steady inflow of San

Juan grizzly sighting and sign reports and recommending appropriate action, this mixed bag of agency and nonagency, professional and lay, pro- and antigrizzly voices (an eclectic assemblage of exactly the sort recommended by the San Juan Grizzly Project) would provide the ideal spawning ground for lucrative dialogue on all aspects of what Beck has so accurately described as the "continuing furor" over the grizzly bear in Colorado.

The Division's Nongame office "felt uncomfortable" providing me with a copy of the grizzly plan in draft form and politely declined to do so. No surprise there, and no matter. I soon came by one elsewhere and learned, disappointingly though hardly unexpectedly, that the large, interdisciplinary, *working* grizzly committee envisioned by Beck had been emasculated by the Division bureaucracy to a three-person panel of agency biologists whose sole task and authority would be to grade grizzly reports. No surprise there, either. Business as usual.

My report of the Grizzly Knoll findings was recorded in mid-August. I sent half of my hair sample to Denver the next day (I kept the other half). It was finally forwarded sometime in September, via Judy Sheppard, to Tom Moore at the Wyoming wildlife forensic lab. In October, Judy sent me Moore's official report, which concluded: "Item No. 1 contains hairs that have characteristics most similar to hairs from an animal in the Ursidae family, bears, most probably black bear. There is overlap of characteristics with grizzly bear hairs, but no silver or colorless tipped hairs were observed, which are common in grizzly bear hairs."

Puzzling, this. Under dissecting microscopes in the Fort Lewis College biology lab, Dr. Bill Romme and I had compared my Grizzly Knoll sample against hairs from the paw of Ernie Wilkinson's 1951 Starvation Gulch grizzly. The known grizzly sample did in fact contain clear-tipped guard hairs, though not in high percentage. The Grizzly Knoll sample showed a similar content of *entirely* clear guard hairs. Under the scope, the cell structure of the clear-tipped and entirely clear hairs appeared identical.

Perplexed that the clear hairs weren't even mentioned in the report, I asked Tom Beck to ask Tom Moore what gives. He did: Moore replied that entirely clear hairs suggested to him a cinnamon-phase black bear; clear-*tipped* hairs, on the other hand, indicate to Moore a roughly 75 percent likelihood of grizzly origin. "That's as definite as we can get it right now."

Seeking a second opinion, I phoned another noted wildlife hair analyst, who said he had looked at a lot of black bear hairs in his time and had never seen a clear one. In his experience and opinion, entirely clear hairs, like clear-tipped hairs, "are strongly suggestive of grizzly."

Not that it really matters, I guess: visual hair analysis, I've been assured repeatedly, is merely an indication, not a scientifically infallible species indicator. Thus, even had the Grizzly Knoll hair been judged "most likely grizzly," while personally exciting, it would be just one more clump of San Juan bear hair on a growing but legally impotent pile.

In late October I met with San Juan National Forest geologist Glen Raby. Glen and I spent a long time studying my slides, projected large on a screen, of the various possible grizzly digs I've stumbled onto in the south San Juans. Glen agreed with the consensus opinion that the old digs above Cub Lake and the fresh (September 1993) overturned clod digs down in Schutz's Hole were "of mechanical rather than natural origin," further confirming the likelihood they were the work of bears. The odd Grizzly Knoll excavations, however, rated a "slightly better than fifty-fifty chance" in Raby's book of being the freak work of ice column frost heaves, "an extremely rare phenomenon but, from the looks of things, a distinct possibility in this instance."

And so it goes. More pieces—some that fit, some that don't—in an increasingly complex puzzle.

If I have gained anything approaching an epiphany in my long search for the truth about the grizzly bear in Colorado—its history and current status—it is that proving a few of the creatures still roam the San Juans is not, or should not be, the ultimate goal for those who care. Rather, the real question to be addressed, the appropriate first concern, is the future of the San Juan ecology—this wild montane landscape which, in one way and another, helps to sustain us all, bears *and* men. If the investigations, observations, and opinions recorded in these pages are capable of accomplishing anything of lasting value, my hope is that it will be to provoke informed, objective, open discussion of the future of wilderness in Colorado. What do a *majority* of the people of Colorado want? And what is *right?*

"In the end," says Doug Peacock, "the very survival of the human species may depend on having wildness in our backyards. Without the enlightenment and generosity to assure those basics, I can't see that we have a chance. By working to save the bear and its tiny wilderness enclaves, we are working to save ourselves. If we can't be big enough to accommodate a species as intelligent, magnificent, and manlike as the grizzly, we probably have no chance of long-term survival ourselves; we'll destroy nature, then we'll destroy ourselves. Humans and bears evolved in identical surroundings, and to transform and destroy the habitat that shaped us both is suicidal."

Here in the San Juan Mountains of Colorado, we have reached that crossroads. Somewhere between the vision of Doug Peacock and the pragmatism of Tom Beck lies an answer.

"Where there was wildness," wrote the late Harry Middleton, a passionate lover of wild trout and wild mountain water, "there was possibility, chance, genuine life full of promise and risk and perplexing uncertainty." And where wildness wants, we walk knee-deep in its absence.

November again, and the little death of winter has descended upon the San Juans.

BIBLIOGRAPHY

PRELUDE

Payne, Roger. "Voices from the Sea." In *Talking on the Water*, ed. Jonathan White. San Francisco: Sierra Club, 1994.

1. "WHERE THE LAST GRIZZLIES ROAM"

Baizel, Bruce (Round River Conservation Studies). Personal communications, 1992–94.
Bass, Rick. Personal communication, 1992.
Peacock, Doug. Personal communications, 1991–94.
Petersen, David L. "Ghost Grizzlies," *Wilderness*, fall 1993.
———. "The Next Last Bear." *Backpacker*, December 1992.

2. THE SEARCHERS

Carlson, LeRoy (U.S. Fish and Wildlife Service). Letter to San Juan Grizzly Project, May 20, 1992.
Moore, Tom (Wyoming Game and Fish Department). Personal communication, 1992.
Murray, John A., ed. *The Great Bear*. Anchorage: Alaska Northwest Books, 1992.
Peacock, Doug. *Grizzly Years*. New York: Henry Holt, 1990.
Servheen, Christopher (U.S. Fish and Wildlife Service). As quoted in letter

from LeRoy Carlson, Colorado state supervisor, FWS, to San Juan Grizzly Project, May 7, 1992.

Sizemore, Dennis (Round River Conservation Studies). Personal communications, 1992–94.

Tolisano, Jim (Round River Conservation Studies). Personal communications, 1992.

3. "BRING 'EM IN, REGARDLESS OF HOW"

Armstrong, David M. "Distribution of Mammals in Colorado." A Monograph of the Museum of Natural History, University of Kansas, Lawrence, no. 3, 1972.

Burdick, Hal (Colorado Division of Wildlife). Minutes of "Grizzly Bear Planning Meeting." Durango, April 6, 1971.

———. "Progress Report, Grizzly Bear Baiting, San Juan." Denver, June 28, 1971.

———. "Progress Report, Grizzly Bear Baiting, San Juan/Rio Grande." Denver, March 1, 1972.

———. Personal communication, 1994.

Cary, Merritt. "North American Fauna, No. 33, A biological Survey of Colorado." Washington, D.C.; Government Printing Office, 1911.

Colorado Division of Wildlife. Nongame wildlife files. Denver.

Cooney, Judd (Colorado Division of Wildlife). "San Juan Grizzly Study, 1971." Pagosa Springs.

Fowler, Jacob. *The Journal of Jacob Fowler.* Edited by Elliott Coues. New York: Francis P. Harper, 1898.

Murray, John A. *Wildlife in Peril: The Endangered Mammals of Colorado.* Boulder: Roberts Rinehart, 1987.

Queal, Cal. "Old Mose." *Colorado Outdoors,* May–June 1970.

Stanford, Dennis (Smithsonian Institution). "Early Man in Southern Colorado." Talk delivered at Fort Lewis College, Durango, April 7, 1994.

Warren, Edward R. *The Mammals of Colorado: Their Habits and Distribution.* Norman: University of Oklahoma Press, 1942.

Zaccagnini, Ronald (Colorado Division of Wildlife). "Is the Grizzly Gone?" *Colorado Outdoors,* July–August, 1975.

Zgainer, Mike (Colorado Division of Wildlife). Personal communication, 1994.

4. THE LAST GRIZZLY SLAYER

Gumbine, R. Edward. *Ghost Bears: Exploring the Biodiversity Crisis.* Covelo, Calif.: Island Press, 1992.

Guthrie, A. B., Jr. Personal communications, 1982–91.

Murray, John A. *Wildlife in Peril: The Endangered Mammals of Colorado.* Boulder: Roberts Rinehart, 1987.

———. Personal communications, 1991–94.

Thomas, Jack Ward (U.S. Forest Service). "Restoring the Agency's Environmental Ethic." Reprinted in *Inner Voice,* vol. 6, no. 1, from *Environmental Leadership.* Covelo, Calif.: Island Press, 1993.

White, Jonathan, ed. *Talking on the Water.* San Francisco: Sierra Club, 1994.

Wilkinson, Ernest. *Snow Caves for Fun and Survival.* Boulder: Johnson Books, 1989.

———. Personal communications, 1993–94.

5. "TORE NEARLY ALL TO PEASES"

Clancy, Liz (Denver Museum of Natural History). Personal communication, 1994.

Colorado Division of Wildlife. Wiseman investigation files and incident reports, 1979–80, Denver.

Cook, Philip St. George. "Some Incidents in the Life of Hugh Glass, a Hunter of the Missouri River." *St. Louis Beacon,* December 2 and 9, 1830.

Flagg, Edmund. "Adventures at the Headwaters of the Missouri." *Louisville Literary News-Letter,* September 7, 1839.

Hall, James. "The Missouri Trapper" and "Letters from the West." *Port Folio* 14 (March 1825).

Hinchman, Steve, and Barry Noreen. "Colorado Mining Industry Strikes Again." *High Country News,* vol. 25, no. 1 (January 25, 1993).

Myers, John Myers. *Pirate, Pawnee, and Mountain Man: The Saga of Hugh Glass.* Boston: Little, Brown, 1963.

Potts, Daniel T. *Early Yellowstone and Western Experiences: Yellowstone Nature Notes,* vol. 21 (September–October 1947).

U.S. Fish and Wildlife Service. Wiseman investigation file, 1979–80.

Wiseman, Ed. Personal communications, 1993–94.

6. "LOTS OF BLACK BEARS BUT NO GRIZZLIES"

Baker, J. A. *The Peregrine.* Moscow: University of Idaho Press, 1985.

Beck, Tom (Colorado Division of Wildlife). "South San Juan Mountains Grizzly Bear Survey, Environmental Assessment." Denver, circa 1980.

————. "South San Juan Mountains Grizzly Bear Survey, Job Progress Report" (January 1, 1981, through December 31, 1981). Denver.

————. "South San Juan Mountains Grizzly Bear Survey, Job Final Report" (January 1, 1982, through December 31, 1982). Denver.

————. Personal communications, 1993–94.

Colorado Division of Wildlife. "Contingency Plan for Captured Grizzly Bear, South San Juan Mountains Grizzly Bear Survey" (draft). Denver, April 20, 1982.

————. "Grizzly Bear Contingency Article." Denver, circa 1982.

————. Project Agreement, Endangered Wildlife Investigations, "South San Juan Mountains Grizzly Bear Survey" (January 1, 1981, through December 31, 1981). Denver.

Thier, Tim (U.S. Fish and Wildlife Service). Personal communications, 1993–94.

Verma, Mool S. (Colorado Bureau of Investigation). Laboratory Report. Denver, June 10, 1982.

7. "SOME MIGHTY BIG BLACK BEARS"

Herrero, Stephen. *Bear Attacks.* New York: Nick Lyon Books, 1985.

Hughes, Dusty. Personal communication, 1994.

Nelson, Richard. *The Island Within.* Berkeley, Calif.: North Point Press, 1989.

Schutz, Dennis. Personal communications, 1991–94.

U.S. Fish and Wildlife Service. Northern Continental Divide Ecosystem Subcommittee. "A Guide to Judging Grizzly Bear Reports." Revised April 1987.

8. THE SNOWSLIDE CANYON GRIZZLY EXPEDITION

Aune, Keith (Montana Department of Fish, Wildlife and Parks). "Report of Laboratory Examination." Sun River, February 4, 1993.

Beck, Tom (Colorado Division of Wildlife). "Black Bears of West-Central Colorado." Colorado Division of Wildlife Technical Publication no. 39. Denver, September 1991.

————. Personal communication, 1994.

Carron, Cary (Colorado Division of Wildlife). Personal communications, 1993–94.

Colorado Division of Wildlife and U.S. Forest Service. "Moose of Southwestern Colorado." Monte Vista, Colorado, no date.

Fischer, Hank. "New Home for the Griz." *Defenders,* winter 1993–94.

Gerhardt, Gary. "Lab Report Backs Grizzly Sighting in San Juans." *Rocky Mountain News,* February 3, 1993.

Kahn, Rick (Colorado Division of Wildlife). Personal communications, 1993–94.

Moore, Tom D. (Wyoming Game and Fish Department). "Laboratory Examination Report, No. 93-3-W-CAF." University of Wyoming, Laramie, January 20, 1993.

9. A GLACIAL INTERLUDE

Clark, Wendy (U.S. Fish and Wildlife Service). Personal communications, 1994.

McIntyre, Rick. Personal communications, 1993–94.

Nelson, Richard. *The Island Within.* Berkeley, Calif.: North Point Press, 1989.

Wedum, Neal. Personal communications, 1993–94.

10. "BLOOD, HAIR, AND THE GROUND TORE UP"

Beck, Tom (Colorado Division of Wildlife). Personal communications, 1993–94.

Kenvin, David (Colorado Division of Wildlife). Personal communications, 1993–94.

LaChapelle, Dolores. "Mountains Constantly Walking." In *Talking on the Water,* ed. Jonathan White. San Francisco: Sierra Club, 1994.

Murray, John A. Personal communications, 1993–94.

Peacock, Doug. Personal communication, 1994.

Schutz, Dennis. Personal communications, 1993–94.

Thier, Tim (U.S. Fish and Wildlife Service). Personal communications, 1993–94.

Twain, Mark. "Ministerial Change." No date.

Wedum, Neal. Personal communication, 1993.

11. THE GRIZZLY AS PREDATOR

Cole, Glen. "Grizzly Bear-Elk Relationships in Yellowstone National Park." 1972.

Errington, Paul L. *Of Predation and Life.* Ames: Iowa State University Press, 1967.

Gunther, Kerry (Yellowstone National Park). Personal communication, 1993.

Jonkel, Jamie. Personal communication, 1993.

Kenvin, David (Colorado Division of Wildlife). Personal communications, 1993–94.

Madel, Michael (U.S. Fish and Wildlife Service). Personal communication, 1993.

Peacock, Doug. Personal communications, 1993.

Petersen, David L. "Griz the Elk Hunter." *Bugle,* spring 1993.

Zgainer, Mike (Colorado Division of Wildlife). Personal communication, 1994.

12. "BRAIN-DEAD POLITICAL HACKS"

Associated Press. "Bad Bears Face Penalty of Death." *Durango Herald,* April 18, 1994.

Beck, Tom (Colorado Division of Wildlife). "Black Bears of West-Central Colorado." Technical Publication No. 39. Colorado Division of Wildlife, Denver, 1991.

————. Personal communications, 1993–94.

Carron, Cary (Colorado Division of Wildlife). Personal communications, 1993–94.

Coloradans United for Bears. "Kill the Mother and the Cubs Die Too." Denver, 1992. (Pamphlet.)

Dentry, Ed. "Anti-hunting Group Snubbed in Colorado." In "Western Adventure." *Rocky Mountain News,* Denver, 1993.

Ewegen, Bob. "A Brain-dead Political Hack Belches the Stupidest Statement of 1992." *Denver Post,* September 21, 1992.

Loker, Cynthia A., and Daniel J. Decker. "The Colorado Black Bear Hunting Controversy: A Case Study of Human Dimensions in Contemporary Wildlife Management." HDRU Series No. 94-4. Human Dimensions Research Unit, Department of Natural Resources, Cornell University (in conjunction with the Terrestrial Wildlife Section, Colorado Division of Wildlife, Denver), Ithaca, New York, 1994.

Smith, Michael. Personal communications, 1994.

13. TASTING THE SOIL

Brown, David E., and Charles H. Lowe, eds. *Biotic Communities of the Southwest.* Fort Collins, Colo.: Rocky Mountain Forest and Range Experimental Station, USDA Forest Service, 1983.

Peacock, Doug. *Grizzly Years.* New York: Henry Holt, 1990.

Tolisano, Jim, and Jim Sharman (Round River Conservation Studies). "Following the Round River." *Wild Earth,* summer 1993.

14. GHOST GRIZZLIES

Beck, Tom (Colorado Division of Wildlife). "Black Bears of West-Central Colorado," Technical Publication No. 39. Colorado Division of Wildlife, Denver, 1991.

————. Personal communications, 1994.

Eyre, Glen (Colorado Division of Wildlife). Personal communications, 1994.

Kahn, Rick (Colorado Division of Wildlife). Personal communications, 1994.

Peacock, Doug. Personal communications, 1994.

Schlarb, Mike. Personal communications, 1994.

Trujillo, Arthur. Personal communications, 1994.

15. "ONLY A MOUNTAIN NOW"

Alliance for the Wild Rockies. "Grizzly Recovery Plan Attacked by Scientists and Conservation Groups." *The Networker,* vol. 6, no. 1 (1994).

Baizel, Bruce, and Dennis Sizemore (Round River Conservation Studies). Personal communications, 1994.

Beck, Tom (Colorado Division of Wildlife). "Black Bears of West-Central Colorado." Technical Publication No. 39. Colorado Division of Wildlife, Denver, 1991.

————. Personal communications, 1993–94.

Carrier, Scott. "Looking for Bears." National Public Radio report, 1993.

Carron, Cary (Colorado Division of Wildlife). Personal communications, 1992–94.

Eyre, Glen (Colorado Division of Wildlife). Personal communications, 1992–94.

Gerhardt, Gary. "Wildlife Official Defends Grizzly Recovery Plan," *Rocky Mountain News,* December 16, 1993.

Grumbine, R. Edward. *Ghost Bears: Exploring the Biodiversity Crisis.* Covelo, Calif.: Island Press, 1992.

Kahn, Rick (Colorado Division of Wildlife). Personal communications, 1993–94.

Leopold, Aldo. "Escudilla." In *A Sand County Almanac.* New York: Oxford University Press, 1949.

Peacock, Doug. Personal communication, 1994.

Povilitis, Tony (Life Net). Personal communication, 1994.

"Recovery Plan Bearly There." *High Country News,* April 18, 1994.

Servheen, Christopher (U.S. Fish and Wildlife Service). Personal communication, 1994.

Shands, Tom. "Groups Challenge Grizzly Plan." *Bear News,* spring/summer 1994.

Soulé, Michael E. Foreword to *Ghost Bears: Exploring the Biodiversity Crisis,* by R. Edward Grumbine. Covelo, Calif.: Island Press, 1992.

U.S. Fish and Wildlife Service. "Grizzly Bear Recovery Plan." Missoula, Mont. 1993.

Wilkinson, Ernest. Personal communications, 1993–94.

Wilkinson, Todd. "Agency Stifles Biologist as Recovery Plan Released." *Bear News,* winter/spring 1994.

Wiseman, Ed. Personal communications, 1993–94.

16. "KNEE-DEEP IN ITS ABSENCE"

Beck, Tom (Colorado Division of Wildlife). Official letter to Judy Sheppard, terrestrial nongame specialist, Colorado Division of Wildlife, April 4, 1994, proposing and outlining a grizzly bear contingency plan.

Berry, Wendell. "A Walk Down Camp Branch." In *Traveling at Home.* Berkeley, Calif.: North Point Press, 1989.

Colorado Division of Wildlife. "Draft Grizzly Bear Contingency Plan." Denver, July 1, 1994.

Moore, Tom D. (Wyoming Game and Fish Department). "Laboratory Examination Report No. 94-43-W-CAT." University of Wyoming, Laramie, September 20, 1994.

Peacock, Doug. Personal communication, 1994.

Schutz, Dennis. Personal communications, 1993–94.

INDEX